KHASI-ENGLISH DICTIONARY

KHASI-ENGLISH DICTIONARY

U. Nissor Singh

GYAN

Published by

Gyan Publishing House
5, Ansari Road
Daryaganj, New Delhi-110002
Phone: 011-47034999, 9811692060
E-mail: books@gyanbooks.com

Distribution Network
gyanbooks.com
India, USA, Canada, UK, Australia, France

ISBN: 978-81-212-0198-8 (HB)

Reprint in India, 2024

First Published, 2013

Printed at: Gyan Press, Delhi.

Khasi-English Dictionary
Author: U. Nissor Singh

KHASI-ENGLISH DICTIONARY

BY

U NISSOR SINGH

EDITED BY

MAJOR P. R. T. GURDON, I.A., U DOHORY ROPMAY, B.A.,

AND

U HAJOM KISSOR SINGH.

PRINTED AT THE EASTERN BENGAL AND ASSAM
SECRETARIAT PRESS.

SHILLONG.

1906.

Agents for the sale of Books published by the Assam Administration.

Agents in India.

(1) Messrs. Thacker, Spink & Co., Calcutta.

(2) Messrs. W. Newman & Co., Calcutta.

(3) Messrs. S. K. Lahiri & Co., Calcutta.

(4) Messrs. A. M. and J. Ferguson, Ceylon.

(5) Messrs. R. Combray & Co., 6 and 8/2, Hastings Street, Calcutta.

(6) Messrs. Thomson & Co., Madras.

Agents in England.

(1) Mr. E. Arnold, 41 and 43, Maddox Street, Bond Street, W., London.

(2) Messrs. Constable & Co., 16, James Street, Hay Market, London.

(3) Messrs. Kegan Paul, Trench, Trübner & Co., 43, Gerrard Street, Soho, W., London.

(4) Mr. B. Quaritch, 15, Piccadilly, W., London.

(5) Messrs. P. S. King & Son, 9, Bridge Street, Westminster, S. W., London.

(6) Mr. B. H. Blackwell, 50 and 51, Broad Street, Oxford.

(7) Messrs. Deighton Bell & Co., Cambridge.

(8) Messrs. Henry S. King & Co., 65, Cornhill, E. C., London.

(9) Messrs. Grindlay & Co., 54, Parliament Street, S. W., London.

Agents on the Continent of Europe.

(1) MM. Friedländer and Sohn, 11, Carlstrasse, Berlin.

(2) M. Otto Harrassowitz, Leipzig.

(3) M. Karl Hiersemann, Leipzig.

(4) M. Ernest Leroux, 28, Rue Bonaparte, Paris.

(5) Martinus Nijhoff, The Hague.

(6) Mr. Rudolf Haupt, Halle-a-S, Germany.

SHILLONG:

PRINTED BY E. HILL, PRESS SUPERINTENDENT, EASTERN BENGAL AND ASSAM.

AUTHOR'S PREFACE.

In bringing out this little book before the public, I beg to say that I have engaged in a work so arduous that I cannot profess to have successfully completed it, but, encouraged by the remembrance that not a few persons have undertaken work of a similar kind in other languages on a small scale at first, I did not shrink from making a like attempt myself. When the work had been finished, and part of it gone through the press, Sir Bampfylde Fuller kindly took notice of it, and at his instance a committee, composed of U Dohory Ropmay, B.A., U Hajom Kissor Singh, and myself, as members, was appointed for revising and enlarging it.

As the Cherra dialect has been selected and introduced by the Welsh Missionaries (and very wisely too) as a standard of the Khasi language, no attempt has been made to insert words of other dialects, excepting in a very few instances.

No pains have been spared to consult as many of the books and local newspapers available, as have been published up to date.

I have great pleasure in acknowledging my personal obligations to the Rev. J. C. Evans, to Major E. R. W. C. Carroll, I.M.S., and to Major P. R. T. Gurdon, I.A., for the kind and valuable assistance rendered by them. I must not omit to mention here my obligations to the members of the revising committee—U Dohory Ropmay, B.A., and U Hajom Kissor Singh—who have devoted much time and thought to the revision work, and to some of my Khasi friends from whom I derived assistance.

In conclusion, I beg to say that, with all that I and the members of the committee have done, there will still be room for further improvements as years pass. I am, however, satisfied that a foundation has been laid for any improvements that may be made in future.

Shillong,
December 1904.

NISSOR SINGH.

EXPLANATORY NOTES.

The reader must first of all make himself acquainted with the letters of the Khasi alphabet, according to which the words have been arranged in this book. These are the letters of the Khasi alphabet :—

a b k d e g ng h i

ʼ j l m n (ñ) o p

r s t u w y

2. The following prefixes, which may be formed with verbs and adjectives to make compound words, have been omitted, excepting in the case where the derivatives so formed bear a special meaning from that of the radicals, *e.g.*, *jingri*—cattle, *jingbriew*—human, *nongwei*—a stranger, *nongra*—a worn-out and useless brass vessel, *iaroh*—to praise, *sngewsih*—to be sorry, *pynhiar*—diarrhœa, export, etc.

Prefixes of the above kind are—

i—(or ih—), ia—, iai—, jing—, kaba—, la—, myn—, nang—, nong—, pyn—, sngew—,

i—, *ih*—, to appear, to look, as, *ibha*—to take a fancy to; *isyn-ei*—to have pity for; *itlot*—to appear weak; *i-raikhoh*—to appear lean or reduced.

ia—, denotes plurality of the subject agreeing with the verb, as, *ki ia kren*—they are talking; *u ia shoh bad u dkhar*—he is fighting with a *dkhar*.

iai—, *nang*—, expresses continuity or progression of action, as, *iai-sneng*—to continue to rebuke; *iai-leit*—to continue to go; *nangthoh*—to be writing, is writing; *nang iaid*—to be going on, is going on.

jing—, when prefixed to a verb or adjective, to form abstract noun, as, *jingbha*—goodness; *jingshái*—light; *jingleh*—action, and so on.

kaba—, a prefix to form a verbal noun and the imperfect participle, as, *kaba sum ka pynkhúid ia ka met*—bathing cleanses the body.

la—, a prefix denoting future time, as, *lasháí*—to-morrow; *lashisngi*—day after to-morrow; *lanymwei*—next season or year.

myn—, a prefix to denote a doer, as, *myntúh*—a thief ; *mynpang*—a patient. In adverbs of time it denotes past time, as, *mynhynne*—a short time ago ; *mynshisngi*—day before yesterday ; *mynnymwei*—last season or year.

nang—, see *iai* above.

nong—, denotes a doer or an inhabitant of, as, *nongkren*—a speaker ; *nong Sohra*—a Cherra-man ; *nong Mylliem*—an inhabitant of Mylliem village.

pyn—, a prefix to form a causative verb, *pynthoh*—to cause one to write ; *pynshong*—to cause one to sit ; *pynsngew*—to announce.

sngew—, a prefix which means to feel, as, *sngewbha*—to be pleased ; *sngewmá*—to be afraid of ; *sngewkwah*—to have a desire ; *sngewtlot*—to feel weak.

A few suffixes have also a significance of their own, such as—dúh, —kái, —sa, —sah, —sat, etc., as :—

Shong-*dúh*—to settle permanently.

Iaid-*kái*—to ramble, to take a stroll.

Leh-*sa*—to be peevish.

Thiah-*sah*—to remain sleeping or in bed.

Shoh-*sat*—to beat in such a way as to reflect cruelty on the part of the person who beats.

3. *The spellings.*—The spellings in this book have been followed according as the people speak or write. In some cases the *y* has been done away with, as in the word *kpa* instead of *kypa*, *kmie* instead of *kymie*, and in some an apostrophe (') has been inserted in its place, as, *k'iuh* for *kyiuh*, *k'iar* for *kyiar*, *k'ing* for *kying*. But in the majority of words both forms of spellings (the old form and the phonetic) have been retained.

4. *Imitatives*, or word-collocations, have been given where necessary, *e.g.*, khutia, *ki, n.* details, odds and ends.

[*Imit.* khutia-khutain.]

5. The meaning of an adverb likely to present difficulty in understanding it, has been given with an illustrative sentence.

6. *Vowel sounds.*

á , â , long, as in 'far'—*jár* (a net), *sár* (to sweep).

à short as in 'fat'—*làt-làt* (a rapid), *màt* (a joint).

Unmarked vowels have generally a short sound.

ABBREVIATIONS AND SIGNS USED IN THIS DICTIONARY.

a., adj.	stands	for	adjective.
ad., adv.	,,	,,	adverb.
abbrev.	,,	,,	abbreviation.
aux.	,,	,,	auxiliary.
Bot.	,,	,,	botany, botanical term.
coloq.	,,	,,	colloquial.
con., conj.	,,	,,	conjunction.
contr.	,,	,,	contraction.
esp.	,,	,,	especially.
fig.	,,	,,	figurative.
Hind.	,,	,,	Hindi.
i	,,	,,	common gender, used as a term of respect or diminution.
Imit.	,,	,,	Imitative.
Imper.	,,	,,	Imperative (verb).
Impers.	,,	,,	Impersonal.
inter., interj.		,,	interjection.
ka,	,,	,,	feminine.
ki,	,,	,,	plural (number).
lit.	,,	,,	literally.
n.	,,	,,	noun.
p., pr., pron.	,,	,,	pronoun.
part.	,,	,,	participle.
phr.	,,	,,	phrase.
pref.	,,	,,	prefix.
prep.	,,	,,	preposition.
suf.	,,	,,	suffix.
u.	,,	,,	masculine.
v.	,,	,,	verb.
i, n.	,,	,,	noun, common gender.
ka, n.	,,	,,	noun, feminine gender.
u, n.	,,	,,	noun, masculine gender.

KHASI-ENGLISH DICTIONARY.

A, the first letter in the Khasi Alphabet; — *int.* oh! ah!

Áb! *int.* the imitation of the cry of a crow.

*Abir, *u*, *n.* red powder used in the Holi festival.

Ak! *int.* ah! ejaculation of disgust at an unpleasant smell.

Aku! *int.* expressing disgust at a bad smell.

Akher-ka-sngi, *ka*, *n.* Domesday.

A-khia, *u*, *n.* (*colloquial*) an earnest man.

*Akôr, *ka*, *n.* behaviour, conduct.

Ada! / Adi! } *int.* Oho! dear me! (expressing acute bodily pain).

*Adda, *ka*, *n.* a stage for changing horses, dak-runners, etc.

Ade, *ad.* may be, perhaps (same as *ide*); [as, "*ade* dum ka bneng kumne ba'n slap, mo."];—*int.* to express surprise or approbation.

Ado! *int.* Oho!

Adong, *ka*, *n.* prohibition;—*v.* to prohibit. [*Imit.* adong-adit.]

Adur! / Adur-lanot! } *int.* woe is me! gracious me!

Adykâr! / Adkâr! } *adv.* thoughtfully, economically, moderately; [as, "bám *adkar*, dih *adkar*."]

Ang, *v.* to open, to crack.

Ang-ang, *adv.* in the open sun; [as, "wat leit shah ha ka sngi *ang-ang*."]

Ang-um, *v.* (*lit.* to open the mouth on account of thirst); to be in a fix.

‡Angel, *u*, *n.* an angel.

Angret, *u*, *n.* a dare-devil (from Hindustani *Angrez*).

Ah, *v.* (*colloquial*) to cut;—*int.* ah!

Ahor, *ka*, *n.* a marshy place, a swamp.

Ai, *v.* to give, to bestow.

---

* Hindi. | ‡ English.

*Aia, *ka*, *n*. Ayah.

Ai-bai-siew, *v*. to give money for buying things at a time, as, on a *hat*-day. [*Imit.* aibai-siew aibai-tda.]

Ai-'baibat, *v*. to pay ready money.

Ai-bainong, *v*. to give wages, to reward. [*Imit.* ai-bainong ai-baini.]

Ai-baishùn, *v*. to give or pay a paltry sum of money.

Ai-bat, *v*. to give one to hold, to entrust with.

Ai-bór, *v*. to authorise, to strengthen, to empower. [*Imit.* aibor ai-sor.]

Ai-bud-nám, *v*. to slander; to defame.

Ai-kái, *v*. to give for a time, to pretend to give.

*Ai-kaiphod, (*legal*), *v*. to give explanation.

Ai-kam, *v*. to give employment. [*Imit.* aikam-aijam.]

Ai-khawdûh, *v*. to leave unlooked or uncared for, to be outcasted.

Ai-khusnâm, *v*. to confer honour for meritorious conduct.

Ai-ksew, *v*. to put a dog on the scent.

Ai-ksûid or ai-ksuid-briew, *v*. to kill or bring disease on a person by the agency of devils. [*Imit.* aiksuid-aikhrei.]

Ai-kum, *kaba*, *n*. a Synteng ceremony which a man performs on leaving his mother's or relative's house in order to go and live with his wife and children. [*Imit.* aikum-aiklong.]

Ai-kylliang, *v*. to give a loan. [*Imit.* ai kylliang-aipalat.]

Ai-dáw, *v*. to give an excuse; to give reason for. [*Imit.* aidaw-ai-dong.]

Ai-ei, *v*. to give freely or gratis.

Ai-ngûh, *v*. to give thanks. [*Imit.* ainguh-aidem.]

Ai-huspai, *v*. to indulge.

Ai-lâd, *v*. to give opportunity, to help. [*Imit.* ailad-ailynti.]

Ai-lait-lân, *v*. to let loose, to give one his own inclination.

Ai-li, *v*. to give one his own way.

Ai-mon, *v*. to give one his own will.

Aiñ, *ka*, *n*. law, statute. [*Imit.* ka aiñ-ka'kanun.]

*Ai-nishán, *v*. to name, to point out, to cite, identify.

Ai-nong, *v*. to give out a work or load to be done or carried on hire. [*Imit.* ainong-aini.]

---

* Hindi.

Aiom, *ka*, *n.* season, time.

Ai-pop, *v.* to charge with, to blame for.

Ai-reng, *v.* to present the horn (bull-fighting); to oppose; to confront.

Ai-rong, *v.* to paint. [*Imit.* airong-airup.]

Ai-sakhi, *v.* to give evidence. [*Imit.* ai-sakhi-ai-satar.]

Ai-sboh, *v.* to manure.

Ai-shah, *v.* to give on credit. [*Imit.* aishah-aisham.]

Ai-siew, *v.* to sell a thing on payment of its cost price. [*Imit.* aisiew-aitda.]

Ai-sniew, *v.* to poison. [*Imit.* aisniew-aismeh.]

Ai-sut, *v.* to give money on interest. [*Imit.* aisut-aibut.]

Ai'ti, *v.* to give up, to hand over, to deliver up.

A-iu, *p.* what.

A-iu-re-aiu, *n.* something.

Alé, *v. imper.* come.

Alhia, *a.* lazy, idle. [*Imit.* alhia-alput.]

Along, *ka*, *n.* a lock-up, a *Hajut.*

Am, *v.* to bite, to plant the teeth in;—*imper. only*, give me.

Ama or Amai! *int.* oh! (in case of a narrow escape).

'amdûh, *ka*, *n.* the wisdom tooth.

Amrang, *ka*, *n.* harsh tone, empty words.

*Ana, *n.* anna ($\frac{1}{16}$ of a rupee).

Ani, *int.* Oh! (whenin pain or surprise).

†Anipot, *ka*, *n.* misfortune.

An-na, *a.* idiotic.

*Antâd, *v.* to guess, to conjecture;—*adv.* by way of conjecture; moderately. *Hind.* andáz.

*Antra, *ka*, *n.* chorus.

Ap, *v.* to wait, to stay for.

Ap-dien, *v.* to guard or watch from behind. [*Imit.* apdien-apbud.]

*Aphing, Aphim, Aphin, *ka*, *n.* opium.

Ap-phira, *v.* to guard as a sentinel.

†Apod, *ka*, *n.* trouble, calamity.

---

* Hindi. | † Bengali.

Ap-thap, *v*, to lie in wait for.

Ap-tûh, *v*. to waylay. [*Imit.* aptuh-apthiem.] ; to wait stealthily.

Ar, *a*. two.

Arban, *a*. two-fold, double.

Arbriew, *n*. two shares, two votes.

Arbaliang, *a*. both sides (of a dispute).

Arbûd, *a*. two folds (of twisted-thread).

Arbyteng, } *ka, n.* a joint (of *two* things).
Arbteng, }

Arkhap, *ka, n.* a cleft, a narrow place between two up-rising mounds, a gorge.

Arkhep, *ka, n.* two occasions.

Arklur, *n*. two crores.

Arkup, *ka, n.* two suits of clothes (said of wrappers or shawls).

Ardeng, *ka, n.* two pairs of ornaments.

Arduna shisuka, *a*, Re. 1 annas 12 ; so also arduna-ar-anna.= Re. 1 annas 14, etc.

Arngut, *a*. two (persons).

Arhajâr, *ka, n.* two thousand.

Ari ! *int*. an ejaculation expressing a sensation of cold.

Arlád-um, *ka, n.* the junction of two rivers. See *sdad, shka*.

Arlak, *ka, n.* two lakhs.

Arliang, *ka, n.* two sides ;—*ad.* into two parts, in halves.

Arliang mamla, *ka, n.* two contending parties.

Armet, *ka, n.* (*lit.* two bodies) hence to be in the family way.

Arpateng, *ka, n.* two steps, two generations.

Arphew, *a*. twenty.

Arpiah, *ka, n.* Rs. 2 annas 8.

†Aro ! *int.* (*colloquial*), there you are !

Arsap, *a*. two-fold, hypocritical.

Arshah, *ad.* doubly, twice as much.

Arsh'ing, *ka, n.* (*lit.* two cowries) hence 2 pice—when used along with annas, as, lái-arsh'ing = 3*a.* 2*p.* Same as *Arshyieng*.

Arsien, *adv.* twice.

Arsut, *adv.* downwards.

---

† Bengali (আর).

Artat, *adv.* besides, at the same time [as, " u trei bad ka siaw *artat*"]; on the way, on passing by [as, " wan khot *artat* ynda phi leit, ho."]

Artatien, *a.* doubtful.

Arteng, *ad.* two occasions.

Artet, *adv.* up, upwards, northwards.

Arwat, *adv.* twice, two folds (of string).

*Asbáb, *ka, n.* luggage.

*Ashâr, *ka, n.* preserved fruits or vegetables, chutney.

Asir, *ka, n.* a toll at Lakhat Bazar in Khyrim. [*Imit.* ka dan ka asir.]

Astor, *ka, n.* the plastering with lime.

At, *v.* to swell, to bulge out, to harbour ill feelings.

*Ata, *u, n.* flour.

*Atád, *ka, n.* a compound of a house.

At-byllen, *v.* to swell as if affected with nettle-rash.

Atbylliang, *kaba, n.* swelling as if caused by a lash of a whip.

At-khu, *v.* to be envious of.

Atkpoh, *v.* to have flatulence. [*Imit.* atkpoh-atsnier.]

At-kuda, *v.* to be formed into a notch.

*Atiar, *ka, n.* instrument, weapon (*Hind.* Hatiar).

Atjalyngkhiang, *ka, n.* a glandular swelling.

Atlukhi, Alukhi, } *a.* scolding, unlucky, obstinate.

Atlybing, Atlbing, } *v.* to swell all over.

Atlyngkding, *v.* to swell (of the abdomen).

Atmiang, *v.* to have the mumps.

At-mytung, *v.* to swell prominently, same as *At-mtung.*

Atnûd, *v.* to feel revengeful, to envy.

At-pateng-pateng, *v.* to form swellings here and there.

At-phyllung, *v.* to roll in waves.

Atsohkhliang, *v.* to have an excrescence on the body.

*Ator, *ka, n.* sweet scent.

*Atoskhana, *u, n.* chimney.

---

* Hindi.

At-top, *v.* to be dropsical.

*Awâj, *Awât, } *ka, n.* voice, sound.

Aw-aw, (ud-), *ad.* importunately (crave). [As, "u úd *aw-aw* kum u b'ym ioh ka ja ba'n bam ruh."]

Awria, *a.* licentious.

B.

B, the second letter in the Khasi alphabet.

Ba, 1. *conj.* that, for, inasmuch as, since.

2. As a *prefix*, it forms *Adj.*, as, *ba*bha.

3. As a *suffix*, it forms a *Relative Pron.*, as, ka*ba*, u*ba*, etc.

4. *v.* to flash, to light [as, "ka leilieh ka *ba*."]

'bâ (*abbrev.* of *kba*), *u, n.* paddy, as, u '*ba*-lum=highland rice.

Babe, *v.* to rue, to repent.

Babha, *a.* good. [*Imit.* babha-bamiat.]

*Baborshi, *n.* a cook.

†Babu, *u, n.* a Baboo, a native gentleman, a writer, a school master. [*Imit.* u Babu-phubu.]

Bak, *ad.* away, sharp [as, "u la leit noh *bak* sha ing."]

Bak-bak, *ad.* heedlessly [as, "u la iaid *bak-bak* khlem kyrtiang dien."]

Bakha, *n.* a son or daughter of a maternal uncle or paternal aunt.

Bakhór, *u, n.* gunpowder.

Bakhrâw, *a.* large, big, great;—*u, n.* a dignitary, a noble.

Bakhrâw-batri, *u, n.* a noble, a person of high family.

Bak-jingbak, *ad.* in spite of opposition, persistently [as, "u shu phet lyndet *bak-jingbak* khlem kren ia nga."]

Bakla, *v.* to err, to make a mistake. [*Imit.* bakla-bakli.]

Bad, *conj.* and;—*prep.* with.

Bád, *v.* to exclude, to make an exception.

Baden, *ka, n.* an irrigated rice field.

Bá-ding, *v.* to light with a torch or lamp.

Badon-ba-em, *n.* a well-to-do person.

Bang, *a.* tasty, savoury, palatable;—*ka, n.* a piece of bamboo with which the Bengalis carry loads by throwing it across the shoulder.

---

* Hindi. | † Bengali.

Bah, *v.* to carry on one's back, to bear;—*u, n.* an older brother (*voc.* case, and a term of respect);—*a.* great, big (generally joined with a Noun in its abbreviated form, as, 'maw*bah*, 'rad*bah*, etc.).

'bâ-hali, *u, n.* same as 'ba-pynthor.

Bah-bang, *v.* to carry loads with a stick across the shoulder, like the Bengalis.

Bahkhala, *v.* to be answerable for, to be responsible for.

Bahkyndong, *v.* to be always carrying.

Bahryndang, *v.* to be vicarious.

Bahtympha, *u, n.* wall-plate.

'bâi, *u, n.* (*abbrev.* of *sbai*), a cowry [this is seen in the names of different varieties of cowrie-shells, as u '*bai*-kúid, u '*bai*-shuti];—*ka, n.* price or value.

Ba-iai, *a.* always, steadfast [as, "ko Pa ba lah ba-*iai*."]

'baibâm, *ka, n.* allowance, diet expenses, stipend. [*Imit.* 'baibam —'bai-dih]

'baibat, *ka, n.* cash, ready-money.

'baikhrong, *ka. n.* toll, tax. [*Imit.* 'baikhrong-'bai musur.]

'baikhiarwait, *ka, n.* redemption money, war indemnity.

Báid (iam-), *ad.* peevishly (cry).

'bâilut, *ka, n.* expenditure, cost. [*Imit.* bailut-baisep.]

'bâi mynrâinkhmat, *ka, n.* compensation for breach of any contract or agreement, *esp.* a marriage contract.

Bâiñ-bâiñ, *ad.* very (soft, as, jem *baiñ-baiñ*).

'bainong, *ka, n.* wages, salary. [*Imit.* 'bainong-'baini.]

Baiong, *v.* to be giddy, to be attacked with headache. [*Imit.* baiong-bangit.]

Ba ioh, *phr.* lest, for fear.

Ba-ioh-ba-kot, *phr.* a well-to-do person.

'bai-seng, *ka, n.* capital, money for carrying on any business.

'bâisngi, *ka, n.* daily wages.

'bâisiew, *ka, n.* money given to meet immediate necessary expenses, as, on a *hat*-day. [*Imit.* 'baisiew-'bai-tda.]

Bait, *v.* to sharpen (a stick).

'baiwâi, *ka, n.* rent.

*Bajawalla, *ka, n.* band (military)—*u*, a bandsman.

---

* Hindi.

*Baje, *ka*, *n*. clock, watch, gong.

Balang, *ka*, *n*. the church; a society (religious);—*a*. gathered, congealed.

Bajubon, *u*, *n*. a kind of bracelet.

Balei? *ad*. why? for what reason.

Balia, *v*. to interfere, to meddle.

'bá-lûm, *u*, *n*. See 'ba.

Bâm, *v*. to eat. [*Imit*. bam-dih.]

Bám-bnai, *v*. to board; to live at another's table for pay.

Bâmbriew, *adj*. cannibal, man-eating.

Bâm-khuti, *v*. to take bribes.

Bám-krang, *v*. to undermine.

Bâm kwâi ha ing U Blei, *phr*. (*lit*.) to eat betel nut in the house of God. This is a form of speech among the Khasis whenever they happen to make mention of a departed relative or friend.

Ba-met, *a*. full (said of tubers and fruits).

Bâm-ngem, *adj*. one who commits secret faults. [*Imit*. bamngem-bamsáp.]

Bâm-hynroh-u-bnai, *kaba*, *n*. eclipse of the moon.

Bâm-hynroh-ka-sngi, *kaba*, *n*. eclipse of the sun.

Bâm-ja-khluit, *v*. (*lit*. to eat scalding cooked rice) hence to be too hasty in doing a thing.

Bám-jajah, *v*. to take cold rice, to have a mid-day meal.

Bâm-jasngi, *v*. to take tiffin or mid-day meal.

Bâm-ñiang-iap, *kaba*, *n*. a disease which attacks the under part of the toes, supposed to be caused by sand getting between the cleavage.

Bâm-ñiangriej, *v*. to be wormeaten (said of fruits).

*Bamon, *n*. a Brahmin.

Bâmpong, *kaba*, *n*. cancer, scrofula.

Bâmplan, *v*. to live from hand to mouth.

Bâmram, *v*. to live in debt, to incur debt. [*Imit*. bamram-bam-shah.]

Bâmrwing, *v*. to eat a thing (fruits, etc.) on the way for personal desire or necessity, [*e.g.*, a traveller who plucks fruits (from a grove belonging to others) on the way for eating there and then and not for taking them home or for selling is said to *bam-rwing*.]

* Hindi.

Bâmsap, *v.* to take bribes; to commit secret faults.

Bám-shiteng-kpoh, *v.* to take half a meal.

Bâmsih, *v.* to eat bad things (*e.g.* the flesh of dead animals, of dogs, etc.).

Bâmtyngka, *v.* to take bribes.

Bâm-tyllan, *v.* to devour; to eat without throwing away anything of it, to eat wholly [as, in the case of a fowl—without throwing away the entrails or feathers.]

Bàn, *v.* to press upon, to treat cruelly, to oppress;—**ka, n.* a *bán* or mantra.

‡Bán, *ka, n.* a dam; a bund.

Ba'n=sign of *Inf. to*;—*prep.* to, in order that.

Ba'n ia, *phr.* rather than.

*Banat, *ka, n.* a woollen cloth. [*Imit.* ka banat-ka patu.]

Ban budkhia, *v.* to stitch.

Bandari, *u, n.* a revenue official in Jaiǹtia Hills in the time of the late Rajas of Jaintia.

*Bandobos, *v.* to make arrangements; to settle.

Bania, *u, n.* a goldsmith.

Banse, *v.* (used negatively) obliged to, to have no other alternative (as, u'm *banse*=he is obliged).

Bàn-snaiap, *kabo, n.* incubus.

Bañiun, *ka, n.* a bog.

Baphoi, *a.* vindictive, captious, easily offended.

Bapli, *a.* pitiable, poor.

'bá-pynthor, *u, n.* lowland rice.

Bár, *ka, n.* outside, surface,—*phr.* leit-*bár*=to answer the call of nature.

*Baranda, *ka, n.* verandah.

*Barandi, *ka, n.* a long cloak; brandy (wine).

†Barobakhor, *u, n.* spices.

*Barobor, *ad.* always, incessantly.

Baroh, *a.* all, every;—*phar*, every one, entirely.

Basa, *u, n.* a village-deity;—*ka, n.* a standing in a market place, a stall,—*adv.* as a lodger, as in the words shong*basa*, thiah*basa*. *u Rynkew-u-basa*, a village deity.

---

* Hindi. | † Bengali. | ‡ English.

Basan, *u*, *n*. a state official in the Khasi Hills; a petty village official in the Jaintia Hills.

Bashala, *a*. not straight, crooked (of planks).

Bashia, *a*. to be particular in the choice of food; fastidious.

Bashla, *v*. to be dazzled.

Basli, *ka*, *n*. a flute.

Bat, *v*. to hold, to catch hold of, to grasp.

'bat, *u*, *n*. (*abbrev*. of kynbat) weed; medicinal plant.

'bat-iambâit *u*, *n*. the sensitive plant.

'Batabak, (shata), *ka*, *n*. a leaf-umbrella.

Batai, *v*. to explain, to make clear. [*Imit* batai-satai.]

*Bato, *v*. to distribute.

Batip, *ad*. knowingly (often ironically, as, u kren *batip*). [*Imit*. batip-banang.]

Batip sngi, *a*. good, well-behaved. [*Imit*. batipsngi-tipnong.]

Bed (same as bet).

†Beng, *ka*, *n*. a big frog.

Beh, *v*. to send away, to expel, to pursue, to seek; as, a *prefix* = about to (as in the words, *beh*shoh, *beh*leh, *beh*thok).

Behbeiñ, *v*. to drive or persecute wrongly. [*Imit*. behbeiñ-beh-khoh.]

Behkha-behman, *a*. helpful to neighbours in time of need.

Behdiengkhlam, *ka*, *n*. a Synteng annual festival to drive away pestilence (cholera).

Behmrâd, *v*. to hunt after wild animals (so also, beh-skei, beh khiat, beh-dngiem, etc.). [*Imit*. behmrad-behmreng.]

Behnongshohnoh, *v*. to pursue in order to murder for the propitiation of *u Thlen*. [*Imit*. behnongshohnoh- behnongshohtuh.]

Behsbâi, *v*. to go about collecting debts.

Behshnong, *v*. to excommunicate (from the village). [*Imit*. behshnong-behtháw.]

Behshoh, *v*. to threaten to beat. [*Imit*. behshoh-behdat.]

Bei, *v*. to help with money,—*ka*, *n*. mother (Synteng).

*Be-ijot (leh), *v*. to dishonour.

*Bei-man (same as b'ymman), *adv*. falsely, untrustworthily.

Beiñ, *v*. to scorn, to despise, to challenge;—*adv*. scornfully, contemptuously, cruelly [as, leh *beiñ*.]

Beiñ-shyntur, *v*. to make a mouth.

---

* Hindi. | † Bengali.

Beit, *a.* straight, right ;—*adv.* uprightly ;—*v.* to agree.

†Bela, *ka, n.* a violin.

‡Ben, *ka, n.* bench, —. *u soh,*—a kind of fruit the kernel of which is cooked and eaten.

Bér, *v.* to sprinkle powder.

Bèr, *adv.* like a flash [as, "nga ioh-i ia ka hamar ba ka bá ka lei-lieh *bèr.*"]

Bet, *v.* to sow ;—*u, n.* sedge ;—also a word put at the end of a sentence and is equivalent to "let me see" [as, "u'n leh a-iu *bet.*"]

Bet-dier, *v.* to be late in the season to sow, late sowing.

Bet-lap, *v.* to sow a seed early in the season.

Bha, *ad.* well ; good, better.

Bhabriew, *a.* beautiful, pretty.

*Bhang, *u, n.* bhang, Indian wild hemp ;—(*khie-*) *v.* to become mad, as from the effect of *bhang.*

Bhah, *ka, n.* share.

†Bhai, *u, n.* a friend.

Bhamet, *a.* healthy, having a good constitution.

Bhár, *ka, n.* a number containing thirty-two (in counting fruits at Cherra and other bazars).

Bha-sngi, *a.* lucky.

Bhek, *ad.* heavily, (as, hap *bhek,* buh *bhek*).

Bhoh, *v.* to desire impudently.

Bhoi, *n.* the inhabitant of the northern lowlands of the Khasi and Jaintia Hills ; an ignorant man.

Bhuk-bhak, *ad.* confusedly (as, ki la bred *bhuk-bhak* la ki jingkit).

Bhum-bham, *ad.* with confusion of noises [as, "nga shu sngew da ka jingsawa *bhum-bham* jong u paitbah."]

Bhur, *ka, n.* (goes along with *pang*) epilepsy ;—*a.* one of a herd (said of wild boars).

*Bhut, *u, n.* a ghost, evil spirit. [*Imit.* u bhut-u soitán.]

Bhut-bhat, *ad.* instantly (as, bam *bhut-bhat*).

†Bia, *v.* to marry.

Biang, *a.* enough,—*ad.* again, a second time ; in peace [as, "khie iaid *biang* ho."]

---

* Hindi. | † Bengali. | ‡ English.

Biangbiang, *ad.* carefully [as, leh *biang biang.*]

Biah, *v.* to spit; to change; to return the excess money in a barter;—*n. ka,* a bundle of 60 *pán* or betel-leaves.

Biahphongrâi, *v.* to infect, to taint, to lay eggs on flesh (by a fly).

Biah-tympew, *v.* to apply a little quantity of lime to a *pan*-leaf folded.

Biar, *ka, n.* a wall (*ekra*); girth.

Biat, *v.* to eat a little at a time (of small pulses).

Bikrompakhiah, *ka, n.* a very large eagle (fabulous).

†Bidesi, *ad.* to a foreign land [as, "bun ki Khasi kiba shongsang ki leit *bidesi.*"]

Bidong, *v.* to be strict;—*ad.* strictly, without indulgence [as, "balei phi kren *bidong* eh ia ki khun."]

Bieit, *a.* foolish, disabled, dumb. [*Imit.* babieit-ba anna.] Same as *biej.*

Bih, *ka, n.* poison.

Bijai, *v.* to become worthless; —*bijaiei, ad.* in vain, for nought.

*Bijâr, *a.* sorrowful, grievous;—*v.* sorry.

*Bilat, *ka, n.* England; Europe.

Bili, *u, n.* an iron instrument for lifting a cooking vessel from the fire; an instrument for punishing criminals, leg-chain. [*Imit.* u bili-u kynda.]

‡Bim, *u. n.* a beam;—*ad.* heavily (as the fall of big timbers or stones), [as, "u maw u hap *bim* hapoh um."]

Bin, *ad.* carefully (to pick), [as, "wat leh khlemakor, da tam *bin* ia ki sohkhawja."]

Bin-bin, *n.* an atom;—*ad.* very small. [As, "ki symbai kiba rit *bin-bin.*"]

Binong-bishon (khun-), *a.* good, noble.

†Bir, *ka, n.* a marsh, a lake.

Bira-biri, *a.* to be in confusion.

Biria, *ad.* jokingly [as, "wat bitar haba nga kren *biria.*"] [*Imit.* biria-birâi].

‡Biskit, *u, n.* a biscuit.

†Biskurom, *u. n.* god of all arts; a Khasi Vulcan.

*Bishâr, *v.* to judge;—*n.* legal proceedings. [*Imit.* bishar-khadar.]

Bishni, *v.* to be envious.

---

* Hindi. | † Bengali. | ‡ English.

*Bisti, *u. n.* a water-carrier, a *bhisti.*

Bit, *a.* fit, proper ;—*v.* to stick ; to resemble.

Bitar, *a.* angry.

Blab-blab (*kren*), *ad.* to jabber.

Blád, *a.* tasteless, unpalatable.

Blait, *ad.* through, across (as, mih *blait*).

Bláit-bláit, (lieh-), *ad.* bloodlessly (white).

Blang, *n.* goat.

Blang-u-bhed, *u, n.* collective name for sacrificial articles brought by ryots to the Nongkrem annual puja. (Bhed=quota of *pan* leaves).

Blar-blar, *ad.* pale [as, "balei ka khmat ka lieh *blar blar* kumne ?"]—*a.* not tasty, colourless, (as, "u shet *blar-blar* ia ka jyntah").

Bláw, (sngew-), *v.* feel lonely.

Blei, *n.* God, a god. [*Imit.* ki blei-ki-dken.]

Blei-thâw, *u, n.* an idol, an image.

Bliat-bliat, *ad.* altogether, completely (as, khoh *bliat-bliat*).

Blir-blir *ad.* pale (as, stem *blir-blir*).

Bloit, *v.* to fall off;—*ad.* suddenly and imperceptibly (as, mih *bloit*).

Blom-blom, *ad.* mutteringly [as, "ki briew ki iakren *blom blom.*"]

Bluit, *ad.* suddenly (as, mih *bluit*).

Blur, *ad.* through, from side to side (as, pei *blur*).

Bna, *v.* to hear, to be informed.

Bnâi, *u, n.* moon, month.

Bneng, *see* byneng.

Bniah, *see* byniah.

Bniap, *see* byniap.

Bniat, *see* byniat.

Bniej, *same* as byniej.

Bnoh, *u, n.* u purlin, a stick with a crooked head.

Bok, *ka, n.* luck. [*Imit.* ka bok-ka rwiang.]

*Bok-bok, *v.* to bother.

Bong-ang, *v.* to stand or sit astride, to straddle.

Bong-knang (raikhoh-, rit-), *ad.* lean and thin. [As, "i briew iba rit *bongknang.*"]

---

* Hindi.

Boh, *v.* to tie behind.

Bohkhaila, *ka, n.* a *dhoti* or a garment for the loins (worn by males).

Boi, *v.* to swarm, to be plentiful.

Boi-boi, *ad.* soft and coming off easily (as, lah *boi-boi*).

*Boina, *ka, n.* earnest or pledge money.

Boiñ-boiñ, *ad.* very soft, yielding (as, jem *boiñ-boiñ*).

Boit, *n.* a fabulous fairy of only a cubit in stature; a Lilliputian; a small boy in the Wár districts.

*Boitha, *ka, n.* a rudder.

‡Bôl, *ka, n.* ball; bowl.

Bór, *ka, n.* power, influence, authority. [*Imit.* ka bór-ka sór.]

§Borkapor, *ka, n.* a kind of coarse cotton cloth. (*Beng.* boro-kapor).

*Borkyndât, *u, n.* a guard for prisoners (from Barkandaz).

Borma, *u. n.* auger; a native of Burma.

*Borti, *ka, n.* a bucket;—*v.* to enlist.

Brah, *ka, n.* the upas tree.

Brái, *v.* like, fond of;—*u, n.* a kind of white mongoose.

Bràì, *ad.* asunder (of a string when snapped [as, "dkut *bràì* u jyrmi."]

Brám, *a.* poisonous (of fungi or fruits).

Bran (iaid), *ad.* quickly, briskly, in haste.

Bred, *v.* to throw away.

Bred-ei, *v.* to throw away as worthless.

Breiñ-breiñ, *ad.* falling softly like a drizzle.

Bri, *ka, n.* a grove, an estate, a farm. [*Imit.* ka bri-ka khyndew.]

Bria, *ad.* slightly, indistinctly (as, thoh *bria*).

Bri-kwái, *ka, n.* a betel-nut grove.

Brin, *ad.* as in a row (as *mih* brin).

Brisoh, *ka, n.* an orange grove (*lit.* fruit grove).

Briw, briew, *n.* a man, woman, person; (*i-*) the apple of the eye—*pl. ki briew*=people.

Broh, *ad.* pitted (generally goes along with *soh*).

Broi (soh), *u, n.* a kind of sour fruit.

---

* Hindi. | ‡ English. | § Assamese.

Broin, *ad.* spotted, (as, thoh *broin*).

Brop, *ad.* unexpectedly, gradually (as, hap *brop*).

Brop-brop, *ad.* in drops.

Brot, *ka, n.* bronze.

Bruh, *see* soh *bruh.*

Brûiñ, *ad.* with large spots (as, thoh *bruiñ*).

Brum-brum, *ad.* with heavy steps of a number of persons; [as iaid *brum-brum.*]

Bsa, *v.* to feed, to nourish. [*Imit.* bsa-btiah.]

Bsap, *v.* to hide, to mix with, to insert.

Bseiñ, *u, n.* a serpent. [*Imit.* ka bseiñ-ka mait.]

Bshád, *u, n.* a civet.

Bsiang, *ka, n.* coal tar, pitch.

Bsiap, *v.* to put between two things; to insert.

Bsiat kti, *v.* to fillip; to snap one's fingers at.

Bsiat-ksai, *v.* to mark a straight line with a thread.

Bsong, *n.* a ferret.

Bsuh, *v.* to push in, to intrude.

Bsut, *v.* to force a way through, to enter.

Bta, *v.* to wash the face, to besmear the face with.

Btái, *a.* weary, tired.

Btaj-btaj, } *ad.* muddily, soft and sticky. [As, "kane ka ja ka
Btej-btej, } jem *btaj-btaj.*"]

Btat, *ad.* snappishly, asunder (as, dykut *btat*).

Bteng, *v.* to join.

Btep, *v.* to cover with earth, to put under ground.

Btet, *a.* a taste like that of an unripe fruit; astringent.

Bthah, *v.* to send word to, to inform, to instruct. [*Imit.* bthah-bthing.]

Bthat, *v.* to break with the hands, to snap.

Bthei, *v.* to explode, to burst.

Bther, *ad.* at random [as, ki shu siat *bther.*]—*v.* to put additional ties.

Bthi, *a.* sticky (of fat).

Bthing, *ka, n.* wax.

Bthong, *n.* a hog-deer.

Bthuh, *a.* mouldy, gray.

Bti, *ka, n.* a kind of tree or wood of reddish colour called *poma* in Bengali.

Btiar, *v.* to feel a stinging pain.

Btin, *v.* to lead by the hand.

Btuid, *v.* to slip ;—*a.* slippery.

Btúr, *v.* to connect or link as a line of argument.

Bukhir, *a.* stingy, niggardly, parsimonious. [*Imit.* u bukhir-u sakhir.]

Bu-âid, *v.* to be intoxicated with liquor. [*Imit.* bu-aid-tang-lang.]

Bùk-bak, *ad.* as quick as possible [as, trei *buk-bak*].

Bûd, *v.* to follow, to imitate ;—*n.* a fold of a thread or rope, as shi-*bud*=one fold, ar*bud*=two-fold, etc.

†Budam, *u, n.* a button.

Bud-du, *u, n.* a carpenter's brace.

Búd-dien, *v.* to track, to follow, to scent.

Búd-markjat, *v.* to follow close to the heels.

Buh, *v.* to put, to place, to appoint.

Buhai, *v.* to provide ; to colonize.

Buhai-shnong, *v.* to colonise.

Buhbot, *v.* to be mindful, to devote one's attention to.

Buhbynda, *v.* to mortgage. [*Imit.* buhbynda-buhbyndop.]

Buhkam, *v.* to engage, to give employment. [*Imit.* buhkam-buh-jam.]

Buh-ktien, (ia-), *v.* to betroth. [*Imit.* buh ktien-buhthylliej.]

Buhkhoh, bukhoh, *ad.* disappointed, aggrieved [as, " u la sngew *bukhoh* shibun eh."]

Buh-ia, *v.* to appoint a time.

Buhnûd, *v.* to cherish revenge, to bear a grudge.

Buhrih, *v.* to hide. [*Imit.* buhrih-buhkai.]

Buh-sngi, *v.* to appoint a day, to postpone. [*Imit.* buhsngi-buh-ia.]

*Bu-iam, *u, n.* a jar (*esp.* one made of porcelain).

Búid, *a.* itching, exciting.

---

* Hindi. | † Bengali.

Buiñ, *v.* to suck.

Búiñ-báiñ, *ad.* with grimaces, contortively, [as, "khih ka khmat *buiñ-baiñ*"].

Buit, *ka, n.* cunningness, cleverness, scheme. [*Imit.* ka-buit-ka-akor.]

Buitti, *a.* inclined to stealing. [*Imit.* buit-ti-buit-jat.]

†**Bujai,** *v.* to explain.

Bula, *u, n.* a mask ; a masquerader.

Bulor, bilor, *u, n.* a bottle.

Bún, *a.* many, much.

Bùn, *u, n.* burnt turf for manure.

Bûn-ktien, *a.* talkative, loquacious.

Bûnshah, *ad.* many times as much.

Bûnsien, *ad.* often, many times.

Búr, *v.* to creep or catch (like fire from one grassy plot to another).

Bùr, *ka, n.* a raft.

Buria, *v.* to give compensation for.

Burom, *ka, n.* honour, glory ;—*v.* to honour. [*Imit.* ka burom-ka surom.

***Buskit,** *ka, n.* gift, a present.

Bydi, *ka, n.* twenty (used in counting fire-wood, etc. same as *bdi*).

Bylla, *v.* to work as a day-labourer ;—*ad.* right through (pierced) [as, "pei *bylla* u khnam."]

Byllai, *ad.* in great numbers, (as, bun *byllai*).

Bylliang, (at-), *ad.* having the marks of stripes. [As, "u sympat ha ba'n da at *bylliang*."]

Bylliat, *ka, n.* a kind of hard wood.

Byllien, *ad.* very numerously, (as, iaid *byllien*).

Byllûd, *v.* to pass so as just to touch anything, to rub gently, to graze.

Byllûn, *ad.* bulgingly, like a cramp, (as, at *byllun*).

B'ym, *phr.* that...not, because it is not. (It is a contraction of ba + ym.)

B'ymdei, *a.* improper, not right. (Ba + ymdei.)

B'ymjukut, *a.* eternal.

B'ymlér, *a.* good for nothing.

---

* Hindi. | † Bengali.

Byna, *v.* to hear, to be informed, (same as *bna*).

Bynái, *u*, *n.* the moon, a month, (same as *bnai*).

Bynda, *ka*, *n.* mortgaged article. [*Imit.* bynda-byndop.]

Byndi, *v.* to mortgage. [*Imit.* byndi-byndop]—*ka*, *n.* a prison.

Byneng, *ka*, *n.* the heaven, the sky, (same as *bneng*).

Bynhei, *u*, *n.* contribution for sacrifice (used along with the word *synñiang*).

Byniah, *ad.* fastidiously, carefully, [same as *bniah*, as, leh *bniah.*]

Byniap, *ka*, *n.* a bush, a thicket, (same as *bniap*).

Byniat, *ka*, *n.* tooth (same as *bniat*).

Byniat-hati, *ka*, *n.* the tusk of an elephant, ivory.

Byniej, *ka*, *n.* a square fish-net drawn by one person and tied from the four corners to a pole, (same as *bniej*).

Byñiup-byñiup, *a.* drizzling (used with '*lap*).

Bynñiaw, *ad.* peevishly, mournfully, (as, leh *bynñiaw*).

Bynoh, *u*, *n.* a pole, a stick with a crooked end;—*a.* curved, bent.

Bynnûd, *v.* to regret.

Bynrap, *v.* to side with, to place together with.

Bynriew, *u*, *n.* human being;—*ad.* in good condition, sound. [As, "mynta ba phi la nang bám te la i *bynriew* bad kumne keiñ phin nang shait irat."]

Bynshet, *v.* to let down a load.

Bynta, *ka*, *n.* a portion, a share, a lot.

Bynthiew, *v.* to spit with violence.

Byr, when used with Adjective=suf.—*ish*, (as, *byr*saw=reddish, *byr*iong=blackish).

Byrdáw, *ka*, *n.* a she-demon, supposed to cause convulsive fits.

Byrngem, *v.* to threaten, to menace. [*Imit.* byrngem-byrngit.]

Byrngia, *a.* to be liking, to be pleasing;—*v.* to while away the time.

Byrngiang, *a.* bitterish (like quinine).

Byrngut, *a.* dusky, evening, murky.

Byrngut-byrnget, *ad.* dimly, indistinctly, (as, shai *byrngut-byrnget*).

Byrhai, *ad.* many and in order, (as, shong *byrhai*).

Byrhien, *ad.* many and in order, (as, iaid *byrhien*).

Byrhuiñ, *ad.* reddish, [as, u soh u saw *byrhuin*].

Byr-ie, *a.* dim, impaired, amblyopic (used with *khmat* to denote imperfect eyesight).

Byr-iong, *a.* blackish.

Byrnep, *ad.* thick with, (as, rben *byrnep*).

Byrni, *ka*, *n.* a sack, a coarse bag. [*Imit.* byrni-byrkhew.]

Byrni-dong, *ka*, *n.* a small sack ; a gunny bag.

Byrshem, *v.* to push in the faggots, to abut, to join together, to come in contact.

Byrship, *a.* knock-kneed.

Byrsieh, *a.* defiling ;—*u*, *n.* a god who presides over or superintends defilement.

Byrta, *ka*, *n.* a notice, an announcement.

Byrtháp, *ka*, *n.* a plank partition.

Byrthen, *v.* to rage (like a big fire), to threaten loudly ; to vociferate.

Byrthiew *or* **pyrthiew**, *u*, *n.* parched pulses ;—*kaba-*, *n.* eruptions.

Byrthit, *a.* fastened to, clinging, viscous.

Byrthit peisa, *a.* niggardly, hard to bring out money for payment ; miserly.

Byrthup, *a.* greyish.

Byrtia, *a.* stingy, hard to pay one's dues.

Byrtong, *ad.* as a sorcerer, (as, kren *byrtong*).

Byrtun-byrten, *ad.* long and entwining, [as, " balei ka met ka at *byrtun-byrten*."]

Bythat, *v.* to snap, (same as *bthat*).

K.

K, the third letter in the Khasi Alphabet.

Ka, *art.* a, an, the ; a sign of the Feminine or Neuter Gender,—she, it. It is also a word put at the end of a sentence for the sake of euphony, [as, " phi'm shim balei *ka*."]

K'a, *ka*, *n.* a Simul tree (see *kya*).

Kaba, 1. *p.* who, which, what ; 2. (*prefix*) used before verbs and Adjectives to form Abstract Nouns meaning *that which is* ; as, *kaba* saw, *kaba* bha.

***Kabáb**, *ka*, *n.* roasted flesh.

Kaba-kái, *n.* plaything, sport, sham, not rea..

---

* Hindi.

Kabo, *v*, to request, solicit importunately (Synteng origin).

Kabu, *ka*, *n*. good luck, opportunity.

‡Kak, *u*, *n*. a cork.

Kâd, *v*. to tear, to rend ;—*ka*, *n*. a place of meeting, a harbour.

*Kada, *ka*, or *u*, *n*. an ass.

Kadiang, *ka*, *n*. left hand, left hand side.

Kâdjatdoh, *kaba*, *n*. cracks on the underpart of the toes.

Kâdlongbneng, *v*. to shoot upward (with an arrow).

Kâd-shyntur, *kaba*, *n*. hare-lip.

Kaei ? *p*. who ? what ?

Kaei-kaei, *n*. a thing, anything.

Kaei-kaei-ruh-em, *phr*. nothing at all.

Kaei-re-kaei, *phr*. something or other, (we know not).

Kang, *v*. to jet out.

K'ang, *v*. to cry, to scream. (Another form of *kyang*.)

Kangár, *a*. gluttonous.

Kah, *v*. to shade, to darken, to screen.

Kahait, }
Kahap, } *v*. to attempt to bite, to snap at.

Kâi, *ad*. for pleasure, for fun, (as, leh *kai*).

*Kaia, *n*. a Marwari.

Kaibri, *ka*, *n*. motions, stools; evacuations.

Kái-khlâw, *v*. to conduct a guerilla warfare.

Kái-kynthei, *a*. licentious.

Kâin, *ka*, *n*. a kind of tree—the bark of which produces eruptions on the skin.

'kâin (*abbrev*. of skain), *u*, *n*. a fly.

'kâin-dait, *u*, *n*. a mosquito.

'kâin-iong, *u*, *n*. a meat-fly.

Kait, *ka*, *n*. a plantain, a banana ; (*Synteng*) scissors.

*Kalai, *u*, *n*. *Matikalai* ;—*v*. to tin.

Kaláiñ, *v*. to whirl round (as with a torch), wield ; wag.

Kalaw, }
Kalew, } *v*. to bite without any success (as with the gums).

---

* Hindi. | ‡ English.

*Kali, *ka*, *n.* a carriage.

Kali-bordi, *ka*, *n.* a bullock-cart.

*Kam, *ka*, *n.* work, necessity, need, [*Imit.* ka kam-ka jam];—*v.* to claim.

Kám, *v.* to stride, to pass over, (same as *jâm*).

Ka'm, *phr.* she or it...... not, (contraction of *ka*+*ym*).

Kamai, *ka*, *n.* income, living. [*Imit.* kamai-kajih];—*v.* to labour, to work for.

Kamai-khynrâw, *ka*, *n.* what one earns while unmarried.

*Kaman, (shong-), *v.* to be on duty in an outpost.

†Kamar, *u*, *n.* a blacksmith.

Kam-bah, *ka*, *n.* a miracle ; a big concern. [*Imit.* kambah-kamsan.]

Kam-karikor, *ka*, *n.* mechanical works.

Kamon, *ka*, *n.* right hand side.

Kamon-u kadiang, *u*, *n.* neighbours.

Kamra, *ka*, *n.* a room.

Kam-ram, *ka*, *n.* duty.

Kamra-shongkái, *ka*, *n.* a drawing-room.

Kam-shnong-kam-tháw, *ka*, *n.* politics.

Kan, *v.* to reserve, to suppress, to hold, to keep silent.

Ka'n, *phr.* she will, it will or shall.

K'an, *v.* to hold one's breath, to bear down, to strain. This is an abbreviated form of *kyan*.

Kane, *a.* this.

§Kani, *ka*, *n.* opium ; a number containing 40 × 10 = 400 (betel nuts).

Kano ? *p.* which ?

*Kano-kano, *p.* any one, any.

Kàp, *u*, *n.* a prong ;—*v.* to join in friendship, to match—invariably preceded by the word *ia* (as, *ia-kap*).

*Kaphur, *u*, *n.* camphor.

‡Kaptan, *u*, *n.* a captain (same as *Koptán*).

Kár, *v.* to stir with, mix with, (said of rice when mixed and cooked with some other grains).

---

* Hindi. | † Bengali. ‡ English. | § Assamese.

Kara, *v.* to earth up.
*Karai, *ka, n.* an iron cooking vessel (for currie).
Karo, *n.* the Garo.
‡Karod, *ka, n.* garrison, guard, guard house.
Karta, *n.* age (more correctly *ka rta*).
‡Kartus, *u, n.* a cartridge.
*Kashari, ka ing ka shari,—*n.* court-house, kutcherry.
Katai, *a.* that in sight but at a distance.
Katba, *ad.* while, as much as.
Katba long, *phr.* be as it may, come what may.
Katei, *a.* that (up there), the said, the aforesaid.
Kathie, *a.* that (down there), the following.
Katne, *ad.* this much.
Katne katne, *ad.* as much as this, so much.
Katno, *ad.* how much ? how many ?
Katno-katno, *ad.* however much.
Katta, *ad.* so much.
Katta katta, *ad.* to such an extent.
Kattei, *ad.* so much (up).
Kattai, *ad.* that much, (referring to a thing at some distance).
Katthie, *ad.* so much (down).
Katto, *ad.* that much (near you).
Katto-katne, *phr.* some, more or less, a certain amount.
Kâw, *ka, n.* a number=1,280 ; (in address) I say, Ho ! hear me.
Kawang, *v.* to throw.
Kâw-kâw, (ia-), *v.* to make a noise or clamour.
Káw-káw-dáw-dáw, *ad.* clamorously ;—*v.* to make a clamour.
Kaweh, *v.* to fan, to wave.
Kawei, *a.* one, certain.
Kawei ka-ar, *p.* some other.
Kawei-pat, *p.* another, other.
Kawiat, *v.* to beat with something small, to lash.
Káw-shiliang-káw-arliang, *ka, n.* a fine.

---

* Hindi. | ‡ English.

Kawut, *v.* same as *kawiat.* (An onomatopœtic form).

Kba, *u, n.* paddy, unhusked rice. [*Imit.* u kba—u khaw.]

Kbâin, *v.* to scatter, to besmear with, (as a little child when eating food).

Kbeit, *u, n.* a kind of hawk.

Kber, *u, n.* a winged white ant.

Kbia, }
Kbong, } *v.* to clutch, to claw.

Kbin-kbin, *a.* small and well cut.

Kboh, *v.* to scratch.

Kbum, *v.* to close up the lips, to shut up, to keep something in the mouth.

Kdang, *v.* to have enough (of food), to feel satisfied, to be replete.

Kdait, *u, n.* reed or ekra.

Kdam, *ad.* violently, with a slam, (as, "u khang *kdam* ia ka jingkhang").

Kdar, *ad.* brightly, brilliantly, [as, "ka bneng ka la rang *kdar* mynta."]

Kdat, *v.* to turn sharp to another direction.

Kdew, *v.* to point out or direct (with the hand).

Kdiah, *v.* to break, to snap (with the hand).

Kdiap, *v.* to walk cautiously, to stalk game.

Kdier, *v.* to straddle(bad sense).

Kdiar, *ad.* transparently, uncloudedly, (said of water or weather).

Kdik-kdik, *ad.* throbbingly, (as, "ka mynsiem ka khih *kdik-kdik*"); longingly, [as " u kwah *kdik kdik* ban ioh-i ia phi"].

Kding-kdang, *ad.* at all, sincerely (used negatively); as, " ngam tip *kding-kdang* ia u."

Kdong, *ka, n.* a corner; an opportunity.

Kdór, *v.* to bend, to curl.

Kdup, *v.* to embrace; to defend.

Keh-keh, *ad.* stammeringly.

'kei, *n.* (*abbrev.* of skei), a barking deer.

'kei-sop, *u, n.* a roe-buck.

Keiñ, (an intensifying particle)=that's it;—*v. imper.* enough, that is all.

Kein-noh, *v.* enough;—*ad.* very (coloquial), [as, " ka jingrunar kaba la *kein-noh.*"]

Kem, *v.* to arrest, to seize; to wrestle; to resemble—when preceded by *ia* ; tending to, showing the signs of, [as, *kem*-synrai, showing the signs of autumn, so also *kem*-tlang, *kem*-pyrem, *kem*-lyiur.]

Kem-*bikâr, *v.* to impress coolies, to arrest indiscriminately.

Kem-ka-lâr, *ka, n.* (poojah term) pieces of broken egg-shell which lie on the left or right hand side of the central biggest broken egg-shell called *ka lieng.*

Kem-khap, *ka, n.* a kimkhap (cloth).

Kem ksûid, *v.* to be affected by evil spirits.

Kem-ktien, *v.* to interrupt, to rejoin.

Kem-iong-rciñ, *kaba, n.* dusk.

Kem-pang, *v.* to become ill.

Kem-puri, *v.* to become ill by the influence of a fairy.

Kêr, *v.* to surround, to enclose.

Kér-kut, *v.* to surround completely; to erect a fort or stockáde.

Kêr-dam, *v.* to hedge round leaving no opening.

Kew, *u. n,* wheat ;—(*voc.* case), husband's sister or brother's wife as addressed by the sister.

Kha, *v.* to give birth ;—*n.* relation from the father's side.

'kha (*case of address*), *i, n.* 1. a paternal aunt ; 2. (*abbrev.* of *doh-kha*), fish.

'khabniang, *u, n.* a pipe-fish.

'khabysein, *u, n.* eel (small).

Khak, *ad.* tightly, firmly, [as, "u bat *khak* na ka kti."]

Kha-ki-man, *ki, n.* neighbours, not being members of one's clan.

Khad, *v.* to shovel ;—*khád,* to perform a sacrifice for the repulsion of an evil-sprit.

Khad-âr, *a.* twelve.

Khad-âr-blang, *ka, n.* the name of a part of the Khyrim State in the Wár country.

Khad-âr-bongthai, *ka, n.* a portion of the Kamrup district on the Khasi Hills border and formerly under the subjection of the Khasis.

---

* Hindi.

Khad-âr-kur, *ki*, *n*. the twelve electoral clans of the Cherra State.

'kha-dki, *ka*, *n*. one of the pieces of fish fried and preserved in closed jars.

Khadduh, *ad.* lastly. [*Imit.* khadduh-khadwai] ;—*a*. youngest, last.

Khat, } *ad*. but, I see (used as a sort of digressive expression),
Khad-ei, } [as, "Phi ong u'm don *khad-ei*, u don du".]

Khad-ja, *v*. to serve out boiled rice. [*Imit.* khadja-khadjhur.]

Khadlâi, *a*. thirteen.

Khâd-tyr-ut, *v*. to drive away an evil-spirit called ka "Tyrut" by means of sacrifices ; to shun, to dislike. [*Imit.* khad-da-ka-tyr-ut-da-ka-smer.]

Khadu, *ka*, *n*. bracelet.

Khang, *v*. to shut, to hinder, to forbid, to prohibit.

'khang, *u*, *n*. (*abbrev.* of tyrkhang) fern.

Khangai, *kà*, *n*. the yolk of an egg.

Khangkdong, *v*. to corner, to surround. [*Imit.* khangdong-khang-lád.]

Khangkhái, (peit), *v*. to scan, to have an eye on, to scrutinize.

Khangkhnam, *v*. (in an archery contest) to prevent an arrow from hitting the target by invoking some deities.

'khangksiar, *u*, *n*. the golden fern.

'khangnar, *u*, *n*. a kind of fern, a tree-fern.

Khah, *u*, *n*. reed ;—*a*. close, thickly set ; to be tainted with (blood, dust, etc.),—*ad*. very often ; [as, "Phim ju kham shem *khah* ia ki dieng kseh shaphang Sohra."]

Khái, *v*. to pluck with the nail.

Kha-ii, *v*. to trade, to buy and sell. [*Imit.* kha-ii-pateng.]

Kháiñ, *a*. rough, coarse.

Khàin, *a*. stunted.

Khaiñshi, *ka*, *n*. scissors ; truss.

Khairim, *ka*, *n*. the Nongkrem State.

Kháit, *u*, *n*. ring-worm ; *ia-*, equal (match), ending in a draw.

Khàit, *ad*. entirely, at once, [as, "u la bam lut *khait*."] [*Imit.* khait-khiej.]

Khait-khait, *a* very poor ; no margin to leave, [as, "u briew u long uba duk *khait-khait*."]

*Khajanshi, *u*, *n.* a treasurer.

†Khala-khala, *ad.* immediately, at once, (as, "wan *khala khala*").

Khalah, *v.* to throw up as with a shovel.

Khal̲âi, *v.* to gamble, to play ; to throw the dice.

Khalâi-wait, *v.* to display one's skill in the wielding of a sword.

Khalas, *v.* to let loose ; to dismiss, to get discharged.

*Khalasi, *u*, *n.* coolies sent to a distance, especially those used for expeditions.

Khalki, *ka*, *n.* a window.

Khalek, *v.* to dance round and round a group of dancing damsels (by men only).

*Khali, *a.* vacant.

*Khalisha, *ka*, *n.* a carpet.

Khalor, *v.* to give birth prematurely, to have an abortion.

Kham, *v.* to close the fist ;—*adj. comp. deg.* corresponding to the *English adj.* ending in *-er* ; more. (As, *kham*bha=better, *kham*jrong=taller.)

†Khamakha, *ad.* without reason ; for nothing.

Khambynriew, *a.* better off.

Kham katto-katne, *a.* considerable (number, quantity, time).

Kham-kynrei, *a.* more abundant.

Khamtam, *ad.* more especially.

Khamti, *ka*, *n.* a measurement from the elbow to the end of the little finger of the closed hand (*i.e.*, about 13 inches).

†Kha-mukur, *u*, *n.* small fish. (*Beng.* magul-mash).

Khan, *v.* to think out ; to consult the spirits by means of an egg, rice, stone, etc.

*Khanasamari, *ka*, *n.* house-tax list, census.

Khanatang, *v.* to relate one's personal experiences ; to recount, to rehearse.

Khan-ktem, *v.* to divine as to the track of hunted game.

Khañia, *a.* stingy, hard to pay off one's dues.

Khanpylleng, *v.* to divine by breaking an egg with a grain of rice.

Khanryntich, *v.* to divine by the swing of a bow.

Khan-shanam, *v.* to divine by the swing of the lime-case.

---

* Hindi. | † Bengali.

Khap, *ka*, *n*. a big drain in a *hali* land or a ditch round a fence; border, side.

Khap, *v*. to fasten, to close; to border on, to gripe.

Khap (bám), *v*. to partake of a feast given to the surrounding land-holders for witnessing the sale of land. [*Imit*. bamkhap-bam-khúm.]

Khap-bria, *a*. having partially closed eyes.

Khapngiah, *a*. crammed, overfull. [*Imit*. khapngiah-khap-uiñ.]

'khapiah, *ka*, *n*. a kind of dried fish. [*Imit*. 'khapiah-khadaiñ.]

Khapnap, *a*. close-fisted, niggardly; hard to part with one's money. [*Imit*. khapnap-khapbit.]

–Khaprip, *v*. to close the eyes; to wink.

†Khár, *ka*, *n*. a mixture of the ashes of burnt plantain folds with some other things used by the Bhoi people to salt their curry.

Khár, *v*. to gather, to pick up; to have looseness of the bowels.

'khar, (*abbrev*. of dkhar), *n*. a foreigner from the plains; one of the clans among the Khasis bearing that name, *e.g.* 'Khar-kongor, 'Khar-ngap-kynta, 'Khar-sawian, 'Khar-shi-iing, etc.

Khara, *a*. of the same good size.

Kharabak, *u*, *n*. the fever-demon.

'kharang, *ka*, *n*. a roasted fish.

Kharâi, *ka*, *n*. a ditch, a trench.

'khar-alot, *u*, *n*. merchant from the plains (on the Sylhet side) who buys wholesale goods from the hill-men, especially potatoes.

'kharkâw, *n*. a villager of the plains, (*lit*. one who lives in a *Gaon*). [*Imit*. kharkaw-kharkor.]

Kharkhar, *ad*. harshly (onomatopoetic), [as, "u kren eh *kharkhar*."]

Khar-kpoh, *kaba*, *n*. diarrhœa or looseness of the bowels.

Khariew, *u*, *n*. a kind of wild climbing plant used for poisoning fish; *Beng*. *Bislot*;—(*Bot*.) *Milletia Pacchycarpa* (*Bth*.).

Kharoi, *v*. to multiply, to increase in population.

Kharpâid, *n*. men mustered for an occasion.

Kharsohlah, *i*, *n*. a dwarf.

†Khas, *ka*, *n*. a land which has not been brought under a regular settlement, a waste land.

* Hindi. | † Bengali.

'kha-sáw, *ka*, *n*. a very common fish in the streams of the Khasi and Jaintia Hills.

Khaseng, *u*, *n*. a species of reed.

*Khashór, *ka* or *u*, *n*. a mule.

*Khashra, *a*. imperfect; preliminary, rough;—*ka*, *n*. a land which borders on the plain districts.

Khasi, *n*. an inhabitant of the Khasi Hills. [*Imit*. u Khasi-u-Khara.]

'khas'ing, 'khasying, } *ka*, *n*. dried fish pounded and mixed with ginger.

Khasynrop, *v*. to give birth to twins; to be twin-born.

Khat, *conj*. but, (*see* khad-ei);—*v*. to drive away devils by divination, as, khát-tyr-ut.

*Khate, *v*. to deduct.

Khat-ei, *conj*. see khad-ei.

Khat-um, *v*. to massage by using water and oil.

Kha-u-man, *u*, *n*. one related by marriage.

Khâw, *u*, *n*. unboiled rice; unhusked rice. [*Imit*. khaw-u-kba.]

Khawa, *v*. to ferry.

†Khawai, *v*. to feast, to entertain. [*Imit*. khawai-dawai.]

Khawait, Khwait, } *v*. to ply the hands like a duck while swimming, to paddle.

Khaw-khaw-daw-daw, *a*. penniless, very poor.

Kháwdúh (ai-), *v*. to outcast (see *kynther jymbuin*). [*Imit*. khawduh-khawtan.]

Kháw-eit, *v*. to be afraid of.

Kháw-iang, *u*, *n*. a certain plant used in fermentation, fermented liquor—(*dei*-), *phr*. affected with wine.

Khawiah, *v*. to reach at and to pull a thing by means of a long stick (such as a rubber ball that has fallen in a well and that cannot be reached with the hand).

Khawoh, *v*. to bale out (water); to bring down or drag a thing with some crooked instrument.

Khawoit, *v*. to beckon with the hand; to paddle.

Kháw-ot, *kaba*, *n*. rice not properly boiled.

---

* Hindi. | † Bengali.

Kháw-pet, *u, n.* rice purchased with money as distinguished from that collected from the field.

Kháwpûd, *a.* cowardly, timid.

Kháwpyrsit, *u, n.* fine particles of rice left after having been crushed and sifted; broken rice.

Khâw-rneng, *u, n.* rice carried to be used on the way.

***Khâwshira**, *u, n.* parched rice; (*Hind. chiwra*).

Khâwtyndep, *u, n.* rice of a yellowish colour supposed to have the power of stupefying people when thrown by the "Nongshohnoh" or Thlen-keepers.

Khek, *ad.* abruptly, suddenly; [as, u ieng *khek.*]

Khengkheng, *ad.* resistingly; [as, "u pyn-oh khengkheng."]

Kheiñ, *v.* to break; to reckon, to value; to have a regard for; to care.

Khein-ba'n khái, *v.* to propitiate the evil-spirits, (see *khein ksúid*).

Khein-briew, *v.* to have some regard for.

Khein-burom, *v.* to be dishonoured, to be put to shame. [*Imit.* kheinburom-kheinsurom.]

Kheiñ kôr, *v.* to value highly, to prize; to esteem.

Kheiñksûid, *v.* to find out by divination the devil who causes the disease or misfortune and to cure that disease or remove that misfortune by propitiating him. [*Imit.* kheinksuid-khein-khrei.]

Kheiñ-kupar, *v.* to be dishonoured.

Kheiñ-kyllûid, *v.* to make a liberal estimate of. [*Imit.* khein kylluid-khein kyrwa.]

Kheiñ-dewthala, *v.* to reckon as worthless.

Kheiñ-doh-ksew, *v.* to become obstinate or desperate.

Kheiñ-dohiap, *v.* to become desperate.

Kheiñ-dûh, *v.* to become reckless, to give oneself up as lost.

Kheiñ-poh, *v.* to under value, to under-rate; to look down upon.

Kheiñ-sbái, *v.* to give an account of an expenditure; to take into consideration (used with a negative expression; as, "nga'm shym *kheinsbai* ia phi.")

Kheiñ-snep, *v.* to care for (used with *ym*).

Kheit, *v.* to pluck, to gather.

†Khejur, *u, n.* date.

* Hindi | † Bengali.

Khem, *v.* to squeeze, to rub and press the body or limbs gently.

Khemdut, *v.* to milk.

Khemmet, *v.* to massage. [*Imit.* khem met-khem phád.]

Khér, *ka, n.* a stockade for capturing elephants; an enclosure for catching fish; a place or district.

*Kheshwan, *u, n.* a driver, a coachman.

Khet, *ka, n.* a throne. [*Imit.* ka khet-ka bishna.]—*v.* to cut down, to sever.

Khet-tiah, *v.* to cut the trees or bamboos and leave them to rot in the same place.

†Khi, *ka, n.* ghee;—*v.* to shave.

Khia, *a.* heavy,—*ad.* with a revengeful spirit, [as, "u la búhnúd *khia* ia u namar ba u la kren pynjah burom."]

Khiah, *a.* healthy. [*Imit.* khiah-nang.]

Khiah-krât, khiahksûid, *v.* to be in a very sound health.

*Khiar, *v.* to be mindful, to pay attention to.

Khiat, *ka, n.* a moss-deer.

Khia-thew, *a.* graceful, elegant, dignified.

Khie, *v.* (*imper.* only) go away; get up (from a recumbent position); to take place, to recur, (as, "La *khie* ka jingpang, la *khie* ka thma ha pdeng u Russia bad u Japan.")

Khie-bhang, *v.* to become mad as if from the effect of *bhang*.

Khie-bhur, *v.* to have epileptic fits.

Khie-ka rasong, *v.* to be fortunate, to be in the height of prosperity.

Khie-khlam, *v.* to become epidemic (used especially with reference to cholera).

Khie-khlieh, *v.* to keep one's head above water, (as "u la dap ram eh u'm lah *khie-khlieh* shuh").

Khie-khynrâw, *v.* to reach the age of maturity.

Khie-kieh, *v.* to stir up suddenly as if for action or on account of some impending danger, generally followed by "*buk.*"

Khie-kyllang, *v.* to be cyclonic.

Khie-ia-iong, *v.* to be stormy.

Khie-im, *v.* to revive; to rally.

Khie-lapeh, *v.* to have abundant leaves but without grain; to grow prematurely.

---

* Hindi. | † Bengali.

Khie-lung, *v.* to bring forth a new shoot.

Khie-rih, *v.* to be attacked with fever.

Khie-sammut, *v.* to have a fancy for; to be capriciously inclined to.

Khiesboh, *v.* to be unusually liberal or kind.

Khie-shoh, *v.* to have fever.

Khie-shylluit, *v.* to bud.

Khie-step, *v.* to rise early. [*Imit.* khie step-khie phyrngáp.]

Khiew, *u*, *n.* a vessel, a pot. [*Imit.* u khiew-u siang.]

'khiew, *u*, *n.* (*abbrev.* of dykhiew) ant, as, u "khiew seiñiong."

'khiew-diengbâi, *u*, *n.* a big red ant (generally living in a nest on a tree).

Khiewja, *u*, *n.* a pot for cooking rice. [*Imit.* khiewja-khiew-jyntah.]

Khiewja-kâi, *i*, *n.* a toy used by children for cooking.

Khiewmutlop, *u*, *n.* (*lit.* an obstinate pot); a thick and wide-mouthed earthen vessel.

Khiewphiang, *u*, *n.* a brazen water vessel.

Khiew ranei, *u*, *n.* a black earthen vessel (so called from its being made in the village of Larnai or Larnei in the Jaintia Hills).

Khiewrynsong, *u*, *n.* another kind of brazen cooking pot.

'khiew-sâw, *u*, *n.* red ant.

'khiew seiñiong, *u*, *n.* a big black ant.

Khiewsla, *u*, *n.* a thin brazen cooking pot.

Khing, (ia-), *v.* to resist.

Khih, *v.* to start, to move, to shake. [*Imit.* khih-ksâr.]

Khih-lyngkhum, *v.* to be unrest by reason of excitement.

Khih map-map, *v.* to quiver.

Khi-lái-núid, *v.* to shave the head in three patches (this refers to a Khasi custom of punishing an evil-doer before his banishment from his country or village).

†Khilki, *ka*, *n.* (same as khalki).

Khilon, *ka*, *n.* an arch.

*Khilonshi, *ka*, *n.* a scaffolding.

Khim, *a.* narrow.

Khir *u*, *n.* a screw.

---

* Hindi. † Bengali.

Khir-khir khar-khar, *ad.* studiously, (as, "u wad dong hi *khir-khir khar-khar* ia nga").

Khir-shi-khir, *ad.* constantly seek a cause far quarrel; [as, "balei phi shu wad dong *khir-shi-khir* ia nga."]

Khla, *n.* a tiger, a leopard. [*Imit.* u khla-u thlen.]

Khlawait, *u, n.* an expert warrior.

Khlâb, *u, n.* a spleen, *esp.* an enlarged one.

Khlak-khlak, (khñiot), *ad.* gaggingly, throttlingly. [As, "u wan ba'n kshot *khlak-khlak* ia nga na ka ryndang."]

Khlád, *v.* to part, separate, secede;—*ad.* apart;—*n.* parts.

Khlang, *ad.* vacantly (looking, as, "u peit *khlang* ia nga").

Khlâi, *v.* to pluck with the thumb or nails (as the grains of maize).

Khlaiñ, *a.* strong, coarse, rough.

Khlait, *v.* to break off, to be dislocated.

Khláit-khláit, *ad.* in tears (bathed). [As, "ei ba kron ba phi iam-*khlait-khlait* kumne."]

Khlam, *ka, n.* a pestilence, a plague *esp.* cholera; a she-devil causing cholera. [*Imit.* ka khlam-ka ngoh.]

Khlam-suid-iap, *a.* having the appearance of one who has lately recovered from an attack of cholera.

Khlâw, *ka, n.* jungle. [*Imit.* khláw-ka btap];—*v.* to draw out, to extract, to dig out.

Khleb-khleb, *ad.* flickeringly, as, "ka sharak ka long *khleb-khleb*."

Khlek, *ad.* glaring with a flash, (as, "ka leilieh ka *bá khlek*").

Khleng, *ad.* showing the white of the eye, (as, "u peit matsoh *khleng*.")

Khleh, *v.* to mix, to pound;—*a.* mixed. [As, "une u briew u *khleh*-lamwir, mo."]

Khlei, *v.* to cast out of the mouth; to spue.

Khleiñ, *ka, n.* lard, fat;—*a.* fatty, rich, oily. [*Imit.* ka khleiñ-ka sbuh.]

Khléj-khléj, *ad.* tearfully, (as, "u iam *khlej khlej*").

Khlem, *prep.* without.

Khlem-akor, *a.* careless, reckless, unmannerly, rude.

Khlem-da-púd, *adv.* unceasingly, always, [as, "u Daniel u duwai *khlem-da-púd*."]

Khlemráiñ, *a.* shameless. [*Imit.* khlemráiñ-khlemsuiñ.]

Khlen-khlen, *a.* muscular, strong. [As, u "briew uba *khlen-khlen* ruh u leit khrong."]

Khlew-khlew, *ad.* staringly, (said of big eyes, as, "u khla u peit *khlew khlew*").

Khliak, *ad.* momentarily, (said of small objects, as, "nga ioh-i *khliak* ia ka skei").

Khliang, *u, n.* the *stomach* of a fowl or bird.

Khliah, *v.* to break off, to pluck.

Khlib-khlib, *ad.* looking fixedly, (as, "u peit *khlib khlib*").

Khlik-khlik, (lieh-), *ad.* cleanly white and tidy. [As, "u riam da ki jain kiba lieh *khlik-khlik.*"]

Khlieh, *ka, n.* the head, the top. [*Imit.* ka khlieh-ka reng.]

Khlieng, *v.* to clean the inside (of a vessel or well) ;—*ka, n.* kite, eagle.

Khlieng-ka-tyngâb, *ka, phr.* hearsay, rumour.

Khling-khling-khlang-khlang, *ad.* (look) round about.

Khlir-khlir, *ad.* clearly, transparently, (as, "ka um ka sngur *khlir-khlir*").

Khlók khlók, *ad.* snortingly.

Khlong, *v.* to pull out of a narrow place.

Khlop, *ad.* there and then (fall), [as, "nga kawang shidieng ia u ksew bad u kyllon *khlop.*"]

Khluit, *a.* hot, boiling hot, scorching ;—*v.* to burn.

Khlup, *ad.* completely, (as, tap *khlup*)—*a.* well covered (wrapper).

Khlúr, *u, n.* a star.

Khlùr, *v.* to come off (as hair.)

Khmat, *ka, n.* eye, face, appearance, end of a thread, subject; one of the points or issues of an argument; every (as, "*khmat* u rangbah briew u dei ba'n mih." Also spelt as 'khymat').

Khmat briew, *phr.* every person.

Khmia-khmia, (sngaid-), *ad.* like a person having a short and thick neck. [As, "ki Babu Dkhar kiba ioh tulop bún ki kylla sngaid *khmia-khmia.*"]

Khmied, *v.* to look up, to lift up the head.

Khmih, *v.* to look, to behold.

Khmihkâi, *v.* to look on as a spectator.

Khmihlynti, *v.* to expect, to look for.

Khmih-matdong, *v.* to eye with suspicion.

Khmih-shain, *v.* to gaze.

Khmih-sian, *v.* to watch.

Khmih-syntiat, *v.* to spy.

Khmihthuh, *v.* to examine, to make out.

Khmot-khmot, *ad.* angrily, (as, "u kren *khmot khmot*").

Khmúd, *u, n.* a squirrel.

Khmuin, *ka, n.* a bud, a protuberant object.

Khmut, *ka, n.* the nose; the tip of anything.

Khnang, *ad.* purposely, intentionally.

Khnangkhning, *ad.* without fail, [as, "wallam soh ia nga *khnang-khning*, ho."]

Khnâi, *ka, n.* a mouse;—*u, n.* biceps.

Khnam, *u, n.* an arrow; a small trap for catching fish (*Synteng*).

Khnap, *ka, n.* cloven hoof;—*v.* to squeeze between the legs.

Khnap-dpei, *ka, n.* the wooden frame of a hearth ; a fender.

Khnek-khnek, *ad.* with a hop, lamely, (as, "u iáid *khnek-khnek* kumba dkoh").

Khñi, *v.* to be on the point of crying.

Khñiang, *n.* worm, insect ; eruptions; parasite.

Khñiot, *v.* to squeeze, to gripe ; to rape.

Khñium, *v.* to grumble, to murmur, to mumble.

Khnok-khnok, *ad.* limpingly, [as, "u iáid *khnok-khnok* ba pang ka khohsiew."]

Khnong, *u, n.* a beam supporting the planks of a floor. [*Imit.* u khnong-u rijied.]

Khñoit-khñoit, *ad.* slowly, [as, "balei phi iáid *khñoit-khñoit* kumba pangkhrew?"]

Khong, *a.* resembling, taking the likeness of. [As, "uno u khynnah u *khong* kpa shibun."]

Khongkhong, *a.* irritable, hot-tempered.

Khongdong, *ka, n.* a turn, a corner ;—*a.* zigzag. [*Imit.* khong-dong-mongdong.]

Khongdong-jat, *ka, n.* the heel.

Khong-ieng, *v.* to open (by means of a lever, etc.).

Khongpong, *ad.* contrariwise, topsy-turvy. [*Imit.* khongpong-khongdeh.]—*n.* a bundle containing 60 *pan* leaves.

Khong-shi, *v.* 20 *pan* leaves.

Khongtoi, *ka, n.* the buttock.

Khongwéng, *a.* like a part of the circumference.

Khoh, *ka, n.* a conical native basket ;—*v.* to skin, to peel.

Khohluh, *ad.* big and round, [as, " u phan uba heh *khohluh-khohluh.*"]

Khohruhram, *a.* rugged, full of stones.

Khohshain, *v.* to come off, (as from the effect of rubbing against a stone, etc.).

Khohsiew, *ka, n.* the knee. [*Imit.* ka khohsiew—ka khohnúb.]

Khohwah, *ka, n.* the calf of a leg.

Khoi, *u, n.* parched rice mixed with molasses.

Khoi Khoi, *a.* easily provoked.

Khoit, *ad.* wholly, entirely. [*Imit.* khoit-khiaj] ;—*contr.* of *kyrkhoit*=a cartillage.

Khoitkait, *ka, n.* the inner part of the banana tree used for curry.

Khôr, *a.* hard, strong (mixture) ;—*ka, n.* a silk, (Assamese=*Gum-cheng*).

*Khorsha, *ka, n.* expenditure; cost of law suit. [*Imit.* ka khorsha-ka borsha.]

Khot, *v.* to call, admit, to accept as a lodger or a husband.

Khra, *u, n.* a pitcher, an earthen water vessel.

Khrái, *v.* to cut across, sever ;—*khrài, ad.* many and small (used with *rit*) [As, " kine ki khún doh kha ki dap *khrài* ha ka pung."]

Khrâi khlieh, *v.* to behead.

Khram, *ad.* with a crash, violently (as, u kyllon *khram*).

Khràn, *ad.* very (healthy), [as, u la koit *khran*=he has recovered completely].

Khráw, *a.* great, big, large ;—*adv.* proudly, arrogantly

Khrâw-batri, *kiba, n.* the great, nobles.

Khreh, *v.* to prepare, to be ready. [*Imit.* khreh-khrum.]

Khrei, *u, n.* used with *ksuid*, in *u ksuid-u khrei*=an evil spirit.

Khrew, *a.* sickly ; to be in a chronic state of illness. [*Imit.* khrew-khriap.]

Khria-khria, (rit-), *ad.* many and small. [As, " ki sla u dieng-kseh ki long kiba rit *khria-khria.*"]

Khriang, *ka, n.* a rapid, a shallow current.

---

* Hindi.

Khriat, *a.* cold.

Khrik-khrik, *ad.* twinkling, sparkling. [As, "ki khlur ki phyrnai *khrik-khrik.*"]

Khriem, *n.* the people of the Nongkhlaw State. Same as *Khyriem.*

Khring, *v.* to pull up or draw out by the hand.

Khrim, *ad.* with a crash.

Khrong, *v.* to beg, to tax, to take a toll;—*ka, n.* a tax, a toll. [*Imit.* ka khrong-ka tlieng.]

Khroh, *v.* to humour, to entice, to cajole. [*Imit.* khroh kjor.]

Khroi, *ad.* a few in number, (as, "ki ia don tang *khroi*)."

Khrón, *v.* te become stiff with cold (especially of the hand); to be benumbed.

Khru, *ad.* like the sound of tumbling, (as, " u ur *khru*").

Khrûd, *v.* to scrape.

Khrum, *ka, n.* a vault, a cellar; the space under the floor.

Khrum-khrum, *ad.* in a business like manner. [As, "u shu leit, *khrum khrum* ba'n kem na iing ia ka syiar."]

Khrún-khrún, *a.* of good size (said of fruits and tubers).

Khru-shi-khru, *ad.* repeatedly [as, " ki iakhih *khru-shikhru.*"]

Khu, *u, n.* a craw or crop.

Khwak, *ka, n.* a small bird about the size of a dove, the cry of which is believed to portend some evil thing about to happen in the village.

Khwâi, *u, n.* a hook (fish);—*v.* to fish, to wind up (a path).

Khwàin. *ad.* straight and long (as, " uba jrong *khwain*").

Khwân, *v.* to covet, to hanker after.

Khwar, *v.* to clean the inside of a hole (as, "*khwar* ia u khiewja").

Khub, *ka, n.* the width of 4 fingers joined together.

Khublei, *v. Imper.* God bless you, peace be with you;—*n.* thanks.

*Khubor, *ka, n.* news, tidings. [*Imit.* ka khubor-ka antor.]

Khuk, *ad.* suddenly, (as, "ia kynduh *khuk*").

Khûd, *v.* to scrape off (with a sharp instrument).

Khung, *u, n.* a cross-beam in a house;—*v.* to wrap or tie up in a cloth.

---

* Hindi.

Khui, *ad.* very (generally used with *khia, at*) [as, "u la khia *khui*"].

Khûid, *a.* clean, holy.

Khûid-ksûid, *v.* to be entirely free from blame.

Khùit-khùit, *a.* offensive ; not well ripe or well cooked.

*Khulom, *u, n.* a pen, a pen-holder ; a wooden sandal.

*Khulom-snêr, *u, n.* a quill pen.

Khulwia, *v.* to waste, to undermine.

Khûm, *v.* to fasten, to tie, to bind.

Khûm-ka jingit, *phr.* to be stunted.

Khum khum, *ad.* actively (engaged) ; in a business like attitude [as, "ki shu wan *khum-khum* bán shoh ia u ha ing."] [*Imit.* khum khum-kham kham ; as, " phi trei a-iu kumne *khum khum kham kham.*"]

Khûm-kpoh, *v.* incapable of doing active work owing to pregnancy.

Khûm-pyrdet, *v.* to bind the hands behind one's back. [*Imit.* khumpyrdet-khum pyrdang.]

Khûm-skum, *v.* to bind a bundle of grass to be used as a target or butt for shooting arrows.

Khún, *n.* a child ; subject. [*Imit.* khun-u-ksiew=child ; u khún-u-hajár=subject.]

Khûn-ki raiot, *ki, n.* subjects.

Khùn, *v.* to bend or drag a thing to one self ;—*ka, n.* murder case.

Khûn-binong bishon, *n.* respectable or honourable persons.

Khûnkha, *n.* a descendant of a male relative. [*Imit.* khunkha-khunlong.]

Khún-khlieng-kpoh, *n.* a pet child.

Khúnkliar wait, *n.* conquered subjects.

Khúnksiew, *n.* a grand-child.

Khûnkur. *n.* respectable and influential people. [*Imit.* khun-kur-khun kmie.]

Khúndir-khúnti, *n.* in Shella, a legal term, meaning children of the first and second wife.

Khúnjeh, *i, n.* a very young calf.

Khûnlung, *n.* a baby, an infant. [*Imit.* khunlung-khunjiap.]

Khúnmaitnia, *ad.* very (small quantity or degree) [as, "tang *khun maitnia* ruh u'm sngap ia nga"].

---

* Hindi.

Khûnpongka, *n.* a bastard, a child of an unknown father.

Khûnrei, *n.* a child of a widow or widower.

Khûn-ruid, *n.* a step-child; nephew or niece. [*Imit.* khunruit-khunjien.]

Khún-soh syiem, *u* or *ka*, *n.* a subject or citizen who belongs to another Syiem or Chief [*e.g.*, Bún na kiba shong ha Mawkhar ki long ki khun *khún-soh syiem*].

Khûnswet, *n.* an orphan. [*Imit.* khunswet-khunmyllung.]

Khûn-tamsneng, *n.* a disobedient child.

Khûn-thepmynsiem, *n.* a pet child.

Khûntrâi, *n.* one's own child; a legitimate child.

Khùr, *v.* to gather up together; to scrape.

Khura, *v.* to search.

Khur-khur, *u*, *n.* the sound of laboured breathing of a dying man.

Khuri, *ka*, *n.* a cup, a bowl; *ka lei khuri*=the household demon of a certain clan (jaid-Dkhar) of these Hills.

Khúr-met *u*, *n.* the outer part of a bamboo or a cane.

Khuslai, *v.* to be anxious, to be aggrieved, to be troubled.

*Khusnám, *ka*, *n.* a name, honour, reputation.

Khuti, *u*, *n.* a short post, a peg;—*v.* (làm-) to play draughts.

Khutia, *ki*, *n.* (*pl.*) odds and ends. [*Imit.* khutia-khulain.]—*ad.* in a very small amount at a time, [as, u "siew *khutia* ia ka ram jong nga"].

Khwiang, *v.* to wind or turn round (when walking).

Khwoh, *v.* to pull a thing by means of a hook or claws.

Khyllád, *v.* to lop off the branches, to prune; (*iaid-*), *phr.* to pass by heedlessly.

Khylláh. *a.* strange, queer, odd. [*Imit.* khyllah-khylliang.]

Khyllái, *ka*, *n.* the kidneys.

Khyllait, (ha), *adv.* out of sight; [as, "ynda *khyllait* ma u ei bán kylli ia nga"]; in the absence of.

Khyllem, *v.* to fall on the side (as a wall); to collapse.

Khyllew, *ad.* vainly, proudly (when praised); as, kren *or* leh *khyllew*.

Khylliah, *v.* to break off, (as, a twig); (*khein-*), to dislocate.

---

* Hindi.

Khylliap, *v.* to fold or wrap ;—*ka, n.* a fold.

Khylliat, *ka, n.* an instrument for pounding a mixture of betel-nut, *pan* and lime, much used by the old people of the Khasi and Jaintia Hills.

Khyllie, *v.* to raise up, to turn out (stone).

Khyllieng, *u, n.* the inner soft part of a bamboo or a cane—the green part or bark having been peeled off.

Khyllong, *v.* to dress the hair into a knot.

Khyndái, *a.* nine.

Khyndái-pateng-ñiamra, *ka, n.* an infernal abyss, hell.

Khyndat, *v.* to throw, to jostle, to push, (same as *kyndat*).

Khyndew, *ka, n.* dust, the earth. [*Imit.* ka khyndew-ka shyiap.]

Khyndiat, *a.* a little, few, very little. [*Imit.* khyndiat-khynsoit.]

Khyndiet, *v.* to lift up; to raise (of a lid); to uncover.

Khyndit, *a.* (same as *khyndiat*).

Khynnah, *n.* a child, a boy or girl. [*Imit.* khynnah-khynlung.]

Khynñiat, *v.* to push.

Khynñing, *a.* squeamish.

Khynñiuh, *v.* to tremble, to shake,—*u, n.* earthquake.

Khynñiuh-rih, *kaba, n.* shiverings caused by fear; paroxysm of fever.

Khynñiuh-u-jumâi, *kaba, n.* an earthquake shock.

Khynra, *v.* to pull down, to break down.

Khynrâi, *v.* to cut and fashion, (generally said of pieces of wood, as, *khynrai* latom).

Khynrat, *ad.* in a hurry, while in a state of confusion, [as, "u phet bad iehnoh *khynrat* ia la ki tiar baroh."]

Khynráw, *n.* a young man or woman; *shongkhynrâw*, to lead a bachelor's or spinster's life.

Khynwin, *v.* to be boisterous or tumultuous.

Khyrdep, *v.* to shut or slam (a door) without fastening it.

Khyrdong, *u, n.* what remains after the grain has been sifted.

Khyrdop, *ka, n.* a gate, a portal.

‡Khyrnit, *ka, n.* the mantel-piece, the cornice.

Khyrwang, *ka, n.* a kind of *eri* cloth with red and white stripes; the name of a Bhoi tribe who inhabit the country near Mynser.

---

‡ English.

Khyrwain, *ad.* tall and handsome (in stature); [as, "u briew uba bha briew *khyrwaiñ*"]. [*Imit.* khyrwaiñ-khyrweh.]

Khyrwait, *v.* to twist, to wring, to strangle. [*Imit.* khyrwait-khyrwiang.]

Khyrwiang, *v.* to go round.

Khyrwit, *v.* to strike, to beat forcibly (with a stick).

Ki, *art. pl.* they.

Kiak-kiak, *ad.* titteringly.

Kiád, *ka, n.* liquor. [*Imit.* ka kiad-ka um.]

Kian, *ka, n.* a charm, a magic; keenness of intelect.

Kiar, *v.* to avoid, to keep clear of.

K'iar (jâin), *v.* to spread over, to extend, same as *kyiar.*

Kiat, *a.* rebellious, wayward.

Kiáw, *i, n.* a grandmother.

Kiaw-kurim, *ka, n.* mother-in-law.

Kiaw-ngap, *ka, n.* queen-bee.

Kie, *v.* to be carried away by water; to drift.

Kie-berong, *v.* to be entirely in the power of (bad sense).

Kieng, *v.* to wear across the shoulder or about the waist as weapons, to sling.

Kieh, *v.* to be excited; to be in an uproar.

Kiei? *p.* who? what?

Kiei-kiei, *n.* things, articles.

Kiew, *v.* to ascend, to go up.

Kiewkhet, *v.* to be enthroned or crowned.

Kiew-langtylli, *phr.* to be so much carried away by flattery as to forget one's real position.

King, *v.* to row; to stir; to be giddy (head).

K'ing, *u, n.* a wasp, a hornet; also spelt as *kyieng.*

*Kil, *u, n.* a vakil, a pleader.

Ki'n, *phr.* they will. (*Ki* + *yn.*)

Kine, *p.* these.

Kino? *p.* which (*pl.*)?

Kino-kino, *p.* any.

---

* Hindi.

Kir, *v.* to strike with a clenched hand (especially vertically) ;—*adv.* at once (as, "la khie ka thma *kir*").

*Kirani, *n.* an Eurasian.

Kir-kir, *ad.* very tender.

Kiri, *u, n.* the title of a king's son (also spelt Giri).

*Kirmit, *ka, n.* an agreement.

†Kiro, *ka n.* a cloth measurement = 2¼ inches.

*Kismis, *u, n.* a raisin.

Kismot, *ka, n.* fate, luck.

Kit, *v.* to carry on the back with a head strap; to bear; to be responsible for; (*Imit.* kit-bah.)

Kita, *p.* those (out of sight).

*Kitâb, *ka, n.* a book.

Kitai, *p.* those (in sight but farther off).

Kit-bru, *ka, n.* an owl.

Kitkhia, *v.* to take deep interest in; to be responsible for.

Kitkhlieh, *v.* to be responsible for.

Kitei, *p.* up there; those; above mentioned.

Kithie, *p.* those (below); down there; the following.

Kit-iapar, *kaba, n.* a very heavy load; (*lit.* to carry so much as to make one walk on all fours).

Kitjingkit, *v.* to carry loads. [*Imit.* kitjingkit-bahjingbah.]

Kitjingmut, *v.* to have the meaning of; to bear the meaning of.

Kitnong, *v.* to carry a load for hire. [*Imit*:. kitnong-kitni.]

Kito, *p.* those (in sight).

Kitpop *or* kitpap, *v.* to be responsible for one's wrong doing.

Kitram, *v.* to be in debt.

Ki tum-ki-tam, *n. pl.* things, furniture.

K'iuh, *v.* to be afraid of, to tremble, (same as *kyiuh*).

Kjai, *ad.* well (dressed);—[as, "haba ki leit khmih kai, ki da riam bha *kjai*."]

Kjam, *a.* cold.

Kjap, *v.* to sip, to suckle;—*a.* bitterly cold;—*v.* absorb.

Kjap-ka stár, *ka, n.* (a poojah term) part of the entrails of a fowl which is not full.

* Hindi. | † Bengali.

Kjat, *ka*, *n.* a foot, a leg.

Kjat-sngi, *ka*, *n.* sun's ray.

Kjéng, *ad.* high up, to a full height, [as, "u kulai uba jrong *kjeng*"].

Kjeh, *v.* to snivel.

Kjit, *v.* to suck, absorb.

Kjit-sim, *kaba*, *n.* a disease of an arecanut which appears as small black patches in the kernel, probably caused by sucking of birds.

Kjóng-kjóng, *ad.* lightly (as the frisking of a deer).

Kjôiñ-kjôiñ, } *ad.* aloft, high up. [As, "u shong *kjoiñ kjoiñ* halor
Kjûiñ-kjûiñ, } ka rynsán."]

Kjôr, *v.* to coax, cajole.

Kjûh, *v.* to fondle, to caress (of an animal).

Kjup, *v.* to suck, draw in by suction.

Kla (sang-), *ka*, *n.* a religious observance of a certain class of the people of the southern lowlands of the Khasi Hills, by which they abstain from all intercourse with outsiders.

Klak-klak, *ad.* chatteringly. [As, "ka briew kaba kren *klak-klak.*"]

Klang, *v.* to blaze, to flare.

Klang klang, *ad.* glitteringly. [As, "ha ri Dkhar, ha ka por l'iur, dap da ka um *klang klang.*"]

Klah, *ka*, *n.* (generally used with Numeral Adjectives), a full arm's length.

Klái, *a.* fit, suitable.

Klán, *v.* to ford, to cross (a stream).

‡Klas, *ka*, *n.* a class.

‡Klat, *ka*, *n.* a glass, a tumbler;—*v.* to turn abruptly to another direction.

Klaw, (peit), *ad.* unremittingly, steadfastly (of big eyes, as, *u peit klaw*).

Klek (bám), *ad.* at once (as, *u nguid klek.*); flaringly [as, "ka ding ka la meh *klek*"].

Klep, *ad.* unawares (as, "u hap *klep* ha ka thliew").

Kler, *v.* to go beyond the bound or limit.

Klet, *v.* to forget, to omit.

Klew, *n.* a peacock.

‡ English.

Klew-klew, *ad.* glitteringly. [As, "ioh-i tang ki khmat ba phyrnái *klew klew.*"]

Kli, *v.* to roll up.

Kliar, *ka, n.* the top.

Kliàw, *ad.* steadfastly, unremittingly (of small eyes), as, khmih *kliaw.*

Kling-lingling, *ad.* all over, [as, "ka madan kaba la dap da ka um *kling-lingling*"].

Klim, *v.* to commit adultery.

Klit (jing), *ka, n.* sleight of hands :—*ad.* very quickly, [as, leh *klit*]

Kliw-kliw, (iong), *ad.* very (black). [As, "ki Negro ki long ki briew kiba iong-synñia *kliw kliw.*"]

Klong, *u, n.* the heart; a bottle-gourd. [*Imit.* u klong-u skáw.]

Kloh, *v.* to push the hand into a hole.

Klói, *a.* ready.

Klói-klói, *ad.* quickly, sharp.

Klói-làn, *ad.* very quickly; [as, "Nga tang shu ioh-i ia u, u la buhrih ia ka wait *kloi-lan.*"]

Klop, *v.* to deceive, to cheat.

Klùm, *v.* to roll up, gather up, to jumble.

Klùn, *v.* to gulp, to swallow up.

†Klùr, *ka, n.* one crore.

Kma, *v.* to wander, to roam about.

Kmang, *ad.* agape, eagerly (as, " u ksew u *peit* kmang").

Kmai, *ad.* at least, if not......at all (as, " *kmai* bym lah eh ruh, ai tang shi paisa").

Kmeng, *ad.* eagerly, (as, when a dog having a long snout is looking at something).

Kmen, *v.* to rejoice ;—*a.* joyful, rejoicing ;—*n.* joy.

Kmie, *ka, n.* a mother.

Kmiekha, *ka, n.* grand-mother (father's side).

Kmie-ki-kpa, *ki, n.* parents.

Kmie-hep, } *ka, n.* grand-mother (mother's side).
Kmie-râd, }

Kmie-nah, *ka, n.* aunt (mother's younger sister).

Kmie-san, *ka, n.* aunt (mother's elder sister).

† Bengali.

Kmir-kmir, *ad.* very (yellow) [as, "balei ba stem kumne *kmir-kmir* kumba dang lah pang?"]

Knang(ia), *v.* to make a bargain for bringing in goods to a place and at a time agreed upon.

Knah, *ka, n.* the cross stick in a bird-trap; the scaffold.

Kneng, (ieng), *ad.* prominently. [As, "nga ioh-i ia u briew ba u ieng *kneng* halor u maw."]

Knêr, *v.* to stretch forth a hand.

Knep-knep, (jhieh-), *ad.* very (wet clothes).

Kñia, *v.* to sacrifice; [*Imit.* kñia-khriam].—*ka, n.* maternal uncle's wife.

Kñiakha, *ka, n.* aunt(father's side.)

Kñia kyntiew, *ka, n.* a sacrifice which the Khasis performed at home to *u blei Synteng* called u Mahet.

Kniah-kniah, (iaid-), *ad.* like the gait of a well-dressed damsel.

Kñi, *u, n.* uncle (mother's side). [*Imit.* kñi-u-kpa.]

Knieh, *v.* to snatch away, ta confiscate. [*Imit.* knieh-knán.]

*Kobja, *ka, n.* a hinge.

Kok, *interj.* there you are! it serves you right!

Kong, *i, n.* an elder brother or sister.

Kongbah, *u, n.* the eldest brother.

‡Kongor, *u, n.* one who marries a princess, *i.e.*, a Syiem's sister or niece.

Kongsan, *a.* chief, greatest.

Koh, *v.* to give chewed food to a child;—*u, n.* an old man (*fem.* =ka iaw).

K'oh, *ka, n.* a concave cut at the head of an arrow to fit the bowstring. Same as *kyoh.*

Kohngûh, *v.* to obey, to nod, to acknowledge.

Kohngûh-samthiah, *v.* to be drowsy; sleepy; to nod (in sleep).

Kohlyngkâi *u, n.* the rhinoceros horn-bill.

Koi, *ka, n.* a fence in the bed of a stream to catch fish, a weir.

*Kóid, *v.* to confine.

*Koidi, *n.* a prisoner.

†Koina, *ka, n.* a virgin; Zenana lady or *parda nishin.*

Koit. *a.* healthy, well;—*adv.* all right, never mind.

* Hindi. | † Bengali. | ‡ Assamese.

Kóit-kóit, } (jem-), *ad.* easily bent. [As, "une u siej u long uba
Kúit-kúit, } jem *kóit kóit.*"]

Kolom, *v.* to plant a twig in the ground to grow.

*Kom, *a.* less, defective.

†Konopâd, *u*, *n.* a kind of necklace.

Kòp, *ka*, *n.* the ear (of corn), the cover; the cuff.

*Kóp, *v.* to vaunt; to be proud of; to challenge. [*Imit.* kop-sop.]

Kóp, *v.* (followed by *da*) to deserve, it serves right.

*Kór, *ka*, *n.* machine, an engine; a resting place built of stones on both sides of a path;—*a.* valuable, precious;—*iakor*, to bid.

Kòr, *u*, *n.* a mole cricket; a kind of reed.

Kòr-kòr. (iaid), *ad.* to walk about like a beggar.

Korbâr, *v.* to meddle;—*n.* business, concern. [*Imit.* ka korbár-ka sorbár.]

Kordit, *ka*, *n.* woe, calamity.

Kordôr, *a.* valuable.

*Korhajir, *v.* to be absent(from duty).

Korni, *ka*, *n.* a trowel.

†Kot, *ka*, *n.* a paper, book; a yard;—*v.* to reach. [*Imit.* ka kot-ka-sla.]

Kotbah, *ka*, *n.* the Bible.

Kot-kot, *a.* illtempered, easily provoked.

Kotkudi, *ka*, *n.* a circular paper kite.

Kot-sada, *ka*, *n.* a blank paper.

Kot-shini, *ka*, *n.* a very thin paper, generally used in making kites and flowers or other ornamentals.

Kot-shonsia, *ka*, *n.* blotting paper.

Kot-thalyngka, *ka*, *n.* a square-kite.

Kpa, *u*, *n.* a father.

Kpa-khâ, *u*, *n.* grandfather (paternal side).

Kpa-hep, *u*, *n.* grandfather (mother's side).

Kpait, *ka*, *n.* track of an animal.

Kpa-nah, *u*, *n.* step-father, uncle (father's younger brother).

Kpa-san, *u*, *n.* uncle (father's elder brother).

---

* Hindi. | † Bengali.

Kpep, *ka, n.* the burning place of a family.

Kpèr, *ka, n.* a garden. [*Imit.* ka kpér-ka phrah.]

Kpieng, *u, n.* a string of beads. [*Imit.* u kpieng-u-ksah.]

Kpong, *v.* to excavate, make a hole;—*n. ka,* a goddess of luck.

Kpoh, *ka, n.* the abdomen, the stomach, family, house.

Kpu, *u, n.* a cake, a loaf.

Kpu-im, *u, n.* dough.

Kpu-rew, *u, n.* flour.

Kput, *ka, n.* revenge, vengeance.

Krak (liat-), *ad.* down (slip into a hole). [As, "ka blang ka liat *krak* ha krem."]

Krád, *v.* to scratch, to scatter;—*ad.* in every direction, off, (as, "u la phet *krad*").

Krang, *v.* to bore, to undermine.

Krâi, *u, n.* a millet.—*v.* to spread.

Kram, *ad.* with a crash (fall); [as, "u la kyllon *kram.*"]

Kram-kram, } (kyllúid-), *ad.* very (roomy or spacious). [As,
Krum-krum, } "hapoh pubon ki ong ka kylluid *kram-kram.*"]

Krek, *ad.* suddenly, (as, " ka ding ka la phyrnai *khrek*").

Kreng-kreng, (ñiar-), *ad.* having big holes in a net work. [As, "kane ka jaiñ kaba ñiar *kreng-kreng.*"]

Krei, *v.* to scatter.

Kreit, *ka, n.* a hard durable kind of wood.

Krem, *ka, n.* a cave. [*Imit.* ka krem-ka-kroh.]

Kren, *v.* to speak. [*Imit.* kren-khana.]

Kren-beiñ, *v.* to revile, to abuse. [*Imit.* krenbeiñ-krenkhoh.]

Kren-bein-blei, *v.* to blaspheme.

Kren-blei, *v.* to be a spokesman for some god (spirit).

Kren-blom-blom, *v.* to mutter.

Kren-bok-bok, *v.* to jabber.

Kren-briew, *v.* to be sociable; to imitate the speech (like a parrot).

Kren-bynñiaw, *v.* to speak in a sorrowful or mournful tone.

Kren-byrtong, *v.* to speak as a sorcerer.

Kren-bythêr, kren-bthêr, *v.* to speak at random; to hint at.

Kren-kâi, *v.* to chat, to gossip.

Kren khñium-khñium, *v.* to mumble. [*Imit.* kren khñium-khñium-kren khñiam-khñiam.]

Kren-khrâw, *v.* to boast, to talk big. [*Imit.* kren khraw-kren hangamei.]

Kren-khutia, *v.* to speak about unnecessary and trifling things.

Kren khyllah, *v.* to speak in an unusual or awkward manner. [*Imit.* kren khyllah-kren khylliang.]

Kren-kulmar, *v.* to speak as if one is in a confused state of mind. [*Imit.* kren kulmar-kren kulmit.]

Kren kunok, *v.* to speak as a seer.

Kren-dathew, *v.* to speak by pondering over the matter, to speak after proper deliberation.

Kren-hangamei, *v.* to speak arrogantly. [*Imit.* kren hangamei-kren hangapa.]

Kren-jakter, *v.* to talk senselessly like an intoxicated person.

Kren-japnej, *v.* to drawl.

Kren-jler, *v.* to tell stories.

Kren-jli, *v.* to speak offensively.

Kren-laitlúid, *v.* to speak out freely.

Kren-lamwir, *v.* to speak as one who is in a deranged state of mind. [*Imit.* kren lamwir-kren lamtham.]

Kren-laplah, *v.* to speak without due deliberation, to overstate.

Kren-lkhit, *v.* to dwell on minor or useless details.

Kren-lyngkut, *v.* to speak bluntly.

Kren-madan, *v.* to speak whatever comes before one's mind.

Kren mynthi, *v.* to speak sarcastically.

Kren-nang-ang, *v.* to have a bad tongue. [*Imit.* kren-nangang-kren-nanghâp.]

Kren-pankwah, *v.* to speak as if one courts for an evil thing.

Kren-pathár, *v.* to speak at random or inconsiderately.

Kren-sa, *v.* to speak sulkily.

Kren-said-lah, *v.* to continue to press a point after one has been beaten in argument.

Kren-salia, *v.* to tease. [*Imit.* kren-salia-kren-salait.]

Kren-satia, *v.* to vex, to annoy.

Kren-siar, *v.* to back-bite.

Kren-sih, *v.* to use indecent language. [*Imit.* krensih-krentla.]

Kren-tain tain, *v.* to rate, to chide.

Kren-thala, *v.* to speak vainly, to speak thoughtlessly. [*Imit.* krenthala-krenthalein.]

Kren-thamula, *v.* to joke, to jest. [*Imit.* kren thamula-kren-thamulein.]

Kren-thawdur, *v.* to speak jocosely. [*Imit.* kren thawdur-kren thawdar.]

Kren-thlia, *v.* same as *kren-satia.* [*Imit.* krenthlia-krenthlait.]

Kren-thuhkhana, *v.* to carry tales about a person. [*Imit.* kren thuh khana-kren thuh khadeh.]

Kren-thurmur, *v.* to speak thoughtlessly.

Kren-wai-wot, *v.* to give a final and blunt answer.

Kren-wei-briew, *v.* to soliloquize.

Kren-woh-nia, *v.* to find fault in an argument.

Krep-krep, (im-), *ad.* fresh (as, "u jhur u dang im *krep-krep*").

Kria, *v.* to sharpen a *daw* with a small piece of whet-stone.

Kriah, *ka, n.* a sieve, a basket. [*Imit.* ka kriah-ka shang.]

Krik-krik (phyrnái), *ad.* brilliantly. [As, "ka rong kaba dang phyrnái *krik krik.*"]

Kring-kring, *ad.* sparklingly (like the surface of water); shining black, [as, "phi sleh aiu kumne ba ka khmat ka phyrnai *kring-kring*"].

Krih, *v.* to spread.

Krim, *ad.* with a crash (as the fall of a wall or a tree).

Krip-krip, *ad.* twitteringly, (as, "u khñiang u par *krip-krip*").

*Krit, *ka, n.* a sword.

Krong, *ka, n.* a bier.

Kroh, *ka, n.* crevices, holes. [*Imit.* ka kroh-ka kram.]

Krop-krop, } (jem-) *ad.* like a broken egg-shell or like a ball
Krup-krup, } made of paper.

Krúd, *v.* to scrape the earth lightly for high-land cultivation.

Krung, *ka, n.* the side, the rip. [*Imit.* krung- ka knab.]

Kruin, *u, n.* a white ant.

Krum, *ad.* with a crash (of large things).

---

* Hindi.

Ksang, *u*, *n*. bile.

Ksangkti, *ka*, *n*. the arm.

Ksang-lbong, *ka*, *n*. the muscle of the thigh.

Ksah, *ka*, *n*. a ring;—*a*. muscular.

Ksái, *u*, *n*. thread, fibre.

Ksaiñ, *u*. *n*, a maggot, a grub.

Ksâid, *v*. to roll on the ground, to sprawl, to make an effort.

Ksam, *v*. to claw. [*Imit*. ksam-kbia.]

Ksan, *v*. to justify, win.

Ksan-rumpei, *phr*. to win the case at home or when not brought before the court.

Ksâr, *n*. a fox.

Ksâw, *v*. to be accustomed to;—*a*. to be lucky;—*ka*, *n*. the goddess of good luck who brings in success in every enterprise, *esp*. in hunting animals.

Kseh, *ka*, *n*. a pine tree;—*u*, a resinous pine wood.

Kseh-blei, *ka*, *n*. (*Bot*.) *taxus baccata*; a kind of pine tree.

Ksem, *ka*, *n*. flatus, wind.

Ksew, *n*. a dog.

Kshâit, *ka*, *n*. a waterfall, a cascade.

Kshêit-kshêit, (lieh), *adv*. very (white), [as, "lieh *ksheit-ksheit* kum ka khoit-kait"].

Kshong, *ka*, *n*. fat next to the skin, (as, "*kshong* sniang").

Kshot, *v*. to squeeze, to press.

Ksi, *ka*, *n*. louse, vermin of the head.

Ksiang, *u*, *n*. an umpire; a mediator; a go-between.

Ksiar, *ka*, *n*. gold;—*a*. golden.

Ksing, *ka*, *n*. a drum. [*Imit*. ka ksing-ka dhah.]

Ksing-ngap, *ka*, *n*. a bee-hive.

Ksiew, *n*. a grand-child (*see* khun-ksiew, para-ksiew, pyrsaksiew).

Ksiew-tun, *n*. a child of a grand-child.

Ksih, *u*, *n*. an otter;—*u*, one who goes through the water ordeal; —*v*. to squeeze on the throat, to throttle, to seize at the throat.

Ksoh, *v*. to cling, to hold on.

Ksúid, *n*. a demon. [*Imit*. u ksuid-u-khrei.]

Ksuit, *ka*, *n*. matter, pus.

Ktak-ktak, (iong-), *ad.* black and adhesive. [As, "na u sh'ing sohpieng ngi lah ba'n ioh ka rong kaba iong *ktak-ktak.*"]

Ktang, *ka, n.* a bamboo pipe in which water is kept; a *chunga.*

Ktah, *v.* to touch. [*Imit.* ktah-shoi.]

Ktah-kti, *v.* to lay hands on.

Ktáit, *v.* to scatter about.

Ktàr-ktàr, *a.* muddy. [As, "ka ktich kaba *ktar-ktar.*"]

Ktem, *ka, n.* a track (of game).

Ktha, *v.* to chew; to have a gnawing pain.

Kthang, *a.* bitter.

Kthang-kti, *uba, n.* one with a heavy hand (*lit.* bitter).

Ktháí, *ad.* well (dressed); [as, "u riam bha noh *kthai* keiñ"].

Kthâw, *u, n.* a grand-father, a father-in-law.

Kthâw kurim *u, n.* a father-in-law.

Kthem, *ad.* well, handsomely (dressed) [as, "u pynnoh bohkhaila noh teh *kthem* kein"].

Kthik, *ad.* still and upright [as, "u ieng *kthik*"].

Kti, *ka, n.* a hand.

Ktiar, *u, n.* a centipede.

Ktik, *v.* to tickle.

Ktich, *ka, n.* mud; paddy-field. [*Imit.* ktich-ka lwer.]

Ktien, *ka, n.* a mouth, a word. [*Imit.* ka ktien-ka thylliej.]

Ktub, ktuk, *v.* to mumble.

Ktúd, *v.* to crawl slowly and with effort as one who is helpless.

Ktuk-ktuk, (iong), *ad.* of a dark and dirty colour, [as, "u briew uba iong *ktuk-ktuk*"].

Ktung, *ka, n.* a small preserved fish; a vetch. [*Imit.* ka ktung-ka ktàp.]

Ktui ktui, *a.* very muddy or dirty (said of water or dress).

Ktur-ktur, *ad.* like a sulphurous glow [as, "phyrnai *ktur-ktur*"].

Kuang, *v.* to roam about. Same as *kwang.*

Kuah, *v.* to court, to wish for anything. Same as *kwah.*

Kuah, (pan-), *v.* to court a wrong or bad thing.

Kuái, *u, n.* areca nut. Same as *kwai.*

Kuar, *ka, n.* a fish trap, generally put in rapids;—*u,* a milkman. Same as *kwar.*

Kubi, *u*, *n*. a cabbage.

*Kublot, *ka*, *n*. a form of agreement; a *kabulyat*.

*Kuboit, *u*, *n*. a small case, a charm; a talisman, amulet.

*Kubur, *v*. to admit, confess.

Kuki, *n*. the Kukis who are also called *Hadem* in the Khasi and Jaintia Hills district.

*Kukri, *ka*, *n*. a dagger, a *khukri*.

Kuda, *ka*, *n*. a cyst.

‡Kudam, *ka*, *n*. a godown; a button.

Kudim-kudim, *a*. very ancient.

Kudom, *v*. to gallop, trot.

Kudu, *a*. tolerably big.

Kuhiw, *a*. shrewish.

Kui, *u*, *n*. a lynx.

Kuju, *ka n*. a sort of flagcolet made from young bamboo.

Kulâi, *n*. a horse, a pony.

*Kulâm, *u*, *n*. a slave.

Kular, *v*. to promise;—*ka*, *n*. a promise. [*Imit*. ka kular-ka madar.]

Kulbut, *ka*, *n*. an arched wooden frame used for supporting a masonry work in an arch.

*Kuli, *u*, *n*. a porter, a bullet, a pill.

Kulia, *ka*, *n*. gonorrhœa (*see* ñiangkulia).

Kulmâr, *ad*. confusedly, disorderly. [*Imit*. kulmar-kulmit.]

Kulong, *a*. very ancient. [*Imit*. kulong-kumah; kulong-kulong.]

Kum, *ad*. like, as, unintentionally, [as, "nga *kum* kren bakla."];—*u*, *n*. a pitcher.

Kumân, *a*. sullen; obstinate.

Kumba, *ad*. as if, about, [as, "ki briew ki don *kumba* 100 ne"].

Kumjuh́, *ad*. the same, all the same, [as, leh—, kren—, kam—*kumjuh*].

Kumne, *ad*. thus; like this.

Kumne kumne, *ad*. at once, immediately.

Kumno? *ad*. how? by what means?

Kumno kumno, *ad*. anyhow, somehow.

Kumno-re-kumno, *ad*. somehow or other.

---

* Hindi. | ‡ English.

§Kushia, *u*, *n*. an eel (big kind).

Kumta, *ad*. like that, so, accordingly.

Kumto, *ad*. like that (as I said).

Kumto-kumne, *kiba*, *n*. persons of less importance, persons of no position.

Kumwei, *ad*. otherwise, [as, nga "ong ia u ba'n leh kumne, hynrei u leh da *kumwei*"].

Kùn, *v*. to reserve, to hold one's breath.

Kuna, *ka*, *n*. a fine, an atonement. [*Imit*. ka kuna-ka kait.]

Kunài, *v*. to be parsimonious, to keep. [*Imit*. kunai-kutin.]

*Kunjari, *ka*, *n*. a tambourine.

*Kunok, *u*, *n*. a seer, a *Ganak*.

Kup, *v*. to put on ; attributable to some demons (in *pujah*) ;—*ka*, *n*. a suit (of clothes). [*Imit*. ka kup-ka sem.]

*Kupar, *ka*, *n*. the forehead, the fate.

Kupar-kâd, *ka*, *n*. an ill luck.

Kur, *n*. a relative (on the mother's side). [*Imit*. ka kur-ka kmie, u kur-u kmie, ki kur-ki kmie].

*Kura, *u*, *n*. a European soldier.

*Kuran, *ka*, *n*. the Koran.

Kurat, *ka*, *n*. a saw.

Kurattia, *u*, *n*. a crocodile.

*Kuri, *n*. number=20.

Kurim, *ka*, *n*. a wife. [*Imit*. Kurim-kupai.]

†Kuro, *ka*, *n*. a league [used with *shi*.]

Kurup, *v*. to distrain, to confiscate, to rob.

Kut, *v*. to come to an end, to resolve, to agree ;—*ka*, *n*. a stockade, a fort.

Kut-jingmut, *v*. to decide, to resolve.

Kut-lâd, *v*. to be at one's wit's end.

Kutok, *a*. very old. [*Imit*. kutok-kutok ; kutok-kudim.]

Kya, *ka*, *n*. simul tree.

Kylla, *v*. to turn, to change.

Kylla-lieng, *v*. to capsize, to be ruined.

Kyllabadur, *ka*, *n*. a large bat, a flying fox.

---

* Hindi. | † Bengali. | § Assamese.

Kylla-kaba-mut, *v.* to repent.

Kyllang, *u, n.* the Kyllang rock in Khadsawphra ; a cyclone.

Kyllain, *v.* to wind, to be inconstant. [*Imit.* kyllain-kyrjaw.]

Kyllain-kyrjaw, *ad.* in a zigzag way.

Kyllain-mongor, *ad.* cross-legged.

Kylla-jaiñ-nep, *phr.* to be destroyed or annihilated.

Kylla-jutang, *v.* to be changing, to be capricious.

Kylla-lyngkot, *u, n.* January.

Kyllán, *v.* to rub, smear.

Kylla-prah, *v.* to perform a somersault.

Kylleng, *ad.* everywhere.

Kyllep, *kaba, n.* a lonely place ;—*a.* capable of covering the whole length—*ad.* unknowingly.

Kylli, *v.* to ask ; (*phah kylli*) to ask for marriage. [*Imit.* kylli-pyr-thew.]

Kylliang, *ad.* as a loan, in return ;—*ka, n.* a loan. [*Imit.* kylliang-palat.]

Kylliang-ktien, *v.* to retort.

Kyllon, *v.* to fall.

Kyllong, *a.* very big.

Kyllúid, *a.* plenty of space, spacious. [*Imit.* kyllúid-kyrwa.]

Kyllum, *ad.* in a lumpsum, as a whole ;—*v.* to gather up in a heap.

Kyllut, *a.* deaf.

Kyn-âd, *v.* to become swollen (as a boil).

Kynbat *u, n.* herb, weed, medicinal plant.

Kynkâw, *v.* to shout, call out.

Kynkhlek, *v.* to brandish, flourish.

Kynkhlok, *v.* to sniff or snore.

Kynkok, *v.* to crow over a person.

§Kynda, *n.* a number=4 ; a rhinoceros ; a form of corporal punishment in the old Khasi Penal Code. [*Imit.* ka nar-ka kynda.]

Kyndâd, *n.* a mole.

Kyndang, *n.* a string of flesh or fish ;—*v.* to raise or turn over as with a lever.

Kyndang-kwah, *phr.* a person who takes a fancy to what it is impossible for him to get.

§ Assamese.

Kyndah-kyndong, *ka, n.* creek and corner.

Kyndár, *v.* to dismantle, break down;—*kyndàr, ad.* like a wide rimmedhat or slouch.

Kyndàt, *v.* to push away forcibly.

Kyndeh, *v.* to palpitate, to pant;—*u, n.* grounded corn or rice.

Kyndiang, *ad.* distinctly, clearly, [as, " nga ioh sngew *kyndiang* haba phi la khot"].

Kyndiah, *v.* to abstain.

Kyndiap, *v.* to be particular in collecting small things or small gain. [*Imit.* kyndiap-kynbiang.]

Kyndiep, *ad.* like a cope, [as, " une u maw u shong *kyndiep* kumba un hap"].

Kyndit, *v.* to be startled, to be surprised.

Kyndit-bynriew, *v.* to regain consciousness, to come to oneself.

Kyndok, *u, n.* sulphur, a lucifer match.

Kyndong, *ka, n.* a corner;—*ad.* carefully (wrapped, said of small things as, "u khung ia ki jain *kyndong*");—(*nong*=) *n.* a villager, a person from an out-of-the-way place. [*Imit.* kyndong-kynshrot.]

Kyndoi-jakpoh, *v.* to go about from place to place in search of work or food.

Kyndon, *ka, n.* step, grade, shelf. [*Imit.* kyndon-ka kynnah.]

Kyndóp, *ad.* like a small projecting coping, [as, "i ing iba rit *kyndop*"].

Kyndung, *ad.* carefully (wrapped, said of a load), [as, "u bah *kyndung* ia la i khun"].

Kyndûh, *v.* to meet with, to strike against.

Kyndùp, *ka, n.* two palm-fuls (made like a bowl).

Kyndùp, *a.* over-hanging.

Kyndùr, *ka, n.* an oven or stove (for baking).

Kynha, *v.* to shout exaltingly, hurraing; to surprise.

Kynhâm, *v.* to give a warning by shouting *hám-hám.*

Kynhied, *v.* to rebuke, to scold, to command.

Kynhói, *v.* to shout by saying *hói-hói.*

Kynhún, *ka, n.* a flock, a herd, a band, a group.

Kyn-iân, *ka, n.* the breadth of a cloth.

Kyn-ieb, *ad.* raised up (as the lid or covering).

Kynieh, *v.* to take by force. Also splet *knieh.*

Kyn-ih, *v.* to crow.

Kynja, *ka, n.* sort, kind, nature ;—*u, ganja.*

Kynjak, *v.* to express regret and surprise (by making a sound of *jk-jk*). [*Imit.* kynjak-kynjik.]

Kynjang, *ka, n.* elevation, height.

Kynjah, *a.* lonely.

Kynjai, *ad.* peacefully, at ease, tranquilly.

Kynjat, *v.* to kick ;—*n.* a pace (used with Numeral Adjective).

Kynjing, *v.* to be fastidious (iaid) ;—*ad.* carefully and on tip-toe (walk).

Kynjih, *v.* to raise one self by standing on the toes, to skip ;—*ad.* with a springy step, (as, iaid *kynjih*).

Kynjlar, *ad.* with a tapering snout, (as, "u thin uba nep ka khmut *kynjlar*").

Kynjnot, *ad.* the appearance of a slender and thin woman [as, "ka tymmen kaba jrong *kynjnot*"].

Kynjóng, *ad.* high up, on the top, (as, "u ieng halor u mawbah *kynjong*").

Kynjoh, *v.* to aim at, to reach, to be ambitious.

Kynjoh-khaskâiñ, *v.* to perform a poojah ceremony before occupying a newly built house ;—*n.* Khasi housewarming.

Kynjóiñ (jrong-), *ad.* up, aloft. [As, "u shong *kynjoiñ* halor u hati."]

Kynjrait, *v.* to pull with a jerk, (as, "u *kynjrait* ia ka kti haba ia khublei").

Kynjri, *u, n.* a chain.

Kynjri-tabah, *u, n.* a silver or gold chain worn across the shoulders.

Kynjri-wahdong, *u, n.* a kind of earing.

Kynjrot, *v.* to pull off bit by bit.

Kynjûh, *v.* to jolt ; to try (the weight or heaviness of a load).

Kynjuiñ, *ad.* safely, aloft, (as, "u don *kynjuiñ* halor u hati").

Kynjut, *v.* to pull out, to feel a throbbing pain.

Kynjut-kti, *v.* to shake hand.

Kynmâw, *v.* to remember ; to recollect ;—*n.* awake, (as, "ynda la shi *kynmáw* hynne mynmiet nga ioh sngew ba ka lynñiar ka briew"). [*Imit.* kynmaw-kyndit.]

Kynmâw-bynriew, *v.* to regain consciousness ; to come to oneself.

Kynnit, *ad.* like a tail lifted up (as, "ka sim ka dem *kynnit* ha ka tnat").

Kynnet, }
Kyn-nut, } (jrong-), *ad.* like a long protuberant object. [As "ka tdong kaba jrong *kynnet*."]

Kynnoh, *v.* to pronounce ; to blame, to find fault with. [*Imit.* kynnoh-kynta.]

Kyn-ói, *v.* to hush, to lull a child.

Kynpha, *v.* to address a male as if he were a female (by using personal pronouns in the feminine gender).

Kynphám, *v.* to help, to assist.

Kynphát, *u, n.* cotton.

Kynphia, *v.* to bluster.

Kynphót, *ad.* like a fop. [As, "u leh ialade *kynphót*."]

Kynphui, *v.* to wish to be unlucky, (especially in arrow-shooting),—*a.* bushy.

Kynphuit, *v.* to spit violently, to decry.

Kynphût, *ad.* improvidently, carelessly [as, "u masi u bam *kynphut* ia u kba"].

Kynphur, *ad.* loosely, (as, "ki mem ki riam phew *kynphur* ha ing").

Kynplam, *v.* to dabble.

Kynrâd, *n.* a master, a lord.

Kynrang, *v.* to undermine, to dig violently.

Kynràm, }
Kynrèm, } *ad.* with long horns pointing in opposite directions or with long moustaches.

Kynran, *v.* to retire, to go backwards.

Kynreng, *ad.* with long horns as those of a stag, obstructingly [as, "nga ioh-ih ia u masi ba u ieng *kynreng*."]

Kynrei, *a.* abundant, common.

Kynriang, *a.* crooked, leaning to one side.

Kynriah, *v.* to remove, to shift.

Kynrih, *v.* to sift with a sieve.

Kynro, *v.* to grope.

Kynrong, *v.* to raise oneself a little from the seat while sitting ; to prop.

Kynrong-sh'ing, *v.* to perform a ceremony for depositing the bones in the common ancestral cairn.

Kynroh, *ka, n.* a wall ;—*v.* to build a wall. [*Imit.* ka kynroh-ka kynram.]

Kynroi, *v.* to stir, agitate.

Kynroi-prie, *v.* to have nausea.

Kynrûh, *v.* to rinse, churn, rumble, shake. [*Imit.* kynruh-kynrang.]

Kynrum, *ad.* confusedly (like debris). [*Imit.* kynrum-kynram.]

Kynrum-kynram, *ki, n.* things lying about in confusion.

Kynrup, *v.* to pounce upon, to seize.

Kynsah, *v.* to strike or push with the elbow.

Kynsâi, *a.* of the best kind, selected, choice, sterling.

Kynsan, *ad.* forcibly, suddenly, [as, "ka miaw ka kynrup *kynsan* trait ia ka khnai."]

Kynsat, *v.* to insert, to stick to.

Kynsha, *a.* lonely, horrid, dangerous.

Kynshah, *v.* to side with ; to be close to.

Kynshait, *v.* to syringe.

Kynshdot, }
Kynshdút, } *ad.* shrewishly, [as, "balei phi leh *kynshdút* kumne."]

Kynshew, *v.* to collect, gather together ; to store up. [*Imit.* kynshew-kyndiap.]

Kynshin, *v.* to dislike eatable things.

Kynshoit, *v.* to instigate ; to abet.

Kynshriang, *a.* graceful, elegant (form).

Kynshu, *v.* to set a dog on.

Kynshur, *v.* to move forward.

Kynsi, *n.* a brother-in-law or sister-in-law ; (*deikynsi*) having relationship not prohibited by Khasi customs to marry.

Kynsia, *v.* to hiss.

Kynsit, *v.* to close the mouth of a pouch by drawing its thread on both sides.

Kynslup, }
Kynslip, } *v.* to suck violently.

Kynslut, *v.* to sniff, snuff.

Kynsnok, *v.* to snore.

*Kynta, *ka, n.* hour,—*v.* to make an unnecessary mention of details.

---

* Hindi.

Kyntait, *v.* to reject, to throw aside.

Kyntang, *a.* consecrated, holy;—*v.* to finish up the fringe of a net-work.

Kyntang-marâm, *u, n.* the spirit of a person who died on the high-way or out-of-doors and whose body lies exposed and unburnt. His attack to people is indicated by a severe headache.

Kynta-lyngkôr, *u, n.* the part of a plough from which the farmer holds and directs the plough-share.

Kyntar, *ad.* like a fox (with a drooping tail).

Kynteit, *v.* to speak or scold with a loud voice.

Kyntem, *ka, n.* the bed of a garden or field; threshing floor.

Kyntem-ñiuh-mat, *a.* lazy, slothful, (*lit.* having long drooping eye-lashes).

Kyntép, } *ad.* with drooping tail like a frightened dog or fox.
Kyntér, }

Kynthak, *ad.* lively, friskily, [as, " ine i khynnah iba smat noh teh *kynthak.*"]

Kynthah, *v.* to foment, to scar; to sting.

Kynthài, *ad.* beautifully (clothed), [as, " u pynnoh ia ka tdong bohkhaila *kynthài*"]; flowingly.

Kynthap, *v.* to be close to or against any object.

Kynthei, *ka, n.* female. [*Imit.* kynthei-khynnah.]

Kynthem, *ad.* with overlapping *dhoti*; flourishing. [*Imit.* kynthem-kynjai.]

Kynthen, *ad.* with a big calf, (as, " u Khasi u don ka khohwah kaba heh *kynthen*").

Kynthêr, *v.* to throw off, to shake.

Kynthêr-jymbuiñ, *v.* to disown a child (by a mother).

Kynthet, *ad.* violently, carelessly, [as, " wat ju shim *kynthet* ia kaei kaei ba sang"];—*v.* to shake off or break off (friendship).

Kynthêw, *ad.* with a long tail; in ragged clothes, [as, " u sim uba jrong u tdong *kynthêw.*"]

Kynthiak, *ad.* like a well dressed little girl, [as, " ine i khynnah iba bha briew *kynthiak.*"]

Kynthiap, *ad.* modestly, (as, " i khynnah i ïeng*kynthiap*").

Kynthih, *v.* to jump up (high),—*ad.* completely, fully, [as, " san snem *kynthih* nga la shong ryngkat bad phi mynta."]

Kynthlâp, *v.* to flap, splash.

Kynthong, *ad.* conspicuously (like a small solitary tree).

Kynthoh, *v.* to make a blotch or mark, to criticise; to comment on.

Kynthróng, } *ad.* crest-like, [as, u spong *kynthrong.*]
Kynthrúng, }

Kynthu, *v.* to give out as decided with a view to win the game.

Kynthung, *ad.* conspicuously (like a big solitary tree).

Kynthun, *ad.* with big, fat calves, (as, "u briew uba heh ka khohwah *kynthun*").

Kynthup, *ad.* modestly, well covered, [as, "nga ioh-i ia u shipai ba u kup la ka brandi *kynthup*"];—*v.* to embrace, clasp, comprise.

Kynthur, *ad.* with loose garments, (as, "u phong ka sopti kaba *kynthur*").

Kynti, *v.* to strike with a clenched fist on the back;—*n.* times, (as, shi*kynti*, once; ar*kynti*, twice);—*ad.* entirely, (as, ioh*kynti*, inherited).

Kyntiak, *a.* well-formed but small; smart.

Kyntiang, *v.* to make a clinging noise.

Kyntik, *v.* to make a dull sound, as if treading heavily on the ground.

Kyntien, *ka, n.* a morsel; a word (generally joined with numerals, Adjectives shi—, ár—, lai—).

Kyntiew, *v.* to lift, to impose, to promote.

Kyntiew-kurim, *v.* to perform a marriage ceremony.

Kyntiew-doh, *v.* to be healed (of a wound).

Kyntiew-iing, *v.* to admit in the house. [*Imit.* kyntiew-iing kyntiew-sem.]

Kynting, *v.* to throw upwards.

Kyntip, *v.* to ask one whether he knows what one is holding or thinking about; to disavow.

Kyntir, *ad.* with a small tail, (as, "u khñiang uba don tdong *kyntir*").

Kynto, *v.* to urge; press.

Kyntong, *a.* like a hillock, [as, "don iwei i lúm iba *kyntong* hajan Mawsmai."]

Kyntoi, *ad.* like a small protuberance.

Kyntoit, *ka, n.* a cluster of houses, a village, a quarter. [*Imit.* kyntoit-kyntiaj.]

Kynton, *v.* to heave;—*ka, n.* a heap, a mound, earthen wall.

Kyntóp (jrong-), *ad.* like a pig tail. [As, "ki *Blue-jackets* ki long ki shipai-lieng ba phong i tupia iba *kyntóp*".]

Kyntu, *v.* to urge, persuade.

Kyntung, *a.* like a hill or mound, [as, "don uwei u marok uba *kyntung* hangtai."]

Kyntui, *ad.* largely.

Kyntuit, *v.* to urge (bad sense), to instigate.

Kyntúp, *ad.* with a long drooping tail like that of a fox.

Kyntur, *v.* to push with the nose ; to burrow.

Kyn-úd, *v.* to sing, to hum ; to intone ; to chant.

Kyn-um, *u, n.* a brother-in-law. [*Imit.* u kyn-um-u iing.]

Kyoh, *ka, n.* (*vide* k'oh).

Kyr-ang, *v.* to crack. *Saw kyrang*, reddish.

Kyr-ah, *a.* ring-shaped (like the ring seen in the tail of a rattle-snake).

Kyr-an, *a.* short but stout.

Kyrbam, *v.* to bite the nether lip.

Kyrbei, *ka, n.* a mantis.

Kyrbeit, *a.* warped, distorted ;—*v.* to strain, to exert. [*Imit.* kyrbeit-kyrthing.]

Kyrkait, *v.* to shout exultingly.

Kyrkhah, *ka, n.* phlegm ;—*v.* to clear the throat.

Kyrkhait, *v.* to gnaw with zest.

Kyrkhoit, *ka, n.* a cartilage.

Kyrkhu, *v.* to bless ; to produce a particular sound (*khu*). [*Imit.* kyrkhu-kyrdoh.]

Kyrkieh, *v.* to be in a hurry ;—*ad.* hastily. [*Imit.* kyrkieh-kyrda.]

Kyrking, *ad.* like a small connecting link or portion between two large bodies ; slender (as, ka " *Isthmus Panama* ka sah sa *kyrking*").

‡Kyrkit, *ka, n.* a cricket, play-ground.

Kyrkoh, *v.* to crow over a person.

Kyrda, *v.* to exert, strive, to use one's strength.

Kyrdan, *ka, n.* step, degree, shelf. [*Imit.* kyrdan-kyrnah].

Kyrdáp, } *ad.* as if wearing something hanging, (as, "u kieng ia
Kyrdép, } ka tráp *kyrdáp*").

Kyrdat, *ad.* dangling, (as, "ka iarong ka sdien *kyrdat* ha ka tyrpeng").

Kyrdem, *v.* to stamp with the foot.

---

‡ English.

Kyrdoh, *v.* to exert.

Kyrdon, *ka, n.* stair, step, degree. [*Imit.* ka kyrdon-ka kyrnah.]

Kyrdot, *ad.* hangingly (like a small ball). [As, "bún ki Khasi ki deng *kyrdot* da ki 'siar-tylli."]

Kyrdûh, *a.* needy, poor, wanting. [*Imit.* kyrduh-kyrtan.]

Kyrdut, *ad.* like a big ball hanging. [As, "nga ioh-i ba ka don kaba atsohkhliang *kyrdut* ha ka shkor u Wár."]

Kyr-eit, *a.* vain, foppish.

Kyrngah, *v.* to shake the head as a sign of disapproval; to be unwilling; to decline. [*Imit.* kyrngah-kyrngang.]

Kyrngang, *ad.* like a lonely boy or truant.

Kyrngaid, *v.* to eat with zest.

Kyrngem, *ka, n.* a fruit-pigeon.

Kyrngiang, *ka, n.* a piece of skin of a pig with the fat adhering to it.

Kyrngong, *ad.* like a modest boy, (as, "u khynnah u shong tipsngi *kyrngong*").

Kyrhai, *a.* abundant;—*ad.* abundantly.

Kyrhieh, *v.* to speak or threaten aloud like a drunkard.

Kyr-iah, *v.* to cut a fish horizontally at short intervals for frying or cooking; to cut at short intervals.

Kyr-iap, } **Kyr-iep**, } *ad.* standing like a diseased fowl. [As, "balei utai u 'khar-káw u ieng *kyriap* ha lyeit dieng?"]

Kyr-iat, *v.* to gnash.

Kyr-iáw, *a.* seasoned, full-grown.

Kyr-ih, *v.* to turn round and round while in a sitting posture; to turn as on a hinge.

Kyrjaw, } **Kyrjúit**, } *v.* to scrub, to rub.

Kyrmen, *v.* to hope.

Kyrnâi, *ad.* in the same place, [as, "u shu shong *kyrnâi* hajuh hi."]

Kyrni, *a.* addicted to, accustomed to.

Kyrñiom, *v.* to roll up (like a cloth when washed); to spoil by rough handling.

Kyrnot, *a.* stubborn, hard, lasting.

Kyr-oh, *v.* to carve in a concave shape, (as the head of an arrow to fit the bow-string).

Kyr-ot, *a.* stubborn, easily provoked.

Kyrpâd, *v.* to pray, beg, supplicate. [*Imit.* kyrpád-kyrpon.]

Kyrpang, *ad.* aside, separately ;—*a.* separate, set apart, particular.

Kyrpong, *ka, n.* the back of the house.

Kyr-sa, *v.* to undermine, (*esp.* in soft earth or sand as a mole does).

Kyrsan-kyrbah, *v.* to call on the gods for the restoration of one's good health or prosperity.

Kyrsan-rngiew, *v.* to call back one's good luck or life by invoking the gods.

Kyrshah, *v.* to put on a piece of cloth in front, (being a part of the dress of women).

Kyrshán, *v.* to uphold, help, to support.

Kyrshung, *a.* having the appearance of a wedge, (as, "u sniang u iaid *kyrshung*").

Kyrshut, *a.* to rub, scour.

Kyrsia, *v.* to squirt ; to spurt.

Kyrsiew, *v.* to call up, to wake up.

Kyrsih, *v.* to go on the haunches, to crawl (as a child).

Kyrsong, *v.* to be swollen (like a boil) ; to come to a head.

Kyrsoi, *v.* to ooze, to come out.

Kyrsúh, *v.* to poke.

Kyrsum, *v.* to wallow.

Kyrteng, *v.* to name ;—*ka, n.* a name.

Kyrtep, *u, n.* an evil-spirit who causes blindness to a man. This affliction is ascribed to the adultery of the father which is visited on his children.

Kyrthái, *v.* to turn round or drive in as with an auger.

Kyrthat, *v.* to sprawl, to writhe.

Kyrthiaw, *v.* to twist ; to maul.

Kyrthom, *v.* to tread heavily on the dust or mud so as to cause damage to crops, etc.

Kyrthup, *v.* to bathe in the dust or sand (as a fowl does).

Kyrtiang, *v.* to turn round.

Kyrtiah, *u, n.* a wind-demon ; a storm mixed with rain.

Kyrtong, *u, n.* a bull, an ox ; a hero.

Kyrtoh, *v.* to leap, to curvet.

Kyrtoh-lyndet, *v.* to rebound, to re-act.

Kyrtúng, *ad.* prominently, bulgingly; [as, phi lah ba'n ioh-i ia u Kyllang nalor u lum Shillong, u tai *kyrtung.*]

Kyrwap, } Kyrwep, } Kyrwop, } *ad.* easily (bent), pliably; [as, "u briew u la jem *kyrwap.*"]

Kyrwat, *ka, n.* a turn (of a path).

Kyrweng, *ad.* loose. [As, "ki Saheb ki ju phong mynmiet ka sopti kaba *kyrweng.*"]

Kyrwiang, *v.* to wind up, to turn round. [*Imit.* kyrwiang-kyrwit.]

Kyrwit, *ka, n.* a round, a turn.

Kyrwoh, *n.* a link, a ring; *aikyrwoh,* to give notice by sending round a ring made of cane or of bamboo, etc.

D.

D, the fourth letter in the Khasi Alphabet.

Da, (1) *prep.* by, with, through: (2) often used to express contingency and to soften a command; [as, "haba phi shim ruh *da* rah biang biang ioh hap."] (3) *v.* to protect.

Dáb, *u, n.* a bullock;—*ka, n.* the handle of a knife.

Dabi, *ka, n.* a small box or case; a claim;—*v.* to lay claim to.

Dabia, *ka, n.* a small box or case.

Dabor, *ka, n.* a basin; a double pice.

Dáb-tari, *n.* a handle of a knife;—*u, n.* a *daftri* or book-binder.

Dak, *u, n.* a sign, a letter; a mark; a postal runner;—*ad.* at once, immediately; [as, "u myrsiang "u la dait ia ka blang, hynrei tang nga shu poi u la iehnoh *dak.*"] [*Imit.* ka dak-ka shin.]

Daka, *ka, n.* a cowrie selected out of a lot for use in gambling.

†Dakáid, *n.* an evil doer; a dacoit.

†Dakhir, *v.* to deposit; entrust; file.

Dakhol, } †Dokhor, } †Dakhor, } *v.* to appropriate; to take possession of.

Dád, *a.* hard, hot tempered, strict.

† Bengali.

Dadien, *ad.* backward; [as, u iaid *dadien.*]

Dang, *ad.* yet, still, just; [as, trei katba *dang* im; khie *dang* step lashai, ho];—*v.* to commence.

Dangkhie, *a.* young, growing. [*Imit.* dangkhie-dangsan.]

Dang-ngir, *ad.* early in the morning.

Dah, *v.* to prepare (pan-leaf and lime);—*n.* preparation (for sacrifice). [*Imit.* ka dah-ka-dong]—*v.* to commence, begin. (*Synteng* to copulate.)

Dahara, } (Jainsem), *n.* an outer garment worn by Khasi women.
Dhara, }

*Dai, *ka, n.* a wet nurse,—*ka dái, n.* a fine. Hindi *dál.*

Daiñ, *v.* to impose (a fine); to cut.

Daiñ-daiñ, *a.* wide, spacious; [as, ki la siang ka rynsan kaba *daiñ-daiñ* halor.]

Daiñdong, *v.* to corner some one in argument.

Daiñ-dor, *v.* to fix the price; to haggle.

Daini-daikot, *ka, n.* a witch.

Dait, *v.* to bite, itch, worry;—*pyndait, v.* to fit.

'dait, *u, n.* (*abbrev.* of kdait) *ekra,* reed.

Dait-doh, *a.* compact, thick.

Dait-thah, *a.* very cold; ice-like.

Da lei-lei, *phr.* at any cost.

Dam, *a.* obliterated.

Da-mar, *phr.* used in contemptuous expressions or in challenging; [as, "*da-mar* une u pran ia leh."]

Dambit, *v.* to stick, to adhere.

Dana, *n.* food, grain (especially given to animals)—*ad.* a bit (used with *shi-*, as, "ym don *shi dana* ruh.")

Danda, *a.* deceiving, cheating, befooling, tricky,—*v.* to joke. [*Imit.* danda-phulit.]

Dap, *a.* full, sufficient, enough.

Dap-hom (ym-), *v.* to be unsatiable.

Dar-dar, *adv.* with quick light steps; [as, iaid *dar-dar.*]

Dara, *ka, n.* a temporary hut; a tent; shelter.

Dá'rap-jot, *phr.* to make a lame excuse.

Dár-lieng, *ka, n.* the trace of a boat in shallow water.

* Hindi.

Dat, *v.* to beat. [*Imit.* dat-shoh.]

Dathew, *ad.* thoughtfully, deliberately ; [as, leh *dathew*; kren *dathew.*]

Dáw, *n.* a cause, an excuse. [*Imit.* ka dáw-ka dong.]

Dáw-dáw (eh), *ad.* tough ; [as, " ka doh ka la eh *dáw-dáw.*"]

Dawa, *v.* to claim.

Dawai, *ka*, *n.* medicine. [*Imit.* dawai-dashin.]

Dkai, *u*, *n.* a kind of small honey-fly.

Dkár, *ka*, *n.* a tortoise.

Dkáw, *ad.* in reserve for an emergency.

Dkhái, *v.* to pull in pieces.

Dkhan, *u*, *n.* a kind of hill-rat or mole.

Dkhap, *ka*, *n.* a tick, (*ixodes*).

Dkhar, *u*, *n.* a non-Khasi. [*Imit.* u dkhar-u-lyngkien.]

Dkhat, *v.* to break off or snap.

Dkháw, *v.* to come off (as hair), to become bald.

Dkhew, *u*, *n.* a kind of gnat.

Dkhi, *u*, *n.* a small kind of wasp.

Dkhiat, *u*, *n.* itch, (*acarus scabiei*).

Dkhiew, *u*, *n.* ant.

Dkhot, *ka*, *n.* a part, a piece, a member, a verse ;—*u*, pieces of meat used in sacrifice. [*Imit.* u dkhot- u dkhái.]

Dkhoh, *ka*, *n.* an owl.

Dko, *n.* the people living in the north-western part of the Khasi Hills, on the borders of the Garo Hills ; the Garos. [*Imit.* u Dko-u Lyngngam.]

Dkoh, *a.* lame. [*Imit.* Dkoh-dkia.]

Dkut, *v.* to snap, break, finish up.

Dkut-mynsiem, *v.* to give up the ghost.

De, *ad.* also, too ; [as, "nga ruh nga'n leit *de.*"]

***Dek**, *u*, *n.* a large cooking vessel, a *dekchi.*

Deng, *v.* to put on (jewels), to adorn with ornaments. [*Imit.* deng-kup.]

Deng-deng, *ad.* with ease ; [as, " ia uba beh u khiew ruh ka rah *deng-deng.*"]

---

* Hindi.

Dei, *v.* to belong to, to hit—*a.* fit, proper, right, related.

Dei-thana, *a.* having some relationship by marriage. [*Imit.* dei thana-dei thakher.]

Dem, *v.* to bend, to lie down, yield, bow, to be deeply engaged in ; —*ad.* constantly ; assiduously ; [as, u *dem* leit, u *dem* wankái.]

Demdiap, *ad.* assiduously, continually; [as, "u iaiwan *dem diap* ha iing."]

Demshylliah, *v.* to be suffering from chronic illness

Den, *ad.* fast, stedfastly ; [as, nga la jan ur hynne hinrei tang ba . nga ioh snoh na u dieng nga la neh *den.*]—*v.* to bund.

Den-den, *ad.* with firm steps (of a child) ; [as, iaid *den-den.*]

Dep, *v.* to finish—*ad.* in full, all.

Der-der, *ad.* lightly, gaily (walk) ; [as, " ki Sohra haba leit Tharia ki iaid *der-der.*"]

'dér-phiang, *u*, *n.* grass dressed for thatching.

*Desi, *a.* country-made.

Det, *int.* pooh ! Tush !

Déw, *int.* a word used in calling a dog—*ka Dew*, *n.* a wave (at sea).

'dew (*abbrev.* of khyndew), *ka*, *n.* earth, dust.

'dewbyrtha, *ka*, *n.* clay.

'dewksang, *ka*, *n.* hard earth.

'dewkynroi, *ka*, *n.* loose earth.

'dewiong, *u*, *n.* coal.

'dewlangni, *ka*, *n.* meadow.

'dewlynnong, *ka*, *n.* an island.

'dewmet, *ka*, *n.* dust ; earth or soil free from sand and stone.

'dewsáw, *ka*, *n.* red earth.

'dewshrah, *ka*, *n.* fallow land ; arable land ; virgin soil.

'dewtrái, *ka*, *n.* solid earth, *terra firma*, (the opposite of '*dew-kynroi*).

Dngang, *ad.* lonely, (as, " u don tang marwei *dngang*").

Dngiang, *ad.* lively, (as, u peit *dngiang*).

Dngiem, *n.* a bear.

Dngong, *ad.* in the same place, steadfastly, (as, u ap *dngong*).

'di, *n.* *abbrev.* of " bdi " *i.e.*, 20.

---

* Hindi.

Diang, *v.* to receive,—*n.* the left.

'diang (*abbrev.* of "pdiang"), *v. imper.* receive it.

'diangti-diangjat, *v.* to receive completely.

Diap, *ad.* carefully, minutely; [as, "phi dei ba'n da tám bha *diap* ia ki sapiet-sapái."]

Diaw, *ad.* low-spirited, disappointed; [as, "balei u leh *diaw* kum-tai."]

*dik, *a.* to become troublesome.

Didiaw, *ka, n.* a long-legged bird; also called "ka Diawoit" from its cry.

Dikdik, *ad.* very, dearly, longingly; [as, "u kwah *dik-dik* ba'n ia shem bad la ki khún."]

Die, *v.* to sell, betray. [*Imit.* die-thied.]

Die-baibat, *v.* to sell for cash.

Die-baitrái, *v.* to sell at a cost price.

Die-khutia, *v.* to sell in retail. [*Imit.* die khutia-khutain.]

Die-dúh, *v.* to sell away; to sell at a loss. [*Imit.* die-duh die-sep]

Dieng, *u* or *ka, n.* wood, tree,—*u.* timber. [*Imit.* ka dieng-ka siej.]

Dieng-bilat, *ka, n.* the gum-tree.

Diengblei, *u, n.* sál tree. (*Bot*). *Shorea Robusta.*

Dieng byllan, *u, n.* a wooden sleeper; a cat's paw.

Dieng bylliat, *u, n.* a hard wood used as posts.

Diengbti or diengbyti, *ka, n.* a red-wood used for making bed-steads, chairs, etc., *poma,* (*Bot.*) *Cedrela toona.*

Diengkáiñ, *ka, n.* a tree whose bark produces a sore if handled. (*Bot.*) *Rhus succedanea.*

Diengkseh, *u, n.* the pine-wood. (*Bot.*) *Pinus Khasya.*

Diengkurlong, *ka, n.* (*Bot.*) *melia composita.*

Diengkya, *n.* (see Kya). (*Bot.*) *Bombay malabaricum*; a cotton tree.

Diengdáw, *ka, n.* a hard dried wood.

Diengdoh, *ka, n.* (*Bot.*) *Buclandia populnea*; a tree with leaves like the betel but thick; a name of one of the Khasi clans.

Diengduh, *u, n.* staff, walking stick. [*Imit.* diengduh-diengshán.]

Dieng-ngan, *ka, n.* a tree which is sometimes dressed for timber. (*Bot.*) *Schima wallichii.*

---

* Hindi.

Dieng-ngai, *ka, n.* the "iron-tree" or *nahor* ; *Nagessor.* (*Bot.*) *Mesua ferrea.*

Diengiap, *ka, n.* fire-wood, dried-wood.

Diengiap-ieng, *ka, n.* a tree which is withered up.

Dieng-iei, *ka, n.* the name of a gigantic tree in Khasi folklore supposed to have grown at the beginning of creation on the hill west of and over-looking the Shillong station. It is said that the tree was of such an enormous size that it over-shadowed the whole earth. [*Imit.* diengiei-diengpict.]

Dieng lamaki, *ka, n.* (*Bot.*) *Symplocus racemosa.* A kind of tree the leaves of which are used in dyeing cloths.

Diengjamynrei, *u, n.* a shrub much used in making *tikia.*

Diengjiug, *u, n.* (*Bot.*) *Quercus spicata.*

Dienglieng, *ka, n.* the name of a tall and straight tree. (*Bot.*) *Betula accuminata.*

Dienglyngngong, *ka, n.* the stump or knob of a tree. [*Imit.* Dienglyngngong-dienglyngngiang.]

Dienglymbong, *ka, n,* a piece of undressed wood, a part of a trunk, a log.

Diengmet, *ka, n.* a term applied to all trees besides pine-trees.

Dieng-ñiangmat, *ka, n.* a shrub whose bark yields a yellow colour and is used as medicine for eye sores ; (*Bot.*) *Berberis Nepalensis* ; a kind of holly.

Diengphasi, *ka, n.* the gallows.

Diengpingwait, *ka, n.* a tree whose bark is of a lively green colour used in making handle for *daw,* etc. (*Bot.*) *Daphnidium pulcherrimum.*

Diengplina, *u, n.* a bolt, a piece of stick for stretching out things (as skins) ; the cross.

Diengphnieng, *u, n.* the bolt of a trap.

Diengpyngkiang, *u, n.* a cross-bar, obstacle.

Dieng-ri, *ka, n.* (*Bot.*) *Quercus dealbata.*

Dieng-rtiang, *ka, n.* (*Bot.*) *Quercus serrata* ; oak.

Diengsawdong, *u, n.* a square piece of timber or post ; a beam.

Diengshalangmat, *u, n.* a rafter.

Diengsahbiar, *u, n.* a batten.

Diengshaindoh, *ka, n.* a piece of wood where flesh is minced, a chopping board ; one who forbears ill-treatment.

Diengshankhung, *u, n.* a truss.

Diengshiah, *u, n.* a brier, a thorn, a bramble.

Diengshynrain, *ka, n.* a dried twig. [*Imit.* diengshynrain-diengshynriah.]

Diengsning, *ka, n.* a kind of oak tree, a Khasi oak, (*Bot.*) *Castanopsis sp.*

Diengsong *ka, n.* a prickly-tree resembling *ka kya* or the simul cree ;(in Assamese) *madar.* (*Bot.*) *Erythrina* ; an instrument made of pieces of wood for punishing criminals ; stocks.

Diengsohbyrthit, *u, n.* a shrub bearing sticky flowers.

Diengsohkynphor, *u, n.* the papaya tree.

Diengsohli-ia, *ka, n.* a tree whose thick bark is used in colouring earthen wares. (*Bot.*) *Myrica Nagi.*

Diengsohiong, *u, n.* a Khasi cherry tree. (*Bot.*) *Prunus ferruginea.*

Diengsohlyngdkhur, *u, n.* the mulberry tree.

Diengsohmanir, *u, n.* a litchee tree.

Diengsohñiamtra, *ka, n.* an orange-tree.

Diengsohpairah, *n.* (*Bot.*) *Sapindus mukorrosi* ; the soap nut. (Hindi) *ritha.*

Diongsohphán, *u, n.* the jack-fruit tree.

Diengsohpieng, *u, n.* the mango tree.

Diengsohphoh, *u, n.* the apple-tree (wild). (*Bot.*) *Pyrus granulata.*

Diengsohpri-am, *u, n.* the guava tree.

Diengsohshur, *u, n.* the wild pear-tree.

Diengsuwali, *u, n.* one of the sticks attached to the big cross-stick of a plough to guard the neck of the ox.

Diengthang, *ka, n.* wood for erecting a funeral pyre.

Diengthlieh, *ka, n.* a split piece of fire wood.

Diengtylláw, *ka, n.* a brand.

Diengtylli, *u, n.* a whole piece of wood.

Die-laka, }
Die-lang, } *kaba, n.* a wholesale.

Die-lilám, *v.* to sell by auction.

Dien, *ka, n.* track, trace, mark. [*Imit.* ka dien-ka búd.]

Dienjat, *ka, n.* foot-print.

Dier., *v.* to be too late.

Ding, *n. ka,* fire. [*Imit.* ka ding-ka theh.]

Dingpyrthat, *ka*, *n.* fire lighted by a flash of lightning.

Dingsuid-tán, *ka*, *n.* will-o'-the wisp, *ignis fatuus*, jack-o'-lantern.

Dih, *v.* to drink [*Imit.* dih-bám.]

Dihduma, *v.* to smoke. [*Imit.* dihduma-dihdukhew.]

Dihe, *a.* big and fat.

Dihia, *a.* fat and heavy.

Diho, *a.* short and fat.

Dób-dób, *ad.* slowly and steadily (child), [as, " i khúnlung i la sdang iaid *dób-dób.*"]

Dok, *v.* to kiss; to correct or counterpoise the balance before weighing things,—*ka*, *n.* a canister.

Dod-dod, Dud dud } *ad.* quiveringly, as an old man (walks); [as, " u la tymmen *dod-dod* mynta."]; very weakly attached; [as, " ka bniat ka la khih *dod-dod.*"]

Dong, *ka*, *n.* corner, quarters, angle. [*Imit.* ka dong-ka kuna.]

'dong (*abbrev.* of tyndong), *ka*, *n.* tube, pipe; [as, ka *dong* tympew.]

Dong, *v.* to roll up *pán* or any leaf in a conical shape (like a *khili*).

Dongkor, *ka*, *n.* the back of the ear.

Dong dong, *ad.* without any difficulty, easily, [as, " ia u khiewphiang ruh u rah *dong-dong.*"]

Dongla, *ka*, *n.* a species of bamboo.

Dong lótlót, *ka*, *n.* a kind of flageolet.

Donglydong, *ad.* completely; [as, " u tyllun *donglydong.*"]

Dongmatang, *ka*, *n.* a right angle.

Dongmatla, *ka*, *n.* a bamboo with diseased joints.

Dongnái, *ka*, *n.* the end of the spinal bone; the coccyx.

Dongnit, *ad.* like the tail of a wag-tail; [as, " i sim iba jrong tdong *dongnit.*"]

Dongrong, *ad.* like a small helpless beetle; [as, kli *dongrong.*]

'dong shimat, *ka*, *n.* a bamboo tube between two joints; a person who cannot keep secrets.

'dongtympew, *ka*, *n.* a *chunga* for *pán* leaf.

Doh, *v.* to kiss. [*Imit.* doh-dait.]—*ka*, *n.* flesh, meat. [*Imit.* ka doh-ka-kah.]

Dohbniat, *ka, n.* the gums at the root of the teeth.

Dohkha, *ka, n.* fish. [*Imit.* dohkha-dohpnat.]

Dohksew, *a.* obstinate, dogged.

Dohkrung, *ka, n.* the rib.

Dohksah, *ka, n.* the muscle.

Dohkyndang, *ka, n.* a string of meat.

Dohdah, *u, n.* the uvula.

Doh-iap, *ka, n.* carrion,—*a.* desperate, reckless.

Dohjem, *ka, n.* the internal soft parts of the body, such as the liver, the lungs, the kidneys, the heart, and other organs in the chest and abdomen.

Dohlen, *ka, n.* the gums without the teeth as those of a baby.

Dohmasi, *ka, n.* beef.

Dohmet, *ka, n.* the lean.

Dohmrád, *ka, n.* venison. [*Imit.* dohmrád-dohmreng.]

Dohniej (kren-), *ad.* in a gentle flow of speech; [as, kren *dohniej.*]

Dohnúd, *u, n.* the liver,—*ka,* heart or mind. [*Imit.* dohnúd-dohnám.]

Dohsatar, *ka, n.* tough flesh (next to the muscle).

Dohshyieng, *ka, n.* bones (with flesh attached to them).

Dohsniang, *ka, n.* pork.

Dohsnieh, *a.* dogged, stubborn.

Dohsohkhia, *u, n.* a piece of bone or cartilage to be found in the chests of cattle.

Dohtaitwait, *ka, n.* odds and ends (of meat).

Dohtdong, *ka, n.* the hump.

Dohthéj, *ad.* with fluency and aptness of speech; [as, " u kren *dohthéj.*"]

Dohthli, *u, n.* a small fish. [*Imit.* dohthli-dohthám.] *Bengali,* জাল মাস।

*Doi, *ka, n.* curd.

Doi-doi, *ad.* as in a swing, to and fro; [as, pawang *doi-doi*]; weak, [as, nga sngew *doi-doi.*]

Doloi, *u, n.* a ruler or chief (in Jaintia Hills); a title of honour.

Dom, *a.* hot tempered, hard;—*ka, n.* a pull (of smoke).

Domriang, *a.* having an angry appearance.

Don, *v.* is, has, exists.

---

* Hindi.

Dón-dón, *ad.* firmly (walk, like a little bird or child) ; [as, " i khúnlung mynta i la iaid *dón-dón.*"]

Don-akór, *a.* well-behaved ; polite, civil.

Donbàk, *v.* to dare (used in challenging or with contemptuous expression).

Donbok, *v.* to be lucky.

Donbór, *a.* powerful, influential. [*Imit.* donbór-donsor.]

Donburom, *a.* honourable. [*Imit.* donburom-donsurom.]

Donkam, *v.* to need, to have business, to be occupied. [*Imit.* donkam-donjam.]

Donduk, *v.* to have complaints or troubles. [*Imit.* donduk-donpap.]

Dondur, *a.* beautiful ; well carved or fashioned. [*Imit.* dondur-dondar]

Don-iktiar, *a.* having authority.

Donráin, *a.* having sense of honour. [*Imit.* donráin-donrem.]

Dop, *ka, n.* the bark or layer as of a plantain tree or bamboo.

Dop-kait, *ka, n.* the bark of a plantain tree.

Dopwái, *ka, n.* the outercrust or cover of an areca-nut tree.

Dór, *ka, n.* price ; [*Imit.* ka dor-ka mur.]—*a.* distorted, curved.

Dorbár, *ka, n.* council. [*Imit.* ka dorbár-ka sorbar.]

*Dorbin, *ka, n.* a telescope ; glasses.

*Dorkhat, *n.* a petition, application. [*Imit.* ka dorkhat-ka dorpat.]

*Dorji, *n.* a tailor.

*Doroga, *u, n.* an Inspector or Sub-Inspector of Police ; a *Doraga.*

*Dorwán, *u, n.* a door-keeper.

†Doskot, *v.* to sign.

†Dostabit, *ka, n.* an agreement on paper ; a bond.

Dpei, *ka, n.* hearth ; ashes.

Du, *ad.* after all, well, really, is n't it ? [as, " ka'm long kumta *du* ? Khat u nang iaid *du.*]

Duwai, or Duai, } *v.* to pray ;—*n.* prayer. [*Imit.* duai-phirat.]

---

* Hindi. † Bengali.

Duwan, or Duan, } *ka*, *n*. an altar. [*Imit.* duwan-dupat.]

Duár, *ka*, *n*. a door, an opening, a *hât* ; a mart. [*Imit.* duar-ka lynti.]

Dubasia, *u*, *n*. an interpreter.

*Dubi, *n*. a *dhobi* or washerman.

Duk, *a*. poor, needy. [*Imit.* duk-suk or ka duk-ka pap.]

*Dukán, *ka*, *n*. a shop, bazaar.

*Dukándár, *n*. a shop-keeper.

†Dukha, *v*. to be in sorrow or anxiety.

Dukhi, *a*. niggardly,—*ad*. with extreme cursing, tenaciously, desparately. [*Imit.* dukhi-dukhait.]

Dûd or Dût, *v*. to make sacrifice for driving away devils.

*Dud, *ka*, *n*. milk.

Dung, *v*. to stab, pierce.

Duh, *v*. to lose, to forfeit. [*Imit.* duh-tan, *or*, duh-sep.]

Duh-(a suffix) which means entirely, once for all, as in the word iap-*duh*, die-*duh*, sah-*duh*.

Duh-buit, *v*. to be perplexed ; to be in a fix. [*Imit.* duhbuit-duhlád.]

Duh-ei, *v*. to lose, to forfeit, to waste.

Duhjingkyrmen, *v*. to be hopeless ; to despair.

Duhái, *phr*. not at all, in the name of (used in speaking anything solemnly as, " *duhai* maharani").

Duhalia, *ki*, *n*. funeral flute-players.

Duhoi, *kaba*, *n*. a cheer (by saying *hoi-hoi*).

*Dui, *n*. two-cowries (in gambling).

Dui-dui, *ad*. to and fro, up and down (big) ; [as, "ka rúh ka khih *dui-dui*."]

Dúid (wah), *ka*, *n*. a rivulet, stream.

Duitara, *ka*, *n*. a harp.

*Dujok, *ka*, *n*. hell.

*Dulan, *ka*, *n*. a brick-house ; masonry building. [*Imit.* ka dulan-ka paki.]

---

* Hindi. | † Bengali.

Dule, *v.* to keep or fulfil one's promise, used only with the negative " ym."

Duli, *ka*, *n.* a palanquin.

†Dulir, *ka*, *n.* document,—*v.* to put to task, punish.

Dulon, *v.* to toil, to plod.

Dum, *a.* dark, ignorant.

†Dúm, *n.* a fisherman. [*Imit.* u dúm-u maswa.]

Duma, *u*, *n.* tobacco. [*Imit.* duma-dukhew.]

Dumadih, *u*, *n.* tobacco for smoking in a *hooka* prepared with treacle.

Dumasla *u*, *n.* tobacco leaf.

Dumbuit, *v.* to be confounded, to be at a loss.

Dum-dngiem, *v.* to be at a loss (*coloq.*)

Duml'oh, or Dumlyoh, } *v.* to be foggy or misty.

Dummiew, *a.* shady, sunless (opposite of *ryngngi*).

Dumok, *v.* to threaten, scold. [*Imit.* dumok-kamok.]

Dún-dún, *ad.* with firm steps (like the walking of a hen).

Duna, *a.* short, faulty, little.

Dup, *aux. v.* may, in order that ; [*as*, minot ba'n *dup* nang.]

Dur, *ka*, *n.* shape, form, picture. [*Imit.* ka dur-ka dar.]

Durblei, *ka*, *n.* an image.

*Duri-pó, *ka*, *n.* a kind of gambling.

*Duriap, *v.* to ponder, think.

Dur-lanot, *int.* good gracious ! bother it !

*Duriaw, *ka*, *n.* the sea.

*Dusmon, *n.* an enemy. [*Imit.* u dusmon-u dandia.]

*Dustur, *ka*, *n.* custom, habit.

†Dusuiñ, *ka*, *n.* a Bengali basket.

Duwai, *v.* to pray, supplicate. [*Imit.* duwai-phirat.]

Duwali, *ka*, *n.* the Kali Poojah festival ; the annual gambling season.

Duwan, *ka*, *n.* an altar. [*Imit.* ka duwan-ka dupat.]

*Duwani, *ka*, *n.* civil suit ; civil court.

---

* Hindi. | † Bengali.

Dyngkhong, *ka*, *n.* a stump (of a tree); [*Imit.* dyngkhong-dyngkhait.]

Dyngngor, *ad.* to be in a stupified state, spell-bound, (as, " u leh biej *dyngngor*").

Dyngheng, *ad.* amazed, surprised ; [as, " u peit lyngngoh *dyngheng.*"]

Dyngong, or Dngong, *ad.* intently, stedfastly ; [as, " u ksew u ap *dyngong.*"]—*u*, *n.* a small bear.

Dympuin, *ka*, *n.* manure (of a *jhum* cultivation).

Dypei, *ka*, *n.* hearth,—*u*, *n.* ashes, same as *dpei.*

E.

E, the fifth letter in the Khasi alphabet.

Ekjakor, *u*, *n.* a devil in the shape of a serpent; a fabulous sea-monster.

‡Eksamin, *ka*, *n.* examination,—*v.* to examine.

Eng-eng, *a.* sound and healthy ; [as, " kumno u briew uba dang *eng-eng* u shu iap ?"]

*Engrej, *n.* the English.

Eh, *a.* hard, difficult, unrelenting,—*ad.* very, exceedingly,—*int.* fie !

Eh-eh, *a.* exceedingly hard or stiff, very tedious.

E-he, *int.* expression of disapproval; expression of triumph and wonder, especially when followed by *heb.* [as, "*e-he heb,* u mareh u kulai."]

Ei=a word used to emphasize or soften the expression; [as, tip-*ei* =who knows ; nga la bthah *ei* ia u =I did instruct him.]

'Ei ? (*contr. u-ei, ka-ei, i-ei*) *pron.* who ? what ? [as, '*ei* kata ba pah ?]

-ei—suffix which means *gratis*, gratuitously ; [as, " u la ai-*ei* ia nga kane."]

Ei-ei, *n.* something, anything.

Ei-ei-ruh-em, *phr.* nothing at all.

Eire, *ka*, *n.* something (already said or understood.)

Eit, *ka*, *n.* stool, dung, excrement, scum. [*Imit.* ka eit-ka ksem.]

Eit-kor, *ka*, *n.* ear-wax.

---

* Hindi. | ‡ English.

Eit-dang, *kaba*, *n.* hard evacuations or faeces.

Eit-masi, *ka*, *n.* cow-dung.

Eit-mat, *ka*, *n.* eye-pus. [*Imit.* eitmat-eitmut.]

Eitmut, *ka*, *n.* nose-pus. [*Imit.* eitmut-eitmat.]

Eit-nar, *ka*, *n.* slag of an iron-furnace.

*Elashi, *u*, *n.* cardamon.

Ém, *ad.* no.

Èm=a word used at the end of a sentence to soften the expression; it is also equivalent to *you know.* [as, " ynda lah bam lah dih *èm*, nga sa leit noh"]. (In *Synteng* it means *there is.*)

Èm (badon-ba-), *a.* well-to-do.

Èn, *v.* to cease from crying; to keep silence.

Èn-ja, *v.* to remain without taking food. [*Imit.* enja-enjhur.]

Èr, *ad.* like the appearance of a sudden burst of flames; [as, " ynda ka ding ka la ieng *èr*, ki sa kyndit."]

Èr-èr, *ad.* in full blaze; [as, " ka ding ka dang meh *èr-èr.*"]

'ér (*abbrev.* of lyer), *ka*, *n.* air, wind, breeze.

'ér-batasi-ér-batamon, *ka*, *n.* a cool refreshing breeze.

'ér-kyllang, *ka*, *n.* a cyclone.

'ér-kyrtiah, *ka*, *n.* a storm mingled with rain.

'ér-iong, *ka*, *n.* a storm. [*Imit.* 'er--iong-'er-ngit.]

'ér-langthari, *ka*, *n.* a whirl-wind.

Ew! *inter.* ejaculation of dismay or surprise = Oh! Ah!

G.

G, the sixth letter in the Khasi alphabet, but very seldom used. It is pronounced *egg.* (এগ্.)

*Gadda (see kadda.)

Garo, *n.* the Garo (same as Karo.)

*Gian (see Kian.)

Giri (see Kiri.)

‡Gospel, *ka*, *n.* the Gospel.

*Gali, *ka*, *n.* same as Kali.

---

* Hindi. | ‡ English.

NG.

Ng, the seventh letter in the Khasi alphabet; it is pronounced *eng*, (ঙ).

Nga, *pron.* I.

Ngak, *ad.* hard; [as, " u wei u lymbub *ngak* ia u wei pat."]; suddenly.

Ngang, *ad.* very (bitter); [as, " nga sngawkthang *ngang* ba nga bam *quinine.*"]

Ngang-ngang, *ad.* obstinately, tenaciously; [as, " La nga ong kumno kumno ruh u shu bat *ngang-ngang* ia u;" " U dieng uba skhem *ngang-ngang.*"]

Ngah-ngah, *a.* as tender as a new born babe; [as, " I khúnlung iba dang *ngah-ngah.*"]

Ngai,
Ngai-ngai, } *ad.* very; soundly (sweet or sleepy); [as, " katba nga nang bam nang bang *ngai-ngai*;" u nongtuh u ong " katta ki la ioh thiah bha *ngai.*"]

Ngai-ngai-ngit-ngit, *a.* weak and dizzy; languid; [as, nga'm sngewshait bha mynta nga shu sngew *ngai-ngai-ngit-ngit* kumno-re.]

Ngain (iong-), *ad.* very (black); [as, " Tang shu buh ia u powder, shu kylla iong *ngain* ka um."]

Ngain-ngain, *ad.* very (dark); [as, " dang dum *ngain-ngain* du, ym pat shái."]

Ngam, *v.* to sink, to plunge.

Nga'm (*contr.* of " nga ym "), *phr.* I.........not.

Ngam-um, *v.* to decide by water-ordeal; to dive.

Nga'n (*contr.* of " nga yn "), *phr.* I'll, I will.

Ngáp, *ka, n.* the cheek.

Ngàp, *u, n.* bee,—*ka*, honey. [*Imit.* u ngàp—u lwái.

Ngáp-ngáp (dang), *ad.* very early in the morning.

Ngàp-tem, *u, n.* a hive-bee, a honey-bee.

Ngàp-tung, *u, n.* a drone.

Ngàp-wieh, *u, n.* a small bee that lives under-ground.

Ngar-ngar, *ad.* lively, green; [as, " phi wallam u soh uba dang im *ngar-ngar.*"]

Ngat, *v.* to fall upon, to fall into or to be caught in a snare.

Ngaw-ngaw (iong-), *ad.* very (black like charcoal).

Ngek, *ad.* to stop short; [as, " nga tang shu dumok u sangeh *ngek.*"]

Ngeng-ngeng, *ad.* drowsily, heavily; [as, " nga sngew ka khlieh ka khia *ngeng-ngeng.*"]

Ngeit, *v.* to believe, to be persuaded.

Ngeit-biet, *v.* to be superstitious, credulous. [*Imit.* ngeit biet-ngeit them.]

Ngem (bám-), *v.* to do wrong secretly, (see *bam-ngem.*)

Ngen, *v.* to disappear, to be suppressed.

Ngen-bnái, *kaba, n.* waning of the moon.

Ngép-ngép, *ad.* with dishevelled hair; when just getting up from bed; [as, " tang shu khie *ngép-ngép* u bamja."]

Ngèr-ngèr, *ad.* indistinctly; dizzily; [as, " nga ioh-i kumba iaid u briew *ngèr-ngèr.*"]

Nget-nget, *ad.* partially and faintly as a passing and vanishing object; [as, " nga ioh-i kein *nget-nget* ia ka rel."]

Ngi, *pron.* we.

'ngi=*abbrev.* of *sngi,* sun, used as a suffix in compound word, as in mih'ngi.

Ngiah, *a.* enough,—*v.* to suffer from ennui. [*Imit.* ngiahshoin.]

Ngiah-ngiah, *a.* very tender or young,—*ad.* daintily; [as, " u leh *ngiah-ngiah* ia lade."]

Ngiam, *v.* to contain, to hold, to be able to enter.

Ngieng, *ad,* nauseous; to be affected with a peculiar sensation; [as, " nga sngew *ngieng* ba'n bám ia ka."]

'ngiem, (*abbrev.* of dngiem), a bear.

Ngih ngih-ngah ngah, *a.* belonging to a far obscure or dismal place.

Ngi'm, *phr.* we...not.

'ngiem-lalu, *ka, n.* a species of large black bear.

Ngi'n, *phr.* we'll, we will.

Ngiñ ngiñ-ngaiñ ngaiñ, *ad.* dark and cloudy.

Ngir-ngir, *ad.* very early in the morning; [as, " u khie hynne dang *ngir-ngir.*"]

Ngong, *ad.* suddenly (meet); [as, " ynda nga ia kynduh *ngong* hajan u sa kren."]

Ngoi-ngoi, *ad.* languidly, weakly; [as, " nga sngew tlot *ngoi ngoi* mynta."]

Ngon, *ad.* down, to the ground, attentively; [as, " u la nguh *ngon* shaphang 'mihngi."]

Ngop, *v.* to sink down.

Ngór, *v.* to prune; to lop off.

Nguk-ngak *ad.* suddenly; [as, " tang shu iakynduh *nguh-ngak* u shu iakem."]

Nguh, *v.* to do homage, to bow, to thank. [*Imit.* nguh-dem.]

Nguhlet-shnong, *v.* to tender apology or ask the pardon of a village Darbar.

Ngùn, *ad.* with the head bent down (*big*), steadily (*walk*); [as, " u shu iaid *ngun* khlem kren."]

Ngur-ngur, *ad.* in the dusk; [as, " ka la sdang miet *ngur-ngur* mynta."]

Ngut, *n.* used when speaking of the number of persons only, as, ar-*ngut*=two persons.

Ngut-ngut (dang-), *ad.* at twilight.

Ngut-ngut-nget-nget, *ad.* indistinctly; [as, " nga'm tip dei u briew ne u mrad namar nga shu ioh-i *ngut-ngut-nget-nget.*"]

H.

H, the eigth letter in the Khasi alphabet.

Ha, *prep.* in, to, into; it is also used impersonally, as, *ha diang*= let me.

Haba, *ad.* when, since.

Habadei-badei, *ad.* sometimes, now and then.

Hak, *ad.* forcibly; [as, u A u la lympat *hak* ia u B.]

Hak-na-hak, *ad.* uselessly, without any cause.

*Hakim, *u, n.* a judge, a Magistrate.

Hadem, *n.* a Kuki.

Hadiang, *phr.* let me see, have, etc....it.

Hadien, *ad.* after, afterwards, behind. [*Imit.* hadien-habúd.]

Haduh, *ad.* up to, as far as, until; [as, "*haduh* katno nga'n iai shah."]

Haei? *ad.* where?

Haei-haei, *ad.* anywhere.

Haei-re-haei, *ad.* somewhere.

---

* Hindi.

Hangamei, *ad.* proud, insolent, haughty. [*Imit.* hangamei-hangapa.]

Hangne, *ad.* here

Hangno? *ad.* where.

Hangno-hangno, *ad.* anywhere.

Hangta, *ad.* there (out of sight); then, thereupon.

Hangtai, *ad.* there (far, but in sight). [*Imit.* hangtai-hangthie.]

Hangtai-tai *ad.* there (very far but in sight).

Hangtei, *ad.* there (up).

Hangthie, *ad.* there (down).

Hangto, *ad.* there (when the place is understood or supposed to be known).

Hái-hái, *ad.* lavishly, extravagantly, (as, "u leh pahuh *hái-hái*").

Hai, *v.* to give out such a sound in playing.

Háin-háin, *ad.* very (red); fresh.

Hai-pa-hai, *ad* slowly.

Hajan, *ad.* near.

*Hajar, *n.* a thousand.

Hajar-katta, *conj.* in spite of, neverthless; [as, "nga la ong ba nga'n ym máp, *hajar katta* ruh lada phi kylla nga'n máp."]

*Hajir, *v.* to present, appear.

*Hajot, *ka, n.* a lock-up; a *Hajut.*

Hajuh, *ad.* in the same place; [as, "u shong *hajuh* hi."]

Hala, *ad.* every

Hala ka jong ka jong, *ad.* separately; [as, "ki la leit ha la *ka jong ka jong* ka iing."]

Halade, *pron.* in one self.

Halai-halai, *ad.* by and by; [as, "ha kaba nyngkong u'm sngewbha ia nga hynrei ynda *halai-halai* u sa ieit."]

*Halla (*Hindi*), *v.* to make a noise.

Hali, *ka, n.* an irrigated rice field; a set of four things.

Halor, *prep.* on, upon, over.

Hamar, *ad.* by or at the time, (as, u wan *hamar* shiteng-synñia= he came just at midnight.)

Hamsaia, *ka, n.* neighbours (legal term).

---

* Hindi.

Hán, *n.* a duck.

Hana, *ad.* so they say, it is said that; (as, " *hana* lashai ka shuti 'sha?")

Hano? *pron.* (to) whom?

Háp, *v.* to fall, to come off, to tally; to agree.

Hapoh, *prop.* under, within, in.

Hapoh-hapoh, *ad.* secretly; clandestinely.

Háp-shop (leit), *v.* to fall into misfortunes.

*Hár, *ka, n.* condition; a pair (generally said of plough-bullocks) —*a.* all kinds of (generally used with *rukom*, as, *hár rukom*).

Hàr-hàr, *ad.* breezy; [as, " wat leit shah khriat ha ka 'er *hàr-hàr* ba ioh pang: sngew pyrhut *hàr hàr*."]

*Hara, *n.* a set or a row or a group of persons or things.

*Harám, *v.* to be unfaithful or ungrateful; to mutiny.

Harieh, *ad.* in secret; [as, " u kren sniew *harieh*."]

Harúd, *prep.* on or by the side of; [as, " ka iing jong u ka don *harud* surok."] [*Imit.* harúd—ha kiar.]

Harum, *ad.* down, below.

†Hat, *ka, n.* a market, especially one situated at the foot of the hills.—*Shi hat*, a period of 4 days.

*Hat-kari, *ka, n.* handcuffs.

Hateng-hateng, *ad.* now and then, (as, " u wan kái *hateng-hateng* ha iing jong ngi"). [*Imit.* hateng-hakhat.]

§Hati, *n.* an elephant.

Hato, *ad.* then; *v. Imper.* let me see, whether or not.

Haw, *int.* why not!—*ad.* publicly.

Hawei-ha-ar, *ad.* elsewhere; [as " ba'n *hawei-ha-ar* ki'm khot basa ia u."]

Haw-haw, *ad.* clamorously,—*n.* the vacuum; the atmosphere.

Hê-hê, *ad.* pantingly; [as, " u la mareh haduh ba u'n da thait *hê-hê*."]

Hek-hek, *ad.* very (odolrous).

Héng-héng, *ad.* with a stentorian sound; [as, " ka ktien jong u kaba sngew *héng-héng*."]

Heh, *v.* take (*imper.* only),—*a.* big, large, great.

* Hindi. | † Bengali. | § Assamese.

Hei, *int.* excuse me; I say; be careful; [as, "*hei* khublei, nga kum dei ho."]

Heit, *ad.* why not? (interogatively only); [as, "kam long kumta-*heit*."]

Hem-hem, *ad.* very (red).

Hen-hen, *ad.* like *kanji*; [as, "nga la shet ia u soh ha ba'n da um *hen-hen*."]

Hep, *i, n.* younger brother or sister (used in calling); dear, a term used by older persons in addressing young people.

Hep-hep kpoh, *ka, n.* the belly.

Hér, *v.* to fly,—(*hèr*) *ad.* awfully, exceedingly; [as, "nga la shepting *hèr* ba nga ioh-i ia u."]

Hér-iap-hér im, *v.* to run for life.

Hèr-hèr, *ad.* strongly (bad smell); too (soft); very (sharp). [as, iwtung *hèr-hèr*; jem *hèr-hèr*; nep *hèr-hèr*.]

Hér-mynsiem, *v.* to be sore afraid.

Hér-syrngiew, *v.* to be at one's wits' end.

Hi, *ad.* and *pr.* self, alone; also used to soften the abruptness of a sentence.

Hiar, *v.* to go or come down, to descend—*ad.* down.

Hiar-iadep, *ka, n.* a flake.

Hiaw-hiaw, *ad.* weakly, softly; asthmatic; [as, "u rangbah ruh u kren *hiaw hiaw* kum ka kynthei."]

Hikai, *v.* to learn, to teach.

Hieng, *v.* having a large bore or hole; dilated.

Hih, *v.* take (*imper.* only).

Hih-i, *ad.* yes (*coloq.*)

Hima, *ka, n.* kingdom, state. [*Imit.* hima-sima.]

Hin, *ad.* finely, thoroughly, flowingly; [as, "tylliat ha ba'n da ni *hin*"; jem *hin*.]

Híp-híp, *ka, n.* the end of the ribs.

Hir-hir, *ad.* longingly, exceedingly; [as, "don ka ri ba sngewtynnad *hir-hir*."]

* Hira, *u, n.* a kind of precious stone, diamond.

* Hiran, *a.* tired.

* Hisa, *ka, n.* a share.

---

* Hindi.

Ho, = please; will you?

Hok, *n.* right, justice, righteousness,—*ad.* uprightly, righteously.

H'óid, *ad.* yes (also written Ha-oid, Ho-oid).

Hóiñ, *ad.* very (red).

Hón-hón, *ad.* like flour which has been mixed with water. [as, "kane ka jingkhleh ka la um eh *hón-hón.*"]

Hor-hor, *ad.* tenderly, softly; [as, "khroh *hor-hor*; jem *hor-hor.*"]

Horkit, *ad.* at any rate, at all cost; [as, "*horkit* ym ju bit harám ia u nongleh bha."] [*Imit.* Horkit-hordang.]

* Hormot, *ka*, *n.* chastity, honour.

Hu, *ka*, *n.* the porpoise.

* Hukum, *ka*, *n.* commandment; order.

Húd, *ka*, *n.* quarter, side; group.—*ad.* *Shihúd*, in one way; [as, "kane ka shu bha *shi-húd.*"]

* Huleng, *n.* ape (black); hoolook.

Hum-hum-ham-ham, *ad.* noisily (talking).

Hunam, *v.* to harp on the same string.

Hun, *a.* satisfied; pleased; contented.

'hur, *u*, *n.* (*abbrev.* of jhur) vegetable.

Huri-hura, *n.* confusion, row.

Hur-hur, *ad.* very, (soft like an over-ripe fruit).

Huspai, (ai-), *v.* to indulge; to give one his own wrong way.

Hynbew, *n.* brother or sister.

Hyndái, *ad.* in olden times. [*Imit.* Hyndái-hynthái.]

Hynmen, *n.* elder brother or sister. [*Imit.* Hynmen-hynbew.]

Hynné, *ad.* a short time ago; after the lapse of some hours.

Hynñiew, *a.* seven.

Hynñiew-skum, *ki*, *n.* the seven families in the beginning of the world. [*Imit.* ki hynñiew skum-ki hynñiew trep.]

Hynnin, *ad.* yesterday.

Hynrei, *conj.* but, though.

Hynriew, *a.* six.

Hynroh, *n.* a frog;—*bám hynroh-u-bnái*, an eclipse of the moon.

---

* Hindi.

I

I, the ninth letter in the Khasi Alphabet.

I, (1) *pron.* an expression of respect or endearment=he, she, it; [as, *I* kong, *I* bah, *I* mei, *I* hep.]; it is also an expression of diminution, as, *I* wait-rit, *I* tylläi.

(2) Prefix=to appear, to look; [as, *i*-sih=to abhor, *i*-bha=to take a fancy to, to like.]

(3) suffix=to get sight of, to see, as in the word *ioh-i*.

Ia, (1) *prep.* to, for, concerning, of; [as, *ia* nga, *ia* kata.]

(2) sign of an *Imper.*=let us, come on, [as, *Ia* kein ngin leit mynta.]

(3) Prefix=sign of plurality or mutuality; [as, " ki *ia* lehkai; u *ia* kren bad kiwei."] (4) time, season; [as, " u la poi ha ka *ia* kaba biang."] (5) reference meaning=regarding, concerning; [as, "*Ia* kaba kwah nga kwah eh tang ba nga'm lah shuh".]

Iabuit, *v*, to conspire. [*Imit.* Iabuit-iasap.]

Iakád-máw, *v.* to cause a split in the religion of the family or clan by erecting a tomb wherein to deposit bones separate from the ancestral tomb ("see máwbah"); to schismatise. [*Imit.* Iakád máw-kád dieng.]

Iakád-jutang, *v.* to break a covenant.

* Iakajia, *v.* to quarrel, to dispute. [*Imit.* Iakajia-ia majia.]

Iakap, *v.* to make friends or join with, to make an alliance with: to have one as one's partner as in dancing.

Iakut, *v.* to make an agreement, to resolve.

'iad (*abbrev.* of kiad), *ka*, *n.* liquor, spirit.

'iad-khar, *ka*, *n.* same as 'iad-pudka.

Iada, *v.* to protect, to defend.

Iadait, *v.* to bite each other, to altercate; to fight (as dogs), to fit.

Iadei, *v.* to agree, to tally, to be unanimous; to be related to; to hit (*pl.*), to touch.

Iadeikha-dei-man, *v.* to have a relationship by marriage.

Iadei-kur, *v.* to have relationship on the mother-side; to be of the same clan.

Iadei-jing-dei, *v.* to have some relationship.

Iadei-jingmut, *v.* to be of the same opinion, to be unanimous, to be friendly with.

---

* Hindi.

'iad-hiar, *ka*, *n*. undistilled liquor which gathers in a pail placed underneath a basket to receive it; wort.

'iad-pudka, *ka*, *n*. distilled liquor; spirit.

'iad-rod, *ka*, *n*. strong liquor.

'iad rong, *ka*, *n*. liquor given by friends when cremating ceremonies are performed.

'iad-tang-snem, (*lit*. liquor consecrated for a year), *ka*, *n*. liquor supposed to have the effect of making people reckless and mad for the time being and of encouraging them to commit murder for the propitiation of "u Thlen."

'iad-thnam, *ka*, *n*. a very strong country spirit.

'iad-um, *ka*, *n*. undistilled liquor taken from a jar; beer.

Ia-ei? *phr*. what for?

Ia-ei-ia-ei, *phr*. for anything.

Ia-ei-re-ia-ei, *phr*. for something.

Iang, *ad*. up (lift), [as, "u la rah *iang* ka wait ba'n pom iạ nga."]

Iáid, *v*. to walk, to go, to proceed [*Imit*. iaid-iẹng.]

Iáid kái, *v*. to take a stroll, to take a pleasure walk. [*Imit*. Iáid kái-iengkái.]

Iáid-ka-ieng, *ka*, *n*. manner of life.

Iáid-káikái, *v*. to walk by swinging the lower part of the body.

Iáid-kán-kán, Iáid-kén-kén, } *v*. to waddle.

Iáid-khnip khnip, *v*. to walk lamely as if pressed with sharp small stones on the soles.

Iáid-kjik kjik, *v*. to walk as if on pins.

Iáid-kynthéw, *v*. to walk with a train or tail.

Iáid-kynthih, *v*. to walk with a springy step.

Iáid-kyrbeit, *v*. to walk by tightening the muscles of the legs.

Iáid-dar dar, *v*. to have a brisk walk.

Iáid-ngeng-ngeng, *v*. to walk as one who is intoxicated.

Iáid-ior-ior, *v*. to walk slowly as a weak person.

Iáid-laitlán, *v*. to walk as if under no restraint; to roam about.

Iáid lammir. *phr*. to lead a profligate life.

Iáid-lyngngeh, *v*. to walk slowly by throwing the head backwards.

Iáid-pawang, *v*. to swagger.

Iáid-shán-shán, } *v.* to walk as one who has been under the in-
Iáid-shon-shen, } fluence of liquor; to stagger.

Iáid-suda, *v.* to go or walk without a load.

Iáid-thnet thnet, *v.* to walk as if one means to knock against everything.

Iáid-tnet-tnet, *v.* to walk as if one is regardless of what the feet might knock against.

Iái, (prefix) *v.* to continue to, [as, *iái* kren, *iái* long, *iái* shong.]

Ia-ieh noh, *v.* to leave off; to divorce.

Iajan, *a.* near each other.—*v.* closely related.

Ialade, *pron.* self, to one's self.

Ialam, *v.* to lead.

Ialap, *v.* to say; preach. [*Imit.* ialap-iariew.]

Ialuh, *v.* to woo, make love, allure, entice. [*Imit.* ialuh-iapah.]

Ialúr, *v.* to court, solicit for marriage.

Iám, *v.* to weep, cry. (Pronounced *yám*).

Iamái, *v.* to quarrel. [*Imit.* iamái-iania.]

Iámbáit, *v.* to easily give way to crying.

Iám-briew, *v.* to lament for the dead.

Ianap, *v.* to devote one's self to.

Iania, *v.* to dispute, quarrel, argue.

Ianoh, *v.* to add a little more quantity than what is bought upon the terms agreed upon;—*v.* (*imper.*) let us be off.

Iapoi, *v.* to cohabit.

Iap (*yap*), *v.* to die, to lose. [*Imit.* iap-im.]

'iap, (*abbrev.* of shyiap), *u, n.* sand; [as, '*iap* lieh,' *iap*-wah.]

Iap-ang, *ad.* (generally used with *rkhie*), to laugh to one's heart's content. [*Imit.* Iap-ang-iaplér.]

Iapah, *v.* to allure, to decoy. [*Imit.* Iapah-ialúh.]

Iapbiej, *v.* to die of accident or as the result of one's own carelessness. [*Imit.* iap-biej-iap them.]

Iapein, *v.* to give for change (money); to barter.

Iapkhlam, *v.* to die of cholera;—*ka, n.* cholera. [*Imit.* iapkhlam-iapngoh.]

Iapkut, *v.* to die because one could not get out of danger as from a burning house or a besieged fort.

Iapduh, *v.* to be annihilated, to die without having any female relative surviving him. [*Imit.* iap-duh-iaptan.]

Iapngiah, *v.* to be much absorbed in anything; to be charmed with. [*Imit.* iapngiah-iapshoiñ.]

Iap-iap, *ad.* thin and light (cloth).

Iap-ieng. *v.* to die in a standing posture as a withered tree.

Iap-iong, *v.* to be attacked with mildew,—*ka, n. kálá-ázár.*

Iap-jyllop, *v.* to die of drowning; to be drowned.

Iapler, *v.* to fall into a swoon, to faint.

Iap-op, *v.* to die of suffocation.

Iap-pongding, *v.* to die with a child in the womb. [*Imit.* iap-pongding-iap-pongruh.]

Iap-shiliang, *ka, n.* palsy.

Iap-snap (i-), *v.* to be of any worth (said of property and used with the negative particle *ym.*)

Iap-snem, *v.* to die of epidemic disease, *esp.* of cholera.

Iap-thái, *v.* to wither; to droop or be sorrowful; to pine away in sorrow.

Iap-them, *ka, n.* cholera.

Iap-thngan, *v.* to die of starvation. [*Imit.* iapthngan-iapjing-it.]

Iap-tram, *v.* to wither.

Iap-tyrsáw, *v.* to faint from hunger. [*Imit.* iap-tyrsaw-iaptyr-sian.]

Iap-tyr-ut, *v.* to die a violent death. [*Imit.* iaptyr-ut-iapsmer.]

Iár (*yár*), *a.* wide, open, extended,—*n.* (*voc.*) friend.—iàr, *ad.* down (fall). [as, "u háp kumba háp ka sla-dieng *iar* na bneng"]; very (thin cloth or paper).

'iar, (*abbrev.* of syiar) *n.* a cock or hen. [Pronounced *eeár.*]

Iarain, *v.* to fondle, to toy, to play or flirt.

Iarap, *v.* to help, to assist.

'iar-kdait, *n.* a small species of fowl.

'iar-khiar, *ka, n.* a bamboo partridge.

'iar-krád-lynti, *u, n.* a cock which is sacrificed previous to the cremation of the dead to act as a *guide* to the departed spirit, (*lit.* "a cock to scratch the way" for the departed spirit).

'iar-lasir, *n.* a kind of cock or hen with yellow feet, the former being much used in cock fighting.

Iarly-iar, *ad.* (falling) like a light thing from a high precipice; [as, " u la háp *iar-lyiar* nalor ka riat."]

'iar-mangkalai, *u*, *n.* a long-legged fowl.

Iarong, *ka*, *n.* a small net bag for putting odds and ends, *esp.* betel-nut, lime, tobacco, etc. [*Imit.* ka iarong-ka iadep.]

Iaroh, *v.* to praise.

'iar-padat, *u*, *n.* a cock which is killed and thrown three times over the Khasi funeral pyre, when fire is set to it.

'iar-ryngkúh, *u*, *n.* a cock.

Iasang, *a.* not sanctioned by the laws and custom of society; tabooing. [*Imit.* iasang-iama.]

Iasáid, *v.* to argue, to debate.

Iasáid-lah, *v.* to hold on a discussion though beaten.

Iasám, *v.* to divide. [*Imit.* iasám-iapiet.]

Iaseng, *v.* to gather, to meet; to hold religious service or meetings.

Iashang, *v.* to associate with, to go near.

Iashah, *v.* to bear with, to side with.

Iashah-iasham, *v.* to have dealing in money matters, *i.e.*, between a money-lender and a borrower.

Iashán, *v.* to hold out; to support.

Iashem, *v.* to meet; to come across.

Iashep, *v.* to suit; (as, " ba'n tupia Phareng uba iong ym i *iashep.*")

Iashet, *v.* to plot against, to betray.

Iashoh, *v.* to fight. [*Imit.* Iashoh-iadat.]

Iashoh-dohkha, *v.* to poison fish in a stream.

Iasiat, *v.* to have a shooting match (with bows and arrows).

Iasiat-shon-shiw, *v.* to tread on one's corns.

Iaslem, *v.* to remain late.

Iasni, *v.* to harbour a revengeful spirit.

Iasnoh, *v.* to connect, to cling.

Iasong, *v.* to prepare and give betel nut, etc., to another; to bundle up. [*Imit.* iasong-iatap.]

Iasop, *v.* to cover; to concentrate one's energy to one object; to throng round a person or thing.

Iasuh-mar-iap, *phr.* to make the last effort in any undertaking by risking one's life.

Iasuit-iashor, *v.* to confirm an agreement by pouring libations of liquor.

Iasùm, *v.* to bathe. [*Imit.* iasùm-iasleh.]

Iasúm, *v.* to throw or cast a spear or pointed ekra at.

Iat, *ka, n.* a piece of wood attached to the plough.

'iat (*abbrev.* of k'iat), *ka, n.* liquor, country spirit; (also spelt *'iad.*)

Iatang, *v.* to make a solemn agreement by oaths.

Iatái, *v.* to sift, to scrutinize, to discuss.

Iatait, *v.* to reject, to disclaim.

Iatáp, *v.* to go beyond the proper limit; to encroach upon.

Iateh-ktien, *phr.* to betroth.

Iatem, *v.* to play on a stringed instrument; to extinguish a fire.

Iatem-ktien, *v.* to interrupt one in the course of his conversation.

Iathád, *v.* to expose; to wash dirty linen in public [*Imit.* iathád-iabád.]

Iatháin, *v.* to interweave; to find an excuse.

Iathàn, }
Iathansi, } *v.* to look to another for the performance of one's own duty; to find an excuse for not doing a thing because others are not doing it.

Iathàp, *v.* to watch for an opportunity, to waylay.

Iathong, *v.* to bet, to wager.

Iathoh, *v.* to commit in writing; to register a marriage. [*Imit.* iathoh-iatar.]

Iathùh, *v.* to tell, to relate.

Iathùhkhana, *v.* to relate as a story; to preach. [*Imit.* iathuh-khana-iathuhkhadeh.]

Iatla, *v.* to quarrel by using obscene words. [*Imit.* iatla-iatlep.]

'iáw (*yáw*), *a.* grown-up, ripe; courageous; an appellation of old women; the *fem.* of *koh* which is an appellation of old men.

Iáwbei, *ka, n.* a primitive ancestress of a clan.

Iáwbei-tymmen, *ka, n.* the grand primitive ancestress of a clan.

Iáwbei-khynráw, *ka, n.* the primitive ancestress of a branch of a clan.

Iáw-paw (shnong ka), *n.* the grave; death, (*lit.* the village on the top of a hill where *ka Iaw-paw* dwells; the story runs that whoever goes into her village never returns.)

Iaweng, *v.* to remove; to be engaged in wrestling, etc.

Iawer, *v.* to call for a companion, to solicit to go along with, to invite.

Iawih, *v.* to be engaged in a struggle; to fight hard.

Iawin, *v.* to make noise.

Ibeiñ, *v.* to despise. [*Imit.* ibeiñ-ikhoh.]

Ibha, *a.* good looking, *v.*—to take fancy to, to be enamoured of. [*Imit.* ibha-imiat.]

Ibiang, *a.* decent-looking. [*Imit.* ibiang-ibit.]

Ibiej, *a.* to look like a fool; absurd. [*Imit.* ibiet-i-anna.]

Ibyn-riew, *v.* to appear to be on the way to betterment.

Ik, *ad.* simultaneously up (to blaze or stir), [as, "ka ding ka ieng *ik*; baroh shishnong ki ieng *ik*."]

*Iktiar, *n.* authority, power.

Ikwah, *v.* to have a desire for a thing from looking at it; to covet.

Id (*or* it), *v.* to tie a baby with a strip of cloth on the back as Khasi women do,—*ka, n.* quarter, side, border. [*Imit.* ka id-ka hima.]

Ide, (same as *ade*).

Ieng, *v.* to stand, to rise up. [*Imit.* ieng-iaid.]

Ieh, }
Iehnoh, } *v.* to leave off, to abandon, to let alone;—*ieh-noh-sansh'-ing*, to divorce (by exchanging five cowries).
Inoh, }

Ieh seh, *phr.* keep off please; let me alone please.

Ieit, *v.* to love. [*Imit.* ieit-thoin.] Same as *iej*.

Iew, *ka, n.* a market. [*Imit.* ka iew-ka hat.]

Iewduh, *ka. n.* the Shillong Bara-Bazar.

Iew-luri-lura, *ka, n.* the market of the beasts in Khasi folklore.

Iew-lyngstieh, *ka, n.* the biggest *hat* in the Nongkhlaw State formerly held at night, the day before the Shillong Bara-Bazar.

Iew-Mawkhar, *ka, n.* the Mawkhar Bazar.

Iew-Mawlong, *ka, n.* the Municipal market at Laban; the name of a Khasi week-day.

Iew-Musiang, *ka, n.* the Jowai *Hat*.

Iew-Shillong, *ka, n.* the Laitlyngkot *Hat*.

Iing (*ying*), *ka, n.* a house. [*Imit.* ka ing ka sem.]

---

* Hindi.

Iing-briew, Iing-ki-briew, (*leit-*) *n.* marriage, (as, "u khun jong nga um pat leit *iing-briew.*")

Ìng, *v.* to be burnt, to catch fire.

'ìng (*abbrev.* of "sh'íng"), *ka, n.* a bone.

'ìng (*abbrev.* of "syìng"), *u, n.* ginger.

I- ngàp, *v.* to appear fascinating or attractive. [*Imit.* i-ngàp-i-bang.]

'ìng-bah, *u, n.* a species of ginger.

Iing-basa, *ka, n.* a temporary lodging, an inn. [*Imit.* iing-basa-iing basuiñ.]

†**Íing-kashari,** *ka, n.* Cutchery; court-house.

Ìngkhong, *v.* to be burnt to cinders; to be exasperated. [*Imit.* ìngkhong-ìngkhait.]

***Íing-kirja,** *ka, n.* a chapel; a church.

Iing-dara, *ka, n.* a temporary shed; a tent.

Ìng-ding, *v.* to get burnt with fire.

'ing-dong, *ka, n.* the back. [*Imit.* ka 'ingdong ka 'ingnap.]

I-ngiew, *v.* to appear dreadful, to appear uncanny.

Iing-jáiñ, *ka, n.* a tent.

Iing-mane, *ka, n.* a temple; a chapel, a church.

'ìng-makhir, *u, n.* a species of small ginger having a more pungent taste than u *'ingbah.*

†**Iing-paki,** *ka, n.* a house with stone-walls and ceiling of concrete cement. [*Imit.* Iing-paki-iingdulan.]

Iing-sád, *ka, n.* the house where a Siem performs family and State sacrifices. [*Imit.* Iing-sád-iingsunon.]

Iing-sáwdong, *ka, n.* (*lit.*) a house having four walls; a house not built after the old pattern of a Khasi-house, but after the English fashion.

Iing-seng, *ka, n.* the house where all the members of a family or a clan perform their sacrifices or transact their business (invariably the house of the youngest sister or niece).

Ìng-thàp, *v.* to be slightly scorched by a flame, to singe.

Iing-trep, *ka, n.* a temporary hut or shed.

'ing-tyrkhong, *u, n.* dried ginger; an old grudge. [*Imit.* 'ing-tyrkhong-ing-tyr-khap.]

Ih, *a.* ripe, well cooked.

---

* Hindi. | † Bengali.

I-hih, (*coloq.*) *adv.* no.

Ih-rod, *a.* not properly ripe.

*Ijár, *v.* to report to the authority *esp.* to the police station,—*ka, n. ejahar.*

I-jew, *v.* to appear hopeless, to be disgusted.

*Ijot, *ka, n.* reputation, honour.

*Ijra, *ka, n.* a long term lease.

*Ilaka, *ka, n.* district or *Ilaka.* [*Imit.* ka ilaka-ka singmana.]

*Ilashi, *u, n.* cardamon.

I-lúb, *a.* attractive, fascinating.

Im, *v.* to live; to be alive; to be safe; unripe, green, not well-cooked.

I'm, *phr.* he or she does not; (I+ym).

*Imán, *ka, n.* regard, honour.

I-mat, *v.* to seem, to appear; to be visible. [*Imit.* imat-imut.]

Im im-peit peit, *ad.* when quite conscious, in *broad* day light, (as, " u shu pyniap ia ka blang *im im-peit peit* mynsngi bah ha pdeng lynti.")

Im-jingmut, *v.* to set one's heart upon, to be alive of.

Im'nong, *v.* to get adequate wages. [*Imit.* im-nong-im-ni.]

Im-sngi, *v.* to have adequate daily wages; to cogitate.

I'n, *phr.* he or she will; (I+yn).

Ine, *pron.* this (diminutive).

Ino, *pron.* which ? (diminutive).

Ino-ino, *pron.* whoever, whichever.

Iong (*yong*), *a.* black.

Iong-ngit, *a.* pitch dark (as night). [*Imit.* iong-ngit-iong-ngáin.]

Iong-reiñ, *a.* dusk, (evening).

Iongsynia, *a.* as black as night.

Iongtili, *a.* as black as a Negro.

Iong-umreit, *a.* beautifully dark (of complexion).

Ioh. *v.* to get, to gain, to obtain, to have, receive. [*Imit.* ioh-kot]; *conj.*—lest, per chance.

---

* Hindi.

Iohkdong, Ioh-dong, } *v.* to get an opportunity. [*Imit.* ioh-dong-ioh-lád.]

Ioh-diang, *v.* to receive. [*Imit.* ioh-diang-ioh-bat.]

Ioh-ei, *v.* to get gratis, to get for nothing; to get by picking up from some place.

Ioh-i, *v.* to see, to get sight of.

Ioh-mon, *v.* to get to do one's own will.

Ioh-nong, *v.* to get profit, to gain; to obtain a reward. [*Imit.* iohnong-iohni.]

Ioh-sa, *v.* to have an alternative; [as, " Nga leit pán ka bainong sngi na u Saheb A. B., hynrei u ong ba u'n ai tang 3 ana, namar b'ym *ioh-sa* (=could not be helped) nga shu shim keiñ.]

Iohsngew, Iohsngow, } *v.* to hear, to feel.

Iohthiah, *v.* to be asleep. [*Imit.* iohthiah-iohdem.]

Iop-iop, *i, n.* pendant, especially attached to an earing,—*ad.* hanging like a pendant.

Iór, *ka, n.* snow. (Pronounced *yór*).

Iòr-iòr, (iaid-), *v.* with slow and weak steps (walk); [as, " balei phi iad *ior-ior* kum uba pang "?]

I-pér, *a.* appearing light-minded or shallow-minded.

Iphér, *v.* to appear awkwardly; appear suspicious; appear strange or different from the ordinary way. [*Imit.* ipher-iphar.]

I-phuh, *v.* to appear cheerful. [*Imit.* iphuh-iphieng.]

Ipoh, *a.* appearing low or servile.

Iphieng, *a.* awe-iaspiring; grand-looking; showy. [*Imit.* iphieng iphuh.]

Ir, *ad.* up (stir, ablaze.)

I-raitong, *a.* appearing poor and ragged.

Irat, *ad.* and so on; onward;[as, " mynta kumne u'n sa nang koit *irat.*"]

I-rngai, *v.* to see something as in a dream or delusion; to hallucinate.

Iriang, *a.* passionate, irritable.

Irmat, *n. pl.* eye-lids.

Ir-shi-ir, *ad.* incessantly, continually; [as, " mynta ki Rus bad ki Jap ki ialeh *ir-shi-ir*".]

Isat, *v.* to appear disgusting, to be irritating. [*Imit.* isat-ijew.]

Isait-met, *a.* appearing loathsome.

*Isbád, *u, n.* steel.

I-shongshán, *a.* having a sinister appearance.

I-shongkun, *a.* having a grave appearance.

Isih, *v.* to abhor, to dislike.

Isnái, *a.* tiresome, wearisome.

Isna-iap, *kaba, n.* wraith.

Isyn-ei, *v.* to have pity or mercy on.

I-syrngiew, *a.* frightful, awe-inspiring.

It (yit), *v.* to examine, to search carefully.—*ka, n.* a looking-glass, a glass.

†It, *u, n.* a brick.—*ka, n.* a quarter, a kingdom, border land.

Ita, *pron.* that (diminutive form of *uta* or *kata.*)

Ithawnang, *a.* comical, funny.

I-thuh, *v.* to know, to make out, to recognise. [*Imit.* ithuh-ithaw.]

I-triem, *a.* dreadful.

Iuh, *v.* to tread upon, to trample.

Iuh-top, *v.* to be tyrannical or despotic.

Iûn-iûn-iân-iân, *a.* weak, (as, "nga sngew *iûn-iûn-iân-iân* ba'm put koit bha.")

Iup, *ad.* completely down, (as, "ka jainkup ka la khlup bha *iup.*")

Iw (*eew*), *v.* to have a smell, to smell.—*u, n.* a person who imitates whatever another does, (as, "u leh kum u *iw.*")

Iw (*yew*), *inter.* fie.

Iw-bih, *v.* to have a pleasant smell.—*a.* sweet smell; aromatic. [*Imit.* iwbih-iwthiang.]

Iwkhong, *v.* to have an unpleasant smell. [*Imit.* iwkhong-iwkhap.]

Iwkyrteng, *v.* to have the smell of a thing bearing that name; (as, "kata ka doh kaba *iwkyrteng* du.")

Iwei, *pron.* one.

I-wit, *a.* appearing obstructive; to be on another's way. [*Imit.* iwit-iwa.]

---

* Hindi. | † Bengali.

Iw-lngáw, *v.* to have the smell of a long unoccupied house.

Iwli, *a.* to have the smell of fresh fish. [*Imit.* íwli-íwhoit.]

Iwpdu, *v.* to have the smell of a putrid fish.

Iw-riem, *v.* to have a very slight bad smell.

Iw-sieng, *v.* to have a pungent snuffy smell. [*Imit.* iwsieng-iwsat.]

Iw-sit, *v.* to have a smell of urine.

Iw-sma, *v.* to have a slight rotten smell.

Iwsyndot myrsiang, *see* syndot myrsiang.

Iw-tung, *v.* to have a stinking smell; to have a putrid smell. [*Imit.* iwtung-iwsat.]

J.

J, the tenth letter in the Khasi alphabet.

Ja, *ka, n.* boiled rice,—[*Imit.* ka ja-ka jhur);—*Int.* ah, oh.

Jabáiñ, *a.* dirty, especially about the mouth.

Jabár, *u, n.* a wild herb.

Jabieng, *ka, n.* the brain.

Jablei, *ka, n.* cooked rice or *pullao* consisting of rice and flesh of fowls sacrificed to a spirit called u blei Synteng—it is cooked and eaten outside the village in the open air.

Jablo, *a.* dumb-like.

Jaboh, *a.* dirty, clumsy.

Jabuit, *u, n.* a kind of herb (of a sour taste).

*Jaka, *ka, n.* place, room. [*Imit.* ka jaka-ka puta.]

Jaka-jaka, *ad.* here and there, in patches, (as, "ki dieng ki shu long *jaka-jaka* ha ki lúm Khasi").

Jakhait-rap, *u, n.* a creeping plant whose leaves—of a sour taste, are used for curry.

Jakhi, *u, n.* a vegetable used in feeding swine.

Jakhir, *ka, n.* rice boiled in sweetened milk.

Jakhlia, *a.* dirty, nasty. [*Imit.* jakhlia-jakhláit.]

*Jakhom, *v.* to be in trouble; wounded.

Jakhyllie, *ka, n.* rice mixed with yeast for extracting liquor but not yet properly fermented, it is generally kept in a basket for one night (see also *jasapung*).

Jaknep, *a.* sluttish.

---

* Hindi.

Jakóid, *n.* a frog.

Jakpoh, *ka, n.* food just enough to sustain one's life; a morsel.

Jakpu, *ka, n.* a lump of cooked rice, sometimes rolled up like a ball usually given to children.

Jakrak, *ad.* in a very careless manner, in ebullition ; [as, "a-iu phi saitthma *jakrak*?"] ; like a babbler.

Jakter, *ad.* like a drunkard who talks with much saliva dribbling from his mouth ; [as, "u briew uba kren bu-aid *jakter*."]

Jaktung, *ka, n.* cooked rice or cooked potato mixed with a certain sort of preserved small fish and used as curry or *chutni.*

Jakyntien, *ka, n.* a morsel.

Jadá, *u, n.* a vegetable.

*Jadu, *ka, n.* charm, enchantment.

Jangjang, *ad.* soon, quickly; [as, "khie leit hynrei iawan *jang-jang*."]

Jangew, *u, n.* a wild herb—of a bitterish taste, much used as a vegetable. [*Imit.* jangew-jathang.]

Jah, *v.* to loose, to be deprived of.

'jah, *abbrev.* of *pjah*=cold, or of *kynjah*=lonely.

Jahar, *ad.* muddily; [as, "ha ka por slap, ka lynti ka ktieh *jahar*."]

Jahare! *Int.* (an exclamation of pity at the loss of a thing or at the change of circumstances)=ah, what a pity!

Jahkwah, *v.* to be satisfied.

Jah-lngáid, *v.* to disappear without any knowledge.

Jahthait, *v.* to find rest; to recover from fatigue. [*Imit.* jahthait-jahjrem.]

Jai, *ad.* slowly, calmly ; carefully; [as, "ka um ha ri Dkhar ka tuid suki *jai*"; "Dung ia u kháw ha ba'n da ni *jai*."]

Jaiáw, *u, n.* a shrub; (*Bot.*) *Artemisia vulgaris.*

*Jaid, *ka, n.* clan, caste, kind. [*Imit.* ka jaid-ka kynja ; ka jaid-ka skér.]

Jaid (ia.) (ba.) } *conj.* since, seeing that.

Jáiñ, *ka, n.* cloth, clothes. [*Imit.* ka jáiñ-ka nep.]

Jáiñkhór, *ka, n.* silk clothes used on festive occasions only. [*Imit.* jáiñkhor-jáiñkhriam.]

Jáiñkhyrwang, *ka, n.* an *eri* cloth with alternate white and red stripes.

---

* Hindi.

Jáiñkup, *ka*, *n*. a wrapper, a cloak; *chadder*.

Jáiñkup-jainsem, *ka*, *n*. garment, clothes (in general).

Jáiñkyrshah, *ka*, *n*. an apron.

Jáiñ-iarong, *ka*, *n*. a net-work cloth.

Jàiñ-jàiñ, *ad*. in pieces, pierced into many holes, [as, "ka masi ka la dait ia ka jáin ba ban da lko *jaiñ jaiñ*."]

Jiáñjri, *ka*, *n*. a waterproof-sheet or cloak.

Jáiñ-mor-mor, *ka*, *n*. a thin cotton cloth.

§Jáiñ muka, *ka*, *n*. a muga or Assam silk.

Jáiñ-pun, Jing-pun, Jym-pun, } *ka*, *n*. a fold in the outer garment of Khasi women for putting in odds and ends.

Jáiñ-ryndia, *ka*, *n*. the *eri* cloth.

Jáiñsala, *ka*, *n*. a cotton cloth.

Jáiñsaipád, *ka*, *n*. a finer *muga* cloth.

Jáiñsai-hon, *ka*, *n*. a cloth made of sunhemp thread or jute.

Jáiñsem, *ka*, *n*. an outer garment of Khasi women worn loosely across the shoulders.

Jáiñ-slieng, *ka*, *n*. a strip of cloth worn by men round the waist. (*Hind.*) *lenguti*.

Jáiñ-sop, *ka*, *n*. a swaddling cloth. [*Imit*. jáiñ-sop-jáiñspaiñ.]

Jáiñspong, *ka*, *n*. a turban; a *pagri*.

Jaipdeh, *a*. lazy, slothful. [*Imit*. jaipdeh-jaisngi.]

Jaitúh, *a*. lazy, indolent. [*Imit*. jaitúh-jaisngi.]

Jaiur, *u*, *n*. a kind of very pungent fruit resembling black pepper

Jájah. *ka*, *n*. cold rice. [*Imit*. jájah-játhngan.]

Jajér, *u*, *n*. a wild vegetable.

Jajew, *u*, *n*. a certain plant of a sourish taste. [*Imit*. jajew-jajap.]

Jalani, *a*. fastidious, over-nice, particular, dandyish.

Jalatyrsim, *ka*, *n*. a kind of *Bon-riha* plant.

Jalia-jaláit, *ad*. poorly, wretchedly, [as, "kiba pli ki shu ia bám *jalia-jaláit* katba ioh".]

Jạli-jạ-um, *a*. kind, gentle, pleasant.

Jalbáin, *ad*. with a dirty or shabby appearance. [as, "balei ba *jalbáin* ka khmat kumne?"]

§ Assamese.

Jalkup *u, n.* a bird so called from its cry of *koop-koop-koop.*

Jaly-eit, *n.* a small-song bird of a green colour.

Jalyngkhan, *u, n.* a wild vegetable.

Jalyngkhiang, *ka, n.* a glandular swelling.

Jalmut, *u, n.* the flower, having a red colour, of a certain tree used in making curry and having a large tuberculous root.

Jalynñiar; *u, n.* a wild vegetable of a bitterish taste.

Jalynnoh, *u, n.* a plant whose leaves are used in making curry.

Jalynshir, *u, n.* a wild vegetable of a bitterish taste.

Jalyòiñ (pyllon-), *ad.* round (said of small things), [as, "ka snepkor kaba pyllon *jalyòiñ.*"]

Jalyùiñ (pyllun), *ad.* round (said of big things, [as, "kaba pyllun *jaly-ùiñ* kum ka shalyntem"].

Jàm, *v.* to make a noise ; [*Imit.* jàm-kieh.]—*ad.* exceedingly, for the most part ; [as, ki la shoh *jàm* ia u ; ki la khleh *jàm* eh u shylap ha ka sorki.]

Jám, *v.* to step, to stride.

*Jamabandi, *ka, n.* rent roll of cultivators.

Jamáw, *u, n.* a sour wild vegetable generally growing on stones.

Jamdor, *ka, n.* a short sword.

Jami-iang, *u, n.* a plant that bears a violet.

*Jamin, *ka, n.* security, bail.

*Jamindari, *ka, n.* an estate.

Jamithiat, *u, n.* a kind of sedge bearing white flowers growing on marshes.

Jamynrei, *u, n.* a shrub much used in making *tikia* and as a tie.

Jamynsleh, *u, n.* the root of a certain mucilaginous plant much used in washing the head, and also as an internal medicine for retention of urine.

Jan, *a.* near.

Janái, *ad.* perfectly, completely ; without fail. [*Imit.* janái-jaton.]

Janor, *ka, n.* the brain.

*Ján-pran, *ad.* very affectionately or dearly, [as, "U Don bad U Mut ki iaieit *ján-pran.*"]

---

* Hndi

Japha, *ka*, *n.* a cooked rice-ball placed over the stones where the bones of the dead are deposited, as a meal for the departed spirit.

Japhrut-japhret, *ad.* in a careless or slip-shod way, [as, "u shu leh *japhrut japhret* tang ban dep."]

Japi, *ka*, *n.* a basket in the shape of a round trunk where precious articles are generally kept ; a casket.

Japieh, *ka*, *n.* a frog of a greenish brown colour found in hill streams.

Japlem, *a.* tasteless (curry).

* **Japri**, *ka*, *n.* a net-work of bamboo placed on the ridges of a roof to prevent the thatch from being blown off by the wind ; a *jaffree.*

Jár, *ka*, *n.* a net ;—*pron.* whoever.

Jàr, *ad.* altogether, entirely, (as, sngap *jàr*=be silent). [*Imit.* jàr jàr-jir jir.]

Jarang, *ka*, *n.* a hole or chink where fish make their dwelling.

Jarain, *u*, *n.* a vegetable of a sour taste.

Jarawaiñ, *ad.* having the appearance of a fine tall man whose dress suits his stature ; [as, "u briew uba jrong *jarawaiñ.*"]

***Jari**, *v.* to enforce ; to execute ; to serve a legal process.

* **Jarimana**, *ka*, *n.* a fine.

Jarut, *ka*, *n.* boiled rice for mixing with yeast to make liquor.

Jarynlúd, *u*, *n.* a wild vegetable.

Jasapung, same as "jakhyllie."

Jasat, *u*, *n.* a plant of a pungent taste which generally grows on wet places.

Jasngi, *ka*, *n.* mid-day meal ; tiffin.

Jashulia, *ka*, *n.* rice cooked in steam or hot vapour.

Jasieh, *u*, *n.* a kind of water-weed.

Jasong, *ka*, *n.* boiled rice packed up in a leaf and eaten by travellers on the way. [*Imit.* jasong-jatap.]

'jat, *ka*, *n.* (*abbrev.* of kjat), foot.

Jata, *u*, *n.* one of the gods of the Syntengs who is also worshipped by many of the Khasis.

Jatbé, *ad.* with some dirty stuff sticking on the lips, [as, "u briew uba *jatbé* ka shyntur."]

* Hindi.

'jat-kmie, *ka, n.* the big toe.

'jat-duh, *ka, n.* the little toe.

Jathang, *u, n.* a wild vegetable of a bitterish taste.

Jathi, *u, n.* a kind of lance.

Jating, *u, n.* a vegetable.

Jatira, *u, n.* a wild aromatic vegetable growing in marshy places and used as medicine for bowel complaints.

Jatmut-jatmat, *ad.* shabbily. [as, "ki briew kiba *jatmut-jatmat* ka khmat."]

Jáw, *v.* to drop, to leak.

Jáwa, *ka, n.* the refused rice after brewing.

Jáwkhláit, *ad.* bathed in tears (as, iám *jáwkhlait*).

Jáw-dúd, *v.* to slaver, to drivel.

Jàw-jàw, *ad.* in wet clothes, (as, "balei phi iaid *jàw-jàw* ha u slap ?")

Jawlia, *a.* very young or tender (as a baby).

Jawliaw, *ad.* in a low spirited or downcast mood, [as, "u leh *jawliaw* ba u sngewrem"]; (fire) which does not burn well.

Jáw-um-mat. *v.* to shed tears. [*Imit.* jáw-um-mat-jáw-um-mut.]

Jawut-jawet, *ad.* perfunctorily, carelessly, [as, "u trei *jawut-jawet* tang ba'n dep."]

Jkap, *ad.* snappishly, [as, "u ksew u dait *jkap* na ka khohwah."]

Jkàr, *ad.* quiveringly, [as, "u sùm *jkàr* ia ka kait."]

Jkéng, *ad.* tall and big, (as, "u briew uba'jrong *jkéng*)."

Jking, *ad.* tall and slender, (as, "u briew uba rit *jking*").

Jkup, *ad.* all at once (to gobble up), [as, "ka dohkha ka bám *jkup* ia u soh"].

Jéng, *ad.* high up (to raise the foot), [as, "u Sikh u'kám *jéng* ia ka kpér."]

Jei, *v.* to lay eggs as fish; to be plentiful.

Jei-jei, *ad.* soft and coming off easily, (as, "kane ka dohkha kaba la pyut *jei-jei.*")

Jem, *a.* soft, easy. [*Imit.* jem-túid.]

Jem-nûd, *a.* gentle, soft hearted. [*Imit.* jemnúd-jémhin.]

Jem-rngiew, *v.* to be deprived of the essential of personality; unfortunate.

Jér, *v.* to name, to christen.

Jer-jer, *ad.* like a jelly.

Jew, *a.* sour, grievous. [*Imit.* jew-sat.]

Jngàng, *ad.* very much, (as, " u la ong rem eh *jngàng*").

Jngái, *a.* far. [*Imit.* ba jngái-ba rwang.]

Jngaiñ-jngaiñ, *ad.* very (deep water).

Jngap, *ad.* (sweet) like honey.

Jngem, *a.* discolouring of the skin ; black and blue.

Jngi, *v.* to swim.

Jngoh, *v.* to look at, to peep in.

Jngum-jngum, *a.* violet-like.

Jngut, *a.* muddy, dirty, obscure.

Jháb-wait, (shi-), *a.* sixteen (children.) ; quiverful.

*Jhád, *ka, n.* steamer, ship.

Jhang-jhang, *ad.* very (loud or clear), [as, " nga ioh sngew ia ka ktien ba ka pyrta *jhang jhang.*"]

Jhám, *a.* gluttonous.

Jhán, *v.* to be in difficulty, to be in haste.

*Jhare, *v.* to cure diseases by *mantras.*

*Jharon, *ka, n.* a duster, a *jharan.*

Jhep, *ka, n.* the after-birth, placenta.

Jhieh, *a.* wet.

Jhop, } *ad.* completely, (as, " wieh ha ba'n da jhieh *jhor* ia ka
Jhor, } jáiñ ").

*Jhula, *ka, n.* a bag, knapsack.

Jhûm, *ka, n.* vapour ;—*v.* to evaporate.

Jhup-jhap, *ad.* simultaneously, [as, " bha ba'n ia bám lang *jhup-jhap* ha kawei ka por."]

Jhur, *u, n.* herb, vegetable. [*Imit.* jhur-u jhep.]

Jia, *v.* to happen ; come up.

Jiap-jiap, *a.* very young, [as, " i syiar iba dang lung *jiap-jiap.*"]

Jiar, *v.* to drain off, to filter.

Jik jik-jak jak (kynjah-), *ad.* very (lonely or dismal.)

Jied, *v.* to choose, to select.

Jied-shiah, *v.* to be overparticular or strict.

Ji-ei, *u, n.* a good rough rider—(Jiei was a man who was notorious for catching stray ponies and riding on them).

---

* Hindi.

Jing=prefix of an Abstract Noun ;—*a.* supreme (*colloq.*), beyond comprehension, (as, "ka jingsniew jong u kaba la *jing*").

Jingat phyllúng, *ka, n.* a wave.

Jingblei, *a.* divine.

Jingbriew, *a.* human, proceeding out of man.

Jingbih-u lasam, *u, n.* an evil-spirit who causes disease of the mouth and teeth.

Jingbuh-jingsat, *ka, n.* furniture.

Jingkha-ar-sien, *ka, n.* regeneration.

Jingkhang, *ka, n.* a door, prohibition.

Jingkhang-iit, *ka, n.* a glazed window.

Jingkheiñ, *ka, n.* arithmetic ; reckoning, estimation. [*Imit.* jingkheiñ-jingdiah.]

Jingkia, *Ji-ngia, } *ka, n.* a bathing or short trousers.

Jingkit, *ka, n.* a load. [*Imit.* jingkit-jingbah.]

Jingngan, *v.* to feel uneasiness or difficulty to pass food into the stomach.

Jing-ngeit-biej, *ka, n.* superstition.

Jing-hiar thma, *ka, n.* expedition.

Jing-iapait, *ka, n.* division (of people) ; split. [*Imit.* Jingiapait-jingiapiet.]

Jingiatip-lem, *ka, n.* conscience.

Jing-it, *ka, n.* a strip of cloth for fastening a baby to the back,—*adv.* fasting ; without food.

Jingjia, *ka, n.* occurrence.

Jinglait-lúid, *ka, n.* freedom ; liberty.

Jingmihpat, *ka, n.* resurrection.

Jingpynbná, *ka, n.* a notice ; proclamation.

Jingpynbúd, *ka, n.* a sequel ; a supplement.

Jingpyrsát-mynsiem, *ka, n.* inspiration (*lit.* exhalation.)

Jingri, *n.* cattle ; domestic animals. [*Imit.* jingri-jingdúp.]

Jingriam, *ka, n.* a dress. [*Imit.* jingriam-jingbeit.] ; snare. [*Imit.* jingriam-jingpah.]

Jingtah, *ka, n.* ointment ; a medicine for rubbing or smearing on the skin ; curry. [*Imit.* jingtah-jingbèr.]

* Hindi.

*Jilla, *ka*, *n.* zillah, district.

*Jilla-kharit, *v.* to banish from the country.

Jillang, *u*, *n.* a kind of Khasi white onion ; the shallot. (*Bot.*) *Allium tuberosum.*

Jillei, *a.* too abundant.

Jin, *ka*, *n.* saddle,—*ad.* to powder ; [as, "tylliat ha ba'n da lwet *jin.*"] ; even to, up to ; [as, " nga tharai ba u'n ioh tang kawei-ar hynrei u ioh *jin* 3 hali"; "*jin* haduh mynta-mynne nga'm tip shuh u poi shano."] ;—*u. n.* a kind of fairy.

Jindat, *ad.* at the same time; also ; [as, " ka um ka la lam *jindat* ia ka khoh ba nga iehnoh harúd wah."]

Jindei, *ad.* too ; too much ; too often ; [as, " ynda iai kren *jindei* u kylla eh noh."]

Jingdeng, } *ka*, *n.* jewel, ornament. [*Imit.* jingdeng-jingkup.]
Jindeng, } Same as *jyndeng.*

Jindem, *ka*, *n.* the refuse of brewery. Same as *jyndem.*

Jindiang, *ka*, *n.* receptacle.

Jindong, *a.* shallow, short.

Jinduh, *ad.* once for all, (as, " u saheb u ai *jinduh* la ka kot ha u.") [*Imit.* jinduh-jintan.]

Jinháw, *ka. n.* gas ; vapour,—*v.* to breathe on.

*Jinis, *ki*, *n. pl.* articles.

Jinjár, *ka*, *n.* trouble. [*Imit.* jinjár-jintrah.] Same as *jynjár.*

Jinjár-trah, *a.* cumbersome ; annoying.

Jinlat, *ka*, *n.* a feast, (*esp.* of pork and rice).

Jinriam, *ka*, *n.* a trap ; a snare. Same as *jingriam.*

Jinrein, *ka*, *n.* vermin on the human body.

Jintang, *u. n.* the stalk. Same as *jyntang.*

Jintah, *ka*, *n.* curry. [*Imit.* jintah-jinbér.]

Jinthut, *v.* to stumble.

*Jira, *u*, *n.* a cumin seed.

Jir-eh, *v.* to feel nausea, to eructate. Same as *jyr-eh.*

Jirthiaw, *v.* to twist.

Jirwit-jirwat, *ad.* in a round about way, not satisfactorily.

Jiw, *ad.* in the habit of, used to ; same as " ju ".

Jiw-jiw-jaw-jaw, *a.* drizling, wet.

---

* Hindi.

*Jiwnom, *ad.* eternally, forever ; same as "junom."

Jiwtang or jutang, *ka, n.* covenant ; arguments. [*Imit.* ka nia-ka jutang."]

Jlang, *ad.* for a long time ; greatly, deeply. [as, "u la leit jah *jlang* sha Dkhar ;" "sngew kynjah *jlang* ;" "sngew kyllut *jlang.*"]

Jlah, *a.* too sweet or bitter.

Jlân, *a.* long ; lengthy : wide.

Jláw, *v.* to howl. Same as *jlew.*

Jláw-ngúid, *a.* greedy, gluttonous. [*Imit.* jlawnguid-jlawhew.]

Jlek, *ad.* up, at once (to gobble). [as, "u bsein u la nguid *jlek* ia ka jakóid."]

Jlen, *ad.* big and tall, gigantic ; [as, "ki ong ba ki Kossack ki long ki briw kiba jrong *jlen.*"]

Jlep, *a.* like the taste or smell of rotten fish ;—*ad.* too much.

Jlep-dohnúd, *v.* to feel bad, to faint.

Jler, *a.* slanderous, vilifying, cavilling.

Jli, *v.* to be sick of ; to be squeamish ; to feel nausea.

Jliang, *ad.* far, deep, (as, "u briew u ngam *jliang* hapoh thwei ; nga tharai ba ngi la iaid jngai *jliang.*")

Jliah, *v.* to lick, to eat up.

Jlih, *a.* even, smooth.

Jlin, *ad.* nicely, comely ; [as, "ki da sád ki da khyllong bha *jlin.*]"

Jlòp, *v.* to wither, to fall off (flower).

Jlúd (sawa-), *ad.* in a long continued tone ; [as, "wei haba la jláw *jlúd* u ksew, kata yn sa iap briew."]

Jmóng, *ad.* out, (as, "u mih *jmóng* ha sla-um.")

Jnang, *v.* to be choked (with a bone.)

Jong, (sign of the Possessive case) of, pertaining to.

Joit, *ad.* at once, up, (used with ieng.)

Jom, *u. n.* the king of Hades.

Jonti, *ka, n.* a net to catch vultures, etc.

Jop, *v.* to conquer ;—*ad.* in drops, (as, "ka um ka jaw *jop-shi-jóp*).

Jór, *ka, n.* the essence or element, semen.

---

* Hindi.

Jot, *a*, destroyed, ruined. [*Imit.* ba jot-ba pei.]

Jráng, *a.* lean (like a man who has just recovered from a severe illness).

Jrái-thied, *v.* to suffer from a sprain.

Jrain-jrain, *ad.* with a crashing sound, like the sound made by volley firing ; [as, "u shu noh *jrain-jrain* shapoh," "ki la siat *jrain-jrain* da ki suloi."]

Jran-um, *v.* to become dried.

Jréng, *ad.* nicely (dressed up). Same as "Jriang."

Jrein, *v.* to fall in drops, to ooze, to drain.

Jri, *ka*, *n.* India rubber, caoutchouc.

Jriang, *ad.* nicely, handsomely ; [as, "u riam bha *jriang* ialade".]

Jri-sim, *ka*, *n.* a Banian tree.

Jrong, *a*, long, tall, high.

Jrùp, *ad.* A dip *cf.* *wieh jrup* to immerse by a dip.

Jrup-jrap, *ad.* at the same time (eat) ; [as, "ki ia bam *jrup jrap.*"]

Ju, *ad.* same as "jiw."

†Juar-bata, *ka*, *n.* a tide.

*Jubáb, *ka*, *n.* a reply, an answer.

Jubân, *ka*, *n.* word, speech, word of honour.

*Jubor, *ad.* by force.

†Juk, *u. n.* a kind of leech,—*ka. n.* an era, age, generation.

Jukali, *n.* a common labourer (rare) ; a coolie who works in mortan.

Juklia (leh-), *ad.* evasively, shufflingly ; [as, "u leh *juklia* ba'n siew ia ka bainong ki briw."]

Jung, *v.* to urinate.

Juhái, *u. n.* a kind of sweet-scented rice.

Júh, *v.* to like, to get tamed; to feel quite at home.

Julai, *v.* to plaster roughly with lime and sand.

*Julap, *ka*, *n.* a purgative medicine ; *jalap.*

Julor, *n.* waste, loss.

*Julum, *ad.* inconsiderately, oppressively ; *zulum* ; [as, leh *julum*, kren *julum.*]

Jumái, *u. n.* earthquake.

Jum-jum, *ad.* full of juice ; [as, "u sohkynphor uba ih u thiang *jum jum.*"]

---

* Hindi. † Bengali.

Junom,
Junom-junom, } *ad.* for ever.
Junom-la-junom,

*Jur, *a.* serious, strong,— *ka, n.* a descent (down hill).

*Jurib, *v.* to survey.

Jút (suh), *n.* false-pains.

*Juti, *ka, n.* shoe.

*Juwari, *ka, n.* a gambling ; a gambler.

Jwái, *v.* to pinch.

Jwár, *ka, n.* a birth-mark ; a horizontal piece of wood attached to the plough.

Jwat, *a.* tough.

Jykáng, *a.* having long and thin legs ; (same as *jkáng*).

Jykéng, *a.* having long and big legs ; (same as *jkéng*).

Jyngut, *a.* muddy, dirty, obscure ; (same as *jngut*).

Jyllád, *ad.* forcibly ; along with ; carelessly ;—*u, n.* a hangman ; [as, " ka long kaba khlem akor ba'n·kám *jyllád* ia ki briew."]

Jyllái (suh), *n.* neuralgia of the stomach.

Jylleng, *ka, n.* the abdomen,—*a.* preponderating too much on one side of the balance—(thread of a paper-kite).

Jyllei, *v.* to be abundant, to be overfull (see "jillei").

Jylli, *ka, n.* a circle, a circumference.

Jylliam, *v.* to wipe out the mouth with the tongue, just as dogs do after having eaten anything. [*Imit.* jylliam-jyllóit.]

Jylliaw, *v.* to fondle, to caress.

Jylliep, *ad.* with drooping eye-lids ; shy-looking (as, peit *jylliep* ; leh *jylliep*).

Jylliep khap-ngain, *ad.* with the eyes cast down ; [as, " ka shad bad ka peit *jylliep-khapngaiñ* kum ka dkoh."]

Jyllóp, *u. n.* a kind of bird who cheers the valley with his song;— Jyllòp *v.* to wither ;—*ad.* by drowning.

Jyllúd, *v.* to wax thread.

Jyllún, *ad.* gracefully, handsomely (said of persons.) [as, ka briew kaba bha briew *jyllún.*] [*Imit.* jyllún lymphúiñ.]

Jymbuiñ, *ka, n.* breast, paps.

*Jymma, *v.* to add, to collect,—*n.* the sum ; total. Same as *jumma.*

Jymmang, *u, n.* the month of May.

Jympa, *v.* to swim.

* Hindi.

Jympan, *ka, n.* a girdle.

Jymphan, *u, n.* a household deity (*see* u phan-u-kyrpád).

Jymphong, *ka, n.* a sleeveless coat.

Jympien, *ka, n.* an under garment worn about the loins by women.

‡Jympor, *u, n.* a jumper or lever.

Jyndam, *ad.* once for all, finally; [as, "u la kren *jyndam* bà phi'n ym buhnúd."]

Jyndat, *ad.* while going past; [as, "ka masi ka la rong *jyndát* ia ka jaiñ."]

Jyndei, *ad.* much, too; [as, "nga la iaishah *jyndei* eh ia u la' u kren bein"].

Jyndem, *ka, n.* fermented rice ready for brewing. (Same as "jindem").

Jyndong, *a.* shallow. (Same as *jindong.*)

Jyndúh, *ad.* finally, once for all; [as, "la tangon haduh ba u'n da iap *jyndúh.*"] (*see* also "jindúh"). [*Imit.* jynduh-jyntan.]

Jynlat, *ka, n.* a feast (*see* jinlat).

Jynrat, *ad.* along (as, "ka l'er ka lam *jynrat* ia ka jáiñ bathád.")—*v.* to uproot.

Jynreh, *kaba, n.* eructation.

Jynsur, *a.* long, reaching down, loose.

Jynteh, *u, n.* a string, bamboo tie.

Jyntia, *a.* to be full of. (Synonymous with *jyllei.*)

Jyrmi, *u. n.* a creeping-plant. [*Imit.* u jyrmi-u jyrthah.]

Jyrhiah, *v.* the effect produced by water passing into the air passage while drinking.

Jyrhoh, *v.* to cough. [*Imit.* jyrhoh-jyrhám.]

Jyrhoh khlúr, *ka, n.* a cough which brings out the phlegm; a peculiar coughing.

Jyrsieh, *v.* to get stuck or get the feet sunk down in mud.

Jyrteng, *a.* lazy, idle, lethargic.

Jyrthiaw, *a.* to twist. (Same as *jirthiaw.*)

Jyrtieng, *v.* to straighten the legs while sitting.

Jyrwait, *v.* to pinch, to twist.

Jyrwit-jyrwat, *ad.* unwillingly, not in a straightforward manner.

‡ English.

L.

L—The eleventh letter in the Khasi alphabet.

La=(1) sign of the Past Tense (as, u *la* leit noh); (2) sign of the Possessive Case, *of*, (as, u la shem *la* ka masi); (3) though, although, (as, *la'* u raikhoh hynrei um tlot); (4) *plus* (+); *into* (×); [as, 5 *la* 5 long 10, *i.e.*, 5 + 5 = 10; ka kynroh kaba 5 *la* 5 *la* 10 pruh, *i.e.*, 5 × 5 × 10 pruh.]

'la, *contr.* of *sla*, a leaf, or of *khla*, a tiger.

'láb, *u. n. contr.* of *khláb*, the spleen.

'la-bam-briew, *n.* a man-eater.

Laban, *n.* a Khasi name for Shillong.

***Lak**=100,000. [*Imit.* ka lak-ka putit.]

Laka *ad.* wholesale (used with *die* and *thied*); *buh la ka*=to stake money in gambling.

'lakait, *n.* the plantain leaf.

***Lakam**, *u*, *n.* a bridle.

'lakúd, *u*, *n.* a kind of orchid.

Lád, *u*, *n.* a way, a means, a road;—*v.* to be overcareful about one's personal toilette; to rub with the sole of the foot in token of contempt.

Lada, *conj.* if.

Ladang, *conj.* when,—*ad.* very (early). [as, *La dang* step-phyr-ngáp u la khie.]

Lade, *pron.* self.

Lang, *ad.* together, in concert; [as, " ngi ia khaii-pateng *lang* bad u"],—*v. i.* to congeal, to solidify.

'lang, *contr.* of *blang*, a goat and of *phlang*, grass.

'langbrot, *n.* a sheep.

Langbyrku, } **Langbyrkaw**, } *ka*, *n.* a green fruit pigeon.

'langkushi, *n.* a big kind of goat.

'lang-lung, *u*, *n.* tender or newly-grown grass.

'langñiuh, *u*, *n.* bearded grass.

'langsah, *u. n.* grass which has not been set fire to for a long time.

'langsohmoh, *u*, *n.* a full-grown he-goat.

'langthohkhlieh, *ka*, *n.* a human victim to be offered to " u Thlen."

---

* Hindi.

Langtati, *ka, n.* a plant which bears a white flower like a lily ; (*Bot. Lilium gigantium*).

Lah, *v.* can, able, succeed.

§**Laha**, *ka, n.* lac, sealing-wax.

Lái, *a.* three.

'lái (*abbrev.* of *tylldi*) *u, n.* a rope ; (2) (*abbrev.* of *tlái*),—*ka, n.* palm.

'lái ktang, *ka, n.* a kind of palm.

'lái-nili, *ka, n. Wallichia* ; a species of palm.

Láiphew-jaid, *phr.* all sorts or kinds.

Lain, *ad.* very (red, like the appearance of one who is excited).

Lait, *v.* to be free, escape ;—*n.* a mistake. [*Imit.* ka lait-ka let.]

Lait kylla, *ka, n.* violation of the sacrificial customs by omission or departure from the old usages ; violation of the ceremonial law.

Lait-ksúid, *v.* to be entirely free from any disagreeable connection, as from the grip of evil-spirits. (*Imit.* lait ksúid lait khrei).

Lait-dár, *v.* to be free to accomplish one's object.

Lait-doh, *v.* to have a sprain.

Lait-ia, *v.* to be free from a period fixed for the observance of certain religious or social ceremonies.

Lait-im, *v.* to be saved.

Lait-lúid, *v.* to be free or be at large.

Lait(na), *phr.* except, besides.

Laitsang, *v.* to be free from a *sang* or taboo,—*ad.* nominally, outwardly; [as, u la thied ia nga tang i sopti sala tang ba'n *laitsang* ; tang shi paisa *laitsang* u'm shym ai.]

Lait-sa-i-sáid, *phr.* narrowly escaped ; [*as, lait-sa-i-sáid* ba nga'n ùr.]

Lait-tháw, *v.* to be free as from an imminent danger,—*kaba, n.* a hair-breadth escape.

La jan, *ad.* nearly, almost.

La jong, *p.* one's own.

La lah, (*aux. v.*) had.

Lali, *a.* slovenly, sluttish, dirty.

'laliar, *ka, n.* a tender top leaf used in sacrifices. [*Imit.* ka 'laliar ka 'lalong.]

---

§ Assamese.

Lalot, *a.* greedy, gluttonous, selfish. [*Imit.* lalot-kangár.]

Lam, *v.* to lead, to bring ; prefix=*ish* (as, *lam*lieh, *lam*iong).

Lama, *ka*, *n.* flag, pennon, banner.

'laman, *n.* the Bengal tiger.

Lamdoh, *v.* to celebrate a marriage ceremony by a feast, (*esp.* of pork.) [*Imit.* lamdoh-lamkah.]

'lamet, *ka*, *n.* a kind of leaf much used in packing things.

Lamhér, *ad.* thoughtlessly, wastefully ; (as, wat leh *lamhér* katba dang ioh.) [*Imit.* lamhér-lamphut.]

Lamjew, *u*, *n.* the internal part of the flesh which lines the spine.

Lamlér, *v.* to lie. [*Imit.* lamlér-lambáit.]

Lamphrang, *v.* to lead, to preface.

Lamwir, *a.* mad, crazy. [*Imit.* lamwir-lamtham.]

Lân(iaid-), *ad.* without any restraint ; [as, ba'n shu iaid *lân* kum phi ym i-dei.]

Làn-làn(khuid-), *ad.* clearly (swept or trampled over) ; [as, ka jaka ba dem ka dngiem ka khuid *làn-làn.*]

Lane, *conj.* or, either.

Lano ? *ad.* when ?

Lano-lano, *ad.* in future, hereafter ; ever.

Lanymwei, *ad.* hereafter, next year. [*Imit.* lanymwei-lanym ár.]

Lap, *v.* to overtake ;—*ad.* in haste, inconsiderately ; [as, "nga la thung *lap* eh ia u phan ; wat ju leh *lap* eh ia kaei kaei."],—láp *kaba*, *n.* in cutting a tree a cut which is a little above the first one is called *kaba láp.*

'lap, (*abbrev.* of slap), rain.

Lapadong, *ka*, *n.* the leaf of a certain plant.

Lapa-iat, *ka*, *n.* a tree bearing small black fruits, a see-saw.

'lap-bah, *u*, *n.* a heavy rain. [*Imit.* 'lapbah-'lapsan.]

'lap-bñiup-bñiup, *u*, *n.* a drizzle.

'lap-kyrtiah, *u*, *n.* rain and storm.

Lape, *v.* to daub, plaster.

Lapér(soh), *u*, *n.* the fruit of a certain small dwarf palm.

'lapeh(sei-), *ad.* with plenty of leaves but without grain or fruit.

Laplah, *ad.* anticipatively, prematurely, [as, "u briew uba leh *laplah* eh ia kaei kaei u kylla kaba mut kloi."]

Laplieng(ym), *phr.* to be in too great a hurry ; [as, "balei phi leh kum ba'm *laplieng* shuh."] [*Imit.* laplieng-lapdár.]

Lapmiet, *v.* to be overtaken by night. [*Imit.* lapmiet–lapiong.]

'lapmynsáw, *u. n*, a sun shower.

Lár(ka), *n.* (omen in egg divination) a piece of the broken shell lying on the right-hand side of the biggest broken central piece called ka "lieng."

Larkam, *a.* useful (used with the negative particle *ym.*) [as, kane ka ba'm *larkam.*] [*Imit.* larkam-larjam.]

Lar-en, *u, n.* a fabulous monster ; a thunderbolt.

Laryndia, *ka, n.* castor-oil plant.

Lasamdoh, *u, n.* the demon who attacks people by bringing in swelling of the neck and hoarseness (the patient is given to drink of the blood of the sacrificed cock or pig).

Lasawia, *ad.* four days hence.

Lasir, *u, n.* a species of grass much used in sacrifices.

Lasháì, *ad.* to-morrow.

Lasháì-lashisngi, *ad.* hereafter ; in future.

Lashibit, *ad.* after a short time, (*i.e.*, after the lapse of some hours.)

Lashisngi, *n.* the day after to-morrow.

Lasiit, *ad.* to-night. (Same as *lasyit*).

‡Lat, *ka, n.* a feast ;—*u, n.* Lord, Governor General.

*Latai, *ka, n.* (Hind.) a thread-roller.

Lati, *a.* oily, greasy.

Lat-lat, *ka, n.* a rapid, a current.

Latohtih, *ka, n.* a tree planted along the edge of a garden to serve as a fence.

Latom, *ka, n.* a top, spinning top, peg-top.

'la-tyrdop, *ka, n.* (*Bot.*) *cinnamomum candatuni.*

'latyrpád, *ka, n.* a bay leaf.

Láw, *v.* to take off, to extract, to undo.

'láw, *ka, n.* (*abbrev.* of khláw), jungle.

'láw-bah, *ka, n.* a big jungle, a dense forest. [*Imit.* láwbah-láwsan.]

'láwkyntang, *ka, n.* a sacred grove.

Lawei, *ad.* hereafter. [*Imit.* lawei-lathai *or* lawei-la-ar.]

---

* Hindi. ‡ English.

Law-law, *ad.* carelessly, superficial, hasty; [as, "u B u long u briew uba *law-law* eh."]

Láwlynnong, *ka, n.* a coppice, bush.

Lbang, *ad.* with the dhoti rolled up; [as, "u tieng ba ioh jhieh, kumta u la kyntiw *lbáng* ia ka bohkhaila."]

Lbér, *u, n.* the month of March.

Lbing(heh-), *ad.* fleshy and big; [as, "u briew uba heh *lbing.*"]

Lbong, *ka, n.* the thigh.

Lboit, *ad.* short and naked; [as, "phim khriat haba phi shah lyngkhuit *lboit* kumne?"]

Lkài, *ad.* plump, (as, "u sniang uba sngaid *lkài.*")

Lker-lker, *ad.* pulpily. [as, "u khynnah uba sngaid *lker-lker.*"]

Lkhang, *ad.* lonely, helpless, (as, "ki iap baroh bad u sah sa marwei *lkhang.*")

Lkhái, *a.* tender, delicate, not tenacious or tough.

Lkhit, *ki, n.* small useless or unserviceable pieces; atoms. [*Imit.* ki lkhit-ki lkhai.]

Lkhoit, *ad.* like a small lump.

Lkhuit, *ad.* resembling a lump; [as, "u kuli tup ki Tibet u long uba tylli *lkhuit.*"]

Lkut, *ad.* like a log; [as, "u bysein uba lyngkot *lkut.*"]

Lko, *a.* utterly broken, crumbling.

Lko-pom, *ad.* completely, (as, "ki la ialeh thyma ha ba'n da *lkopom.*")

Lkur-lkur, *ad.* dumpling-like; [as, "une u khynnah uba sngáid *lkur-lkur.*"]

Ldang, *ad.* lying on the back and helpless (as, "ka dohkha ka pér *ldang*").

Ldai,
Ldet,
Ldit,
Ldoi,
Ldui, etc., } *ad.* dangling; [as, "ka tuta ka sdien *ldai*; ka sim ka ngat *ldet* ha ka shangkhawiah; ki sdien ia u bol *ldoi*; ka kylla-badur ka sdien *ldui* ialade," etc.]

Ldat, *ad.* hanging (as a bird); [as, "ka la ngat ka sim *ldat* ha ka shangkawiah."]

Lding(at-), *ad.* lying with a swollen abdomen; [as, "at ka kpoh *lding.*"]

Ldui, *ad.* hanging (said of big things ;—as, " u lwai u sdien *ldui* ha shiteng riat").

‡**Led,** *u, n.* a lead pencil.

'leng, (*abbrev.* of pylleng) *ka, n.* an egg.

Léngléng, *ad.* wildly, aimlessly ; [we speak of the flight of an alarmed butterfly and say—" ka hér *léng-léng* " ; also of a poisoned fish as, " ka jngi *léng-léng.*"]

'lengkha, *ka, n.* fresh egg.

'lengkpoh, *ka, n.* an egg placed over the navel of a dead person and which is broken on the funeral pyre.

'leng-iew, *ka, n.* old egg or that which is sold in the hat ; bázar egg.

'leng-ra, *ka, n.* an egg left unhatched by a hen.

Leh, *v.* to do, to perform, to act.

Lehbeiñ, *v.* to maltreat, to ill-treat. [*Imit.* lehbeiñ-lehkhoh.]

Lehkái, *v.* to play, to make sport of.

Lehkhynráw, *v.* to play a bachelor or spinster, to dress nicely like a young man or a young woman. [*Imit.* lehkhynráw-lehkhyndeiñ.]

Lehdiaw, *v.* to be dejected or cast down.

Leh-eh, *v.* to handle roughly, to deal hard with.

Leh-jalani, *v.* to be fastidious regarding dress or toilette.

Leh-mushlia, *v.* to meddle with. [*Imit.* Leh mushlia—leh-mushláit.]

Lehmynleh, *v.* to affect to do ; to feign, to pretend.

Lehnoh-ei, *a.* vain, useless ; [as, " ka long kaba *lehnoh-ei* ba'n kynjat ia ki speh "] ,—*v.* to waste.

Leh-palat, *v.* to do more than what is right or proper ; to transgress. [*Imit.* lehpalat-lehpaliang.]

Lehráin, *v.* to be ashamed of. [*Imit.* lehráin-lehsuiñ.]

Lehrit, *v.* to be unassuming or humble.

Lehroh, *v.* to make a show of,—*adj.* pretentious, fond. [*Imit.* lehroh-lehmeng.]

Lehrong, *v.* to make a display or a show of anything. [*Imit.* lehrong-lehrup.]

Lehsa, *v.* to be in the dumps, to sulk.

Lehsang, *v.* to do or act anything that is immoral, profane or indecent. [*Imit.* lehsang-lehma.]

---

‡ English.

Lehsat, *v.* to do anything by way of vengeance or self-mortification. [*Imit.* lehsat-lehjew.]

Lehse, *ad.* probably, perhaps.

Lehsih, *v.* to have dirty habits ; to be untidy.

Lehsting, *v.* to make light of the matter, to be unmindful.

*Leh-tamsa, *v.* to make a show or to have a *tamasha.* [*Imit.* lehtamsa-lehtamhoi.]

Leh-thamula, *v.* to make sport of ; to cut practical jokes. [*Imit.* leh-thamula-leh-thamuleiñ.]

Leh-thawlir, }
Leh-thawnang, } *v.* to mimic ; to do something odd.

Lei ? *ad.* why ? for what reason ?—*ka, n.* a flour paste.

'lei, *n.* (*abbrev.* of *blei*), a god.

Lei-lei, (*phr.*), 1. So much (the better) [as, "ba'n da phi lah *lei-lei* ba'n iaid shi sngi, kata la bit eh"];
2. at any rate, any how (when preceded by *da*) [as, "da *lei-lei* nga'n ym harám ia phi"];
3. without any cause (when preceded by *khlem*) [as, "u la dumok ia nga *khlem lei-lei.*"]

'Leikhuri, *ka, n.* the household god of a certain clan of the Khasis.

'Leikbyrdop-'leikharái, *ka, n.* the goddess who is supposed to guard over the gate of or entrance into a village in time of war.

Leilieh, *ka, n.* lightning.

'Lei-muluk, *ka, n.* the goddess who takes care of a village or state.

'Leisád-'leisunon, *ka, n.* the guardian goddess of a Siem, clan, (*esp.* in the time of war).

Leit, *v.* to go, to proceed ; to fit.

L'eit, *ka, n.* the bottom, the foot, the buttock. Same as *lyeit.*

Leit-bár, *v.* to answer a call of nature.

Leit-bhih, *v.* to go and beg.

Leit-kái, *v.* to go out for a walk, to go on a visit. [*Imit.* leitkái-leitiáid.]

Leit-ka-wan, *ka, n.* journey, travel, (*esp.* for trading purpose.)

Leitkha-leitman, *v.* to get married (said of a man).

---

* Hindi.

Leitkhyndew, *v.* to go out to answer a call of nature. [*Imit.* leitkhyndew-leitmynshem.]

Leit-dur, *v.* to suit, to be fit. [*Imit.* leitdur-leitdar.]

Leit-hapshop, *v.* to fall into an unlucky condition, to be unfortunate.

Leit-ing-briew, *phr.* to get married (said of a man).

Leit-lamdoh, *phr.* to celebrate a marriage ceremony by giving a feast. [*Imit* leitlamdoh-leitlamkah.]

Leit-lát, *v.* to enter the wind passage (as water when drunk).

Leitrúd, *v.* to go out to answer a call of nature.

'lei-umtong, *ka*, *n.* the goddess who looks after drinking water.

Lem, *ad.* together, along with, (as, leit-*lem*) ;—*v.* (in spinning tops) to be out of the circle.

Len, *v.* to deny.

'len, *u*, *n.* (*abbrev.* of u *thlen*), a big snake ; [as, *'len*-lúm, *'len*pula.]

Len-len, *ad.* smooth and bare ; [as, "phi'n snoh phi'n. bat nangno haba khúid *len-len* u máw."]

'lenpula *u*, *n.* a big mountain snake ; a python.

Lep, *ad.* furiously ; (*as*, " u la bitar *lep* ia u ") ; flaringly.

Lér, (1) *ad.* once, by chance ; [as, "nga iohsngew ba u la pyrshang *lér* ba'n kem ia u," "la shu lait-*lér* ba'n dei na ka khlieh."

(2) useless (used with the negative particle *ym*, as, " kane ka jingpyrshang jong phi ka ba'm *lér* ").

(3) creepingly (as a serpent does); [as, " u bsein u la pár *lér* sha sañium."]

L'er, *ka*, *n.* wind, air. Same as *lyer*.

L'er-kyllang, *ka*, *n.* a cyclone.

L'er-kyrtiah, *ka*, *n.* a storm mixed with rain.

L'er-langthari, *ka*, *n.* the whirlwind.

L'er-synrái, *ka*, *n.* a soft breeze which blows in autumn.

'let (*abbrev.* of klet), *ad.* amiss, (as, "nga la kum kren *'let*")—*ka*, *n.* transgression, wrongs."

Lew, *ad.* intensely ; [as, " shit *lew*."]

Lew-lew, *ad.* while it is hot (of eatables or temper).

Léw-lit ! *Int.* beware !

Lngáw (iw), *a.* having a peculiar smell, as that of an unoccupied house.

Lngen, *kaba, n.* a gentle flow of a stream.

Lngér, *ad.* throughout the whole length (used with *shi*—).

Lngiar, *v.* to make delay, to be dilatory.

Lngiej, *v.* to be greasy.

Lhen, *ad.* stagnantly; [as, "ka um ka lang *lhen*."]

Lhep, *ad.* very (oppressive or hot); [as, "ka shit *lhep*."]

Lhin (hin-), *ad.* completely, all over (covered with water); [as, "ka um ka dap *hin-lhin*."]

Lhiẹh, *a.* becoming more severe (applicable to a sore only).

Lhiej, *u, n.* a grass with sharp blades.

Lhon, *ad.* like the water of cesspools; [as, "ka um ka lang *lhon*."]

L'hoh, *a.* emanating bad smell (as from the body or clothes of a dirty fellow).

Lhop, *a.* without free access of fresh air; close, stuffy.

Li, *adv.* like the smell of a fish (used with *iw* = smell).

'li, (*abbrev.* of *dohthli*), *n.* a small fish, (as, '*li*jarang, '*li*siaw, '*li*por).

Liak, *ad.* at a glance, (as, "nga ioh-i ia ka khmat jong u tang *liak*").

Liang, *ka, n.* side, party.

'liang (*abbrev.* of pliang), *ka, n.* a plate.

'liangdieng, *ka, n.* a wooden plate.

Liam, *ad.* towering, exceedingly; [as, "ka rynñeng jong u ka palat *liam* ia kiwei baroh."]

Lian, *ad.* used negatively only with *ym*=much more; more than; [as, "nga tharai ba ym *lian* 1,000 u briew uba khmih kái."]

Lian-khún, *a.* having children one after another in a short lapse of time.

Liap-liap, *ad.* lappingly; [as, "ka miaw ka jliah *liap-liap* ia ka du."]

'liar-kait, *ka, n.* the topmost plantain leaf.

Liar-ngot, *a.* broken, as a young bamboo; (hence) stunted, short.

Liat, *v.* to fall through.

Liat-khún, *v.* to have a miscarriage.

Liat-lor, to slip off, to have an abortion.

Liaw, *ad.* for a short time (to look), glancingly; [as, "u shu peit *liaw* sha nga bad u dem noh."]

Lieb, *ad.* at a glance (look); [as, "nga tang shu peit *lieb*, nga la ihthuh ia ka jinglong jong u."]

Lied, *v.* to dismantle, unroof.

Lieng, *ká*, *n*, a boat, a ship, a canoe. [*Imit.* ka lieng-ka phan.]

'lieng, (*contr.* of khlieng), *n.* a kite.

Liengkynda, *ka*, *n.* a boat, a dug-out, a canoe.

Liengiapom, *ka*, *n.* a man-of-war.

'liengjathang, *ka*, *n.* a spotted eagle.

Lieh, *a.* white.

Lieh-khleiñ, *a.* white, like porcelain.

Liem, *v.* to lie on the back (said of cowries); to be a match for (used with *ia*).

Lien (iáid-), *ad.* like many people walking; [as, "u paitbah u la iáid *lien* sha kyrkit."]

'liew (*contr.* of thliew), *ka*, *n.* a hole.

'liewlep, *ka*, *n.* a pitfall.

'liewlong, *ka*, *n.* a natural pit, abyss.

Ling-ling, *ad.* swiftly, agilely; [as, "khie leit hynrei wat jah ia wan *ling-ling* ho."]

Lih! (*vulgarism*) *n.* friend! my friend! [as, "balei *lih* me jah?"]

*Lilam, *ka*, *n.* auction.

Lilipenpen, *a.* having nothing, empty handed.

Lin, *ad.* to the brim, all over, altogether; [as, "ka madan baroh ka la dap *lin* da ka um."]

Lin-lin (jlih), *ad.* very (smooth); [as, "kane ka snieh ka long kaba jlih *lin-lin.*"]

Lip, *v.* to go out, to be extinguished.

'li-pòr, *n.* a kind of small fish.

Lir, *u*, *n.* indigo,—*v.* to meddle.

Lir-lir, *ad.* creepingly (of small things); [as, "i bsein iba rit i par *lir-lir.*"]

---

* Hindi.

Lit, *v.* to sharpen.

L'iur, *ka, n.* the rainy season.

Liw, *ad.* sulky (to look). [As " u peit *liw* ia nga kumba u bitar eh."]

Liwliw-lawlaw (thngan-), *ad.* cravingly, uncomfortably; [as, "ynda la koit na kaba pang, ju thngan *liwliw-lawlaw.*"]

Ljang,
Ljeng,
Ljing,
Ljóng,
Ljung, } *ad.* hanging down; [as, " ki sdien ia ka doh *ljang.*"]

Lmang, *ad.* with the head cut off; [as, " balei phi ot pynlyngkot ia la u diengduh *lmang*?"]

Lmam-lmam,
Lmem-lmem,
Lmum-lmum, } *ad.* full of flesh (as, u khúnlung u sngáid *lmam-lmam*"); fatty.

Lmeh-lmeh, *ad.* fresh, lively; [as, "ka dur jong u briew uba iap mynsáw ka shu i *lmeh-lmeh* hi."]

Lmet-lmet, (stem), *ad.* very (yellow), golden colour; [as, "u briew uba stem bhabriew *lmet-lmet.*"]

Lmit-lmit, *ad.* yellowish, (as a person suffering from liver complaint; [as, "ki briew kiba don khláb ki stem *lmit-lmit.*"]

Lmoin,
Lmuin, } *ad.* short or bob-tailed.

Lok, *n.* a friend; husband or wife. [*Imit.* u lok-u-jor.]

Long, *v.* is, exist, become, —*u, n.* a fox-glove.

Lóng-lóng (khih-), *ad.* madly, wildly; [as, " u sarong, hynrei ynda mudui ki briew un sa khih *lóng-lóng*"]; aimlessly.

Long bneng (khmied), *ad.* upwards; [as, " khmih la ka lynti wat ju khmied *longbneng* ioh jinthut."]

Longbteng, *ka, n.* an inheritance.

Longbynriew, *ka, n.* humanity. [*Imit.* longbynriew—manbynriew.]

Longkha, *ka, n.* the goddess who presides over the relationship by marriage.

Longkur, *ka, n.* the guardian goddess of a *kur* (clan).

Longra, *v.* to grow sparsely here and there,— *a.* consisting of small hard lumps of earth.

Longrynieng, *ka, n.* being.

Longshuwa-manshuwa, *u, n.* ancestor; predecessor.

L'oh, *u*, *n*. cloud, mist. Same as *lyoh.*

Loi-loi, *a*. mild, soft-hearted, innocent.

Lo-lo, *a*. superficial, shallow-minded.

L'oiñ (pyllon-), *ad*. nicely or beautifully (round). Same as *lyoin.*

Loit, *v*. to untie, undo, to take off.

Lop, *v*. to cut off, to knock down (the teeth); break off (said of the blade of an axe or cutting instrument).

Lór, *ka*, *n*. the surface, external part.

'lor (suffix)=prematurely (as, kha*lor*=abortion).

Lorni, *a*. meddlesome, tale-bearing. [*Imit.* lorni—lorháp];—*n*. a shrike.

Lot, *v*. to go in a hole (gambling).

Lpa, *ad*. already, beforehand.

Lpan, *ad*. stoutly (body) (as, u loit lyngkhuit *lpan*).

Lpen, *ad*. like a serpent while lying, (as, "u bseiñ u dem *lpen* ha lynti").

Lphóng, *ad*. like a small straight post or tree.

Lphúng, *ad*. like a big straight post or column; (as, "ka dieng-lieng ka long ka dieng kaba beit *lphúng*").

Lping, *ad*. indolently, lazily (as, "u sniang uba la heh eh u shu thiah *lping*").

L'sheng, } *ad*. like the appearance of anything long when hung;
Lshung } [as, "nga ioh-i ba ki wah *lsheng* ia ka lbong masi."]

Lshúiñ, *a*. oval.

Ltar, } *ad*. at full length [as, "ka long kaba khlem akor ba'n
Lter, } jyrtieng *lter* ia ki kjat"].
Ltir, }

Ltóin, } (jrong-), *ad*. long and 'round at both ends [as, "bún
Ltúin, } phi'n shem ki maw kiba jrong *ltóin* ha rud-wah"].
Ltáin, }

Luab-luab (jem.), *ad*. flexibly (bent), (as, "ka kti ka kjat jong u ka jem *luab-luab*").

Luar, *u*, *n*. small bamboo string or tie.

Luar-ding, *ka*, *n*. a furnace. Same as *lawar ding.*

Lúb, *a*. moderately big, good sized; *i-lúb*=attractive.

‡**Lukiar** (ki), *n*. the 44th Gurkha Regiment (once the Sylhet Light Infantry).

‡ English (a corruption of the phrase "look here!").

Luksan, *v.* to suffer loss.

Luk-u-lak, *u, n.* common people.

Lúd, *a.* young.

Lueng, *ad.* like a serpent (as, "u bseiñ uba jrong *lueng*").

Luen, *ad.* big and long (as, "u bseiñ u dem *luen*").

Lung, *a.* young, tender.

Lung-lung-leng-leng, *ad.* cursorily (as, "nga shu khmih *lung-lung-leng-leng* ia ka kot jong phi").

Lúh (ia-) *v.* to woo.

Lui-lui, *a.* innocent, harmless.

Luiñ, *ad.* point-blank, (as, "u tang shu thew *luiñ* da ka suloi, ki la khaweit").

Lúiñ, *a.* blunt.

Lúm, *u, n.* a hill, a mountain; outside the village.

Lúm-Mangkashang, *n.* the Himalayas.

Lùm, *v.* to gather, to collect.

Lùn, *n.* a tadpole.

Lún, *u*, to throw stones, to pelt with stones.

Lupula, (see *'Lenpula*).

Lúr, *v.* to plough; (*ia-*)—to woo, to court.

'lúr (*abbrev.* of khlúr),—*u, n.* a star.

Lur, *v.* to push forward (the firewood).

'lúr-dih-duma, *u, n.* the comet.

Luri-lura (ka Iew-), *ka, n.* the market of beasts (connected with the history of the dog in Khasi folk-lore).

'lur-mangkara, *u, n.* the brightest star.

'lúr-miet, *u, n.* the evening star.

'lúr-shái, *u, n.* the morning star.

Lushia, *v.* to finger, to handle, to meddle.

***Lut**, *a.* spent, exhausted,—*ka, n.* a currency note.

Lut-phut, *a.* squandering [*Imit.* lutphut—lut sha].

***Luta**, *u, n.* a goblet, a brass cup; the proboscis, the trunk (of an elephant).

Lute, *v.* to spoil, to plunder.

Lyaiñ, *ad.* short and wide (as, "u briew uba lyngkot *lyaiñ*").

---

* Hindi.

Lyar, *ad.* short and round (as "u khiew uba pyllun *lyar*").

Lykhit, *ki*, *n.* small useless things or details. [*Imit.* ki lykhit—ki lkhai.] Same as *Lkhit.*

Lyeit, *ka*, *n.* the bottom, the foot, the buttock.

Lyér, *ka*, *n.* wind, air (see also *l'ér*).

Lyng-a, *a.* hot, uncomfortable, uneasy [*Imit.* lyng-a—pisa].

Ly-ngang, *ad.* lonely, (as, "u shong tang marwei *ly-ngang* ha lúm.")

Lyng-án, *ad.* short and stout (in stature) (as "u briew uba lyngkot *lyng-án.*")

Lyngáit, / **Lngáit**, *v.* to disappear without knowledge.

Lyngba, *pr.* through,—*ad.* throughout.

Lyngbiang, *a.* without earrings or ornaments or handle (as, "ka wait kaba *lyngbiang*").

Lyngka, *n.* the name of a second day in a Khasi week; Ceylon.

Lyngkár, *ad.* without care, at random (as "wat pyllait *lyngkár* ia ki masi ioh dait u khla").

Lyngkdang, *ad.* lying helpless on the back [as, "ka dohkha ka pér *lyngkdong.*"]

Lyngkdong, *ka*, *n.* the occiput; nape of the head.

Lyngkha, *ka*, *n.* a field [*Imit.* lyngkha—ka risai].

*__Lyngkhason__, *ka*, *n.* a frame of wood or bier for carrying the dead body to the cremating place.

Lyngkhot, *ka*, *n.* a piece [*Imit.* ka lyngkhot—ka lyngkhái.]

Lyngkhúh, *v.* to happen by accident;—*n.* an evil spirit [*Imit.* lyngkhúh-pakhuh].

Lyngkhuùid, *a.* naked [*Imit.* lyngkhùid—lyngbiang].

Lyngki, *a.* barren.

Lyngkien, *ka*, *n.* a meadow, a *maidan*;—*a.* spilling all over, flowing, copious,—*a.* level with.

‡**Lyngklad**, *ka*, *n.* longcloth.

Lyngknap, / **Lyngkniap**, / **Lyngknep**, *ad.* like a piece of slate on the ground (as, "ynda nga iit shitom nga shem ia ka tyngka kane *lyngknap* ha khyndew"); flat.

Lyngknot, *ka*, *n.* a low wooden stool.

Lyngkór, *ka*, *n.* a plough; an anchor.

Lyngkot, *a.* short;—*n.* a piece (used with *shi*, ar, lai, etc.)

---

* Hindi. ‡ English.

Lyngkraug, }
Lyngkrangreit, } *ad.* with things scattered here and there (as "phi itynnad kumno ba'n ieh noh *lyngkrang* ia ki-ei ki-ei?").

Lyngkrang, }
Lyngkreng, } *ad.* helplessly (lying on the back), (as, "ynda la bu-aid u thiah *lyngkrang* ha surok").

Lyngkut, *a.* short, laconic; even (number).

Lyngkyrneng, *u, n.* an ear ornament.

Lyngkyrwiang, *ka, n.* the point on the head where the hair appears to end (generally on the top).

Lyngdáu, *u, n.* (used along with u *pyngrem*), a man of great influence—*u. Pyngrem-u-Lyngdán*, a statesman.

Lyngdhang, *a.* shallow and flat.

Lyngdoh, *n.* a priest.

Lyngdúm, *a.* bareheaded.

Lyngdykhur, *n.* a dove. Same as *Lyngdkhur*.

Lyngeng, *ad.* having a big head, lonely (as "u briew uba heh ka khlieh *lyngeng*"). (Same as *Lngeng*).

Lyngen, *a.* slow, gently flowing (stream). (Same as *Lyngen*).

Lyngér, *n.* full or whole length. (Same as *Lynger*.)

Lyngngai, *ad.* in ecstasy of joy, in an unconscious state, (as, "u la shong sngewbha *lyngngai*").

Lyngngam, *n.* the name of the hill-tribe in the north-west of the Khasi Hills.

Lyngngeh, *ad.* with the head thrown backwards, (as, "u ioh thiah *lyngngeh* ha ka shuki").

Lyngngeit, *ad.* with the whole weight of the body (sitting),—*v.* to thrust down.

Lyngngiah, *ad.* with the head thrown backwards, (as, "u leh *lyngngiah* ia lade").

Lyngngoh, *v.* to be perplexed; to be astonished. [*Imit. Lyngngoh*-lyngngain.]

Lyngngon, *ad.* closely shaven (small), [as, u khi *lyngngon* ia la ka khlieh.]

Lyngngot, *n.* a block of wood.

Lyngngùn, *ad.* closely shaven (big); with the head exposed (*esp.* to the rains); [as "u iaid *lyngngun* ha u slap khlem khein ei ei."]

Lynghoh-khohwah, *ka, n.* the back part of the leg just under the knee.

Ly-ngiar, *v.* to be late. (Same as *Ingiar*).

Lyngiej, *a.* oily. (Same as *Ingiej*).

Lyng-ien, *ad.* half-reclining, like the walking of a big man with a big belly [as, "u S'iem, *k,* u iaid *lyngien lyngien* ha Sòr."]

Lynglit, langlit, *n.* a species of parrot.

Lynglùn, *ka, n.* a lump.

Lyngrah, *u, n.* white-ants.

Lyngráw, *u, n.* a young bull.

Lyngrom, *ad.* in a small group (standing) (as "ki ia ieng *lyngrom* ha ka juh ka jaka").

Lyngrum-lyngram, *ad,* carelessly or in such a way as to obstruct the passage (as "ki shu buh *lyngrum-lyngram* ia ki dieng").

Lyngskór, *u, n.* a Prime Minister.

Lyngsnap,
Lyngsnep,
Lyngsnej,
Lyngsniap,
Lyngsnop,
Lyngsnup, } *a.* flat.

Lyngter,
Lyngkter, } *a.* lazy, indolent.

Lyngthen, *ad.* bulky and without proportion, (as, "u briew uba heh *lyngthen*").

Lyngthohdoh, *ka, n.* the back of the neck.

Lyng-úh, *a.* thick, raging; densely smoky,—*v.* to rage (as fire).

Lyng-úin, *ka, n.* the circumference.

Lyng-ur, *ad.* like a big ring or ball (as "shna ka syngwiang kaba pyllun *lyng-ur*").

Lyngwit, *ad.* revolvingly, (as, "tang dei kuli, u khla u la shád *lyngwit* bad u kyllon artat").

Lyhar, *ad.* carelessly and with the whole weight of the body (to sit). Same as *Lhar.*

Lylon, *ad.* like a ball (small); (as, "ba'n khuai dohkha shu kli *lylon* da ka ja"). Same as *Llon.*

Lymbher, *ad.* in a heap, (as, " ki lum *lymbher* ia u 'dewiong ha madan ").

Lymbher-tait, *ad.* carelessly ; scattered about, (as, " ki iehnoh ia kiei kiei *lymbher-tait* ").

Lymbhor. *ad.* like a sleeping baby, (*as*, " i khúnlung i iohthiah *lymbhor*.")

Lymbiang, *ad.* without any earring or ornament or handles. (Same as *Lyngbiang*).

Lymbit, *ka*, *n.* a bat ; mica.

Lymbnep, *ad.* thickly, (covered, as with scabs or eruptive disease) ; (as, " u ñiang thylliew u rben *lymbnep*").

Lymboit, *a.* almost naked.

Lymbung. *ad.* in a heap or group, (as, " ynda la lah shoh ia u kba, ki shu lum *lymbung* ia u skum ").

Lymbup, *v.* to push with the shoulder.

Lymda, *conj.* unless.

Lymmang, *ad.* without dress or ornaments, [as, " ka isih shibun ba'n khet noh ia u khlieh diengduh *lymmang*."]

Lymmen, *ka*. *n.* palm or sole deprived of wrists or toes.

Lymmúh, *ka*, *n.* a branch or a twig with green leaves.

Lympat, *v.* to dash to pieces, to throw down.

Lympeh, *ad.* fine and long (as, "ka dohkha kaba *lympeh*").

Lympen, *ad.* naked, destitute, listless,—*n.* the trunk (of a tree etc.)

Lymphiang, *u*, *n.* a bundle of grass dressed like a sheet for thatching.

Lymphiar, *ad.* with the abdomen hanging down ; [as, "ki dkhar kiba riwbha ki hiar ka kpoh *lymphiar*."]

Lymphóiñ, } *ad.* smooth, sleek ; [as, "i khunlung iba bha briew
Lymphúiñ, } *lymphoiñ*."]

Lymphop, *v.* to wash as a piece of cloth by beating on a flat stone ; to wash down.

Lympung, *ka*, *n.* a place or enclosure where dancing is performed, a stage.

'lymuiñ, *a.* without tail. (Same as *lmuin*).

Lymum-lymum, *ad.* fat, corpulent ; [as, " u khunlung uba sngáid *lymum-lymum*."]

Lymun, *a.* liking (applicable to eatable things). Same as *Lymun*.

Lyndang, *ad.* on the back (to lie). [*Imit.* Lyndang-pyllup.]

Lyndet, *ad.* beyond, behind,—*v.* to transgress, to forsake.

Lyndúm, *a.* bare-headed, bald.

Lynnái, *u*, *n.* a reed.

Lynniang, *u*, *n.* a plant the root of which is of a bitterish taste and which is eaten with pán and areca nut.

Lynniap, *ka*, *n.* a slice.

Lynñiar, *v.* to cry aloud, to weep. [*Imit.* lynñiar-lympat.]

Lynnong, *ka*, *n.* a portion, a chapter,—*a.* isolated.

Lynráw (si-), *u*, *n.* a young bull or ox.

Lynruh-lynram, *ka*, *n.* things lying disorderly.

Lynrum, *ad.* disorderly.

Lynrum-lynrah, *ka*, *n.* rubbish, a débris.

Lynshér, *v*, to plant in, to ram in, to hurl down.

Lynshop, *v.* to dash or plunge down (as a hill stream does to any floating object).

Lynstong, *u*, *n.* sward, sod, turf.

Lyntang, *ka*, *n.* a plank. [*Imit.* ka lyntang-ka thaboh.]

Lyntait, *ka*, *n.* the swallow.

‡Lynten, *ka*, *n.* a lantern.

Lynter, *ka*, *n.* a line, a length.

Lynter-tait, } *ad.* all along, over and over the same state of
Lynter-tuid, } things; [as, "ba'n shu iai leh ia kajuh-pa-kajuh *lynter-tait* ka'm long kaba i-tynnad"], careless.

Lyntháw, *v.* to dash to pieces.

Lyntheng, *ad.* with big calves; [as, "u briew uba heh ka khohwah *lyntheng.*"]

Lynthem, *v.* to throw stones (big); to stone; to pelt.

Lynthér, *v.* to throw stones constantly at any place, to spatter,—*ad.* without due consideration; [as, kren *lynthér*, leh *lynthér.*]

Lynti, *ka*, *n.* path, way. [*Imit.* lynti-syngkieng]; a trip [as, shi*lynti* ar*lynti*, etc.]

Lynti-bah, *ka*, *n.* a main path. [*Imit.* lynti-bah lynti-san.]

Lynti-khasi, *ka*, *n*, a foot-path; a short-cut.

Lynti-khlieh, *ka*, *n.* the parting of the hair.

---

‡ English.

Lyntied, *v.* to strike forcibly, to patter.

Lyóin, *ad.* round (small); [as, "ka lyngknot kaba pyllon *lyoin.*"]

Lyphur, *u*, *n.* a beam or post over which a wall-plate rests (in Khasi houses).

Lwa, *u. n.* a vessel made of plaited canes and daubed over with India-rubber for holding liquor.

Lwái, *ka*, *n.* wild honey,—*u*, a wild bee;—*ad.* like water in a pool.

Lwait, *a.* fainting, weak.

Lwár, *u*, *n.* a small bamboo tie.

Lwar-ding, *ka*, *n*, a furnace.

Lwat-lwat, *ad.* turning round and round; [as, "u khnam uba peh u iaid *lwat-lwat.*"]

Lwet, *a.* broken, powdered, useless.

Lwit, *a.* very finely broken or pounded.

Lwoi, *ad.* like a cesspool, in a small group; [as, "ka um ka lang, *lwoi*;" "ki shipai ki ialang shi kompani *lwoi.*"]

M.

M—The 12th letter of the Khasi Alphabet.

Má, *adj.* dangerous, frightful;—*I ma*, *n.* a maternal uncle (used in the case of address).

Ma—, (a prefix) used with the Personal Pronoun to emphasise it, as, *ma*nga (it is I), *ma*phi (it is you), etc.

'ma, (an *abbrev.* of "thma"), *ka*, *n.* a battle, campaign (as, ka *'ma* haramnimok—a mutiny).

Ma-bah, *i*, *n.* a great or grand maternal uncle;—*ka*, a great battle.

Mak-mak, *ad.* harshly, heedlessly; [as, kren *mak-mak*, leh *mak-mak.*]

Makia, *v.* to beg; to go from door to door.

*Makna, *ad.* gratis, for nothing, used also to emphasize meaning of words, (as, " Lada phi kohnguh *makna* ruh um rat ai eiei.")

Mád, *v.* to taste.

*Madan, *ka*, *n.* a plain, a *maidan.* [*Imit.* madan—madiah.]

Madei-mata, *adv.* roughly, [as " u shu leh *madei-mata* tang ba'n dep."]

Mang, *v.* to give just enough of anything.

---

* Hindi.

Má-nga, (*Pers. Pron.*). It is I ; I, myself.

Mangkara, (lúr), *u, n.* the brightest star.

Mangkariang, (sá), *a.* affected with a parasitic disease (trees); (*fig.*) to be envious of ;—*u, n.* a wasp ; parasitic plant.

Mangkarong, *ka, n.* a show, a display.

Mangkashang (u lúm-), *u, n.* the Himalayas.

Mahadei, *ka, n.* the title of a S'iem's wife ; Queen.

*Mahajon, *n.* a merchant, a trader.

Mahám, *v.* to warn.

†Mahet, *u, n.* one of the demons worshipped by the Syntengs' and also by many of the Khasis.

†Mahu, *ka, n.* an ornament for the arms.

*Mahut, *n.* an elephant-driver.

Mái, *v.* to scold ; to call one by bad names. [*Imit.* mái-nia, mai-tim.]

*Maia, *ka, n.* *maya*, mystery.

Ma-ián, *ka, n.* resemblance, likeness ;—*a.* mysterious [*Imit.* maián-maiot ; maián-saián.]

Máiñ, *ka, n.* features, mien ;—*u,* a kind of fish.

'máiñ, - (*abbrev.*) of tmain), *u. n.* moustache.

Màiñ, *ad.* to the brim.

'máiñker, *u, n.* whiskers.

Máiñmoh, *u, n.* beard.

Máiñksiar-maiñ rupa, *ka, n.* earnings sufficient to buy gold and silver.

Mait, *u, n.* a mosquito ;—*v.* to clear, to cut off.

Maitang, *v.* to declare solemnly ; to abstain from doing the like ;—*ad.* never ; (as, "nadulı ba ki theh um ia u, *maitang* um ju leit thiah shuh"). [*Imit.* maitang-maitait.]

Maiun-maian, *ad.* faintly ; [as, " nga shu kynmáw *maiun-maián* ia la ka jinglong khynnah."]

*Maji, *n.* a sailor.

‡Majistor, *n.* a magistrate.

Mala, *ka, n.* the story (of a house).

*Malai, *ka, n.* cream.

*Mali, *n.* a gardener.

---

* Hindi. | † Bengali. | ‡ English.

Maloi, *ka*, *n*. a cocoa-nut shell; anything that looks like a half sphere.

Maloi-khlieh, *ka*, *n*. a skull.

*Malom, *ka*, *n*. ointment.

Malumala, *ad*. roughly, not properly, [as, " leh *malumala*, kren *malumala*."]

Mama, *i*, *n*. a maternal uncle.

*Mamla, *ka*, *n*. a contending party.

Mân, k*a*, *n*. a cannon. [*Imit*. ka tup-ka-mân.]

Màn, *a*. each, every ;—*v*. to grow, to thrive.

Mán-mán,'*ad*. obstinately, (as, "balei me sngàp *mán-mán* haba khot ?")

*Mana, *v*. to forbid.

Mane, *v*. to worship, to submit,

†Manik (máw-), *u*, *n*. a kind of precious stone. [*Imit*. u moin u-manik.]

Manir, (soh-), *u*, *n*. the *lichi* fruit.

Mano ? *p*. who ?

Mano-mano, *p*. whoever, anyone.

Mano-re-mano, *p*. somebody

Máp, *v*. to forgive.

*Maphot, *ad*. for nothing, [as, " wat ju bám *maphot* ia ka jong ki briew."]

‡Maphusor, *n*. *mafassil*; tour.

*Mapik, *a*. moderate, middling. [*Imit*. mapik—adkar.]

*Már, *n*. articles, goods. [*Imit*. ka már-ka mata.]

Már-már, *ad*. at once; without loss of time, [as, "phah briew *már-már* ba'n leit kumne sha Sohra."]

Màr (a prefix), equally ; just, [as, ia sám ia kine shiphew tyngka *màr* biang hapdeng jong phi.]

Marbúd-marbúd (iaid-), *ad*. closely, apace (follow), [as, " nga ioh-i phi ia iaid *marbúd-marbúd* bad U Saheb bishar."]

Markháit, *a*. ending in a draw (of a match).

Markhap, *a*. alongside of, adjoining to.

Markhmat, *ad*. face to face [as, " phi dei ban da ia ong *mar-khmat*."]

Mar-kti, *ad*. hand to hand, [as, " Ki Jap. bad ki Rus. ki la ialeh *markti* ha Nanshan."]

---

* Hindi. | † Bengali. | ‡ English.

Markylliang, *ad.* in return, tit for tat ; [as, " wat ju ialeh *markylliang* ia u kpa ba sang."]

Mardór, *ad.* with all haste, at once [as, " phi dei ban leh *mardór* ia kane."]

Marjan, *ad.* close, near, [*Imit.* marjan-marpa.]

Mar-mlien, *v.* to continue to do the same thing (bad habit or what offends others), to get into the habit of.

Marshak, *a.* exactly equal or alike, matching.

†Marte-marte, *ad.* there and then, [as, " haba phi la iakut-dor phi dei ban shim noh *marte-marte* ia ka mar."]

Marwei, *a.* alone ;—*ad.* lonely.

Masi, *n.* a cow ; a bull ; an ox.

Masi-bordi, *u, n.* a bullock ; a large cow or bull.

Masi-khar, *n.* a small cow brought from the plains.

Masi-khynna, *n.* a Khasi cow, invariably of a better quality than the Assamese or Sylhet cow.

Masi-kyrtong, *u, n.* a bull.

Masi-dáp, *u, n.* a castrated bull ; a bullock.

Masi-lynrâw, *n.* young bulls (*esp.* for trading purposes).

Masi-prùt, *n.* a mithan (Zool.) *Bos frontalis.*

Masi-pyllait rong, *u, n.* a bull that is dedicated and set at large on certain funeral occasions and given away to any one who can catch or kill him : the horns of such a bull are covered with a thin sheet of gold or silver ; a sacred bull.

Masi-támrong, *u, n.* a term applied to a " masi-pyllait-rong " after having been let loose or caught.

Mastieh, *v.* to dance with the sword ;—*n.* a running dance with the sword. [*Imit.* mastieh-ryngkang.]

†Maswa, *u, n.* a fisherman.

Mat, *ka, n.* a joint, a knob. [*Imit.* ka mat-ka pung.]

'mat (*abbrev.* of khmat), *ka, n.* an eye.

Matang, *ka, n.* a carpenter's square ; a right angle.

'mat-blang, *ka, n.* eyes like that of a goat.

'matkylliang, *ka. n.* a child, a representative.

'mat-dong, *ka, n.* the corner of the eye.

'mat-iar, *kaba, n.* amaurosis, amblyopia ; dimness of sight at night.

---

† Bengali.

'mat-iong, *ka*, *n*. the iris.

Matla, *ka*, *n*, a diseased bamboo joint or knob from which there is no shoot.

'mat-lieh, *ka*, *n*. the white of the eye.

Matsohlah, *ka*, *n*. the ankle.

Matlah, *a*. blind;—*n*. a blind person. [*Imit*. matlah—matpei.]

Mattah, *ka*, *n*. a snail; (*med*.) a corn.

Mat'ti-mat'jat, *ki*, *n*. the joints of the fingers and toes, the hands; marks or traces of work.

Máw, *u*, *n*. a stone. [*Imit*. u máw-u dieng.]

Máwbah, *u*, *n*. a big stone or rock. [*Imit*. máwbah-mawsàn]; a big ancestral bone repository or cairn.

Máwbri, *u*, *n*. a boundary stone.

Máwbynna, *u*, *n*. a memorial stone, a monolith.

Máwbyrsiew, *u*, *n*. one of the three stones set on end in the hearth between which fire is kindled for cooking purposes.

Máwkait, *u*, *n*. one of a set of memorial stones which stands at the extreme left-hand side.

Máwkñie, *u*, *n*. in a set of memorial stones, the tallest one in the middle is so called.

Máwkórdór, *u*, *n*. a precious stone.

Máwksing, *u*, *n*. in a set of memorial stones, the one situated in the extreme right-hand side is called " u mawksing."

Máwkynroh, *u*, *n*. a stone for building purposes.

Máwkynthei, *ka*, *n*. a large flat stone or slab supported by four small stones set on end; a cromlech.

Máw-ïap, *u*, *n*. sand-stone (pronounced *máw-eeáp*).

Máw-jabieng, *u*, *n*. the head or middle stone in an arch; a key-stone.

Máwlaitlyngkot, *u*, *n*. a soft white claystone found near the village of Laitlyngkot.

Máwleiñ, *u*, *n*. quartz.

Máwlong, *u*, *n*. a big stone or rock. [*Imit*. máwlong-máwteh.]

Máwlyngnâi *u*, *n*. a stone set in ornaments.

Máwpún, *u*, *n*. a bridge made by throwing a single stone, also a name given to the stone itself.

Máwpyrsut, *u*, *n*. iron-ore.

Máw-ramsong, *u*, *n*. a limestone rock. [*Imit.* máwramsong-máwramteh.]

Máwria, *u*, *n*. gravel, metal.

Máwshamok, *u*, *n*. a flint-stone.

Máwsh'ing, *u*, *n*. a stone enclosure resembling a box for depositing the bones of the dead; a stone cairn (same as *máwshyieng*).

Máwshun, *u*, *n*. limestone.

Máwshut-wait, *u*, *n*. a whetstone.

Máwsiar, *u*, *n*. a hone, a whetstone.

Máwsohriew, *u*, *n*. granite, from which stones for grinding job's tears are generally made (hence the name).

Máwshynrut, *u*, *n*. a very hard kind of stone used as a whetstone, and found in the Nongstoin State.

Máwthoh, *u*, *n*. a slate-pencil.

Me, *p*. thou (applicable to male only), this word is not used in polite society, but is used in addressing God.

Merg, *a*. proud, insolent.

Meh, *v*. to blaze, to catch fire, to kindle.

Mei, *i*, *n*. mother.

Meikha, *i*, *n*. a paternal grandmother.

Mei-hep, *i*, *n*. a maternal grandmother; also a respectful appellation of an old woman.

Mei-húm-ia ka mei! *inter*. gracious me! by jingo!

Meirád, *i*, *n*. a maternal grandmother.

*Mem, *ka*, *n*. a European lady.

Mem-mem (s'áid-), *ad*. lukewarm (water).

'men (*abbrev*. of "tymmen"), *n*. an old man or woman.

Me'n, *phr*. thou wilt; abbreviation of *me yn*.

Men-kjat, *ka*, *n*. the front part of the sole.

Men-kti, *ka*, *n*. the upper portion of the palm.

'men-suh-syntiew, *ka*, *n*. an old woman given to matchmaking, a pimp.

Mér, *v*. to grow well; to sprout.

Mèr-mèr, *ad*. very (yellow); [as, "ka 'tiew lasubon ka stem *mèr-mèr*."]

---

* Hindi.

Met, *ka, n.* a body, person; [*Imit.* ka met-ka-phát.]—*a.* full, good.

Met-iáw, *a.* of mature age (from 40 to 50 years of age).

Met-sáwdoh, *a.* of a brown complexion (applicable to persons only).

*Mi (*abbrev.* of "jyrmi"), *u, n.* a creeper.

Miang, *ka, n.* the angle of the lower jawbone; also the swelling of the jaw gland; mumps.

***Miaj,** *ka, n.* a stipulated period.

Mian, *ad.* slowly.

Miar, *ad.* to the brim, [as, "wat theh um ha ba'n da dap eh *miar.*"]

Miaw, *n.* a cat.

Miaw-wa, *u, n.* a tom-cat which roams about.

Mikhli, *v.* to jumble, to mix up.

'mied, *v.* to raise up one's head.

Mieng, *ka, n.* a piece of bamboo or iron musical instrument, which is made to vibrate close to the mouth, producing high or low tones according to the way the mouth is more or less opened.

***Miej,** *ka, n.* a table.

Miet, *ka, n.* night.

Mih, *v.* to rise, to issue.

Mih'ngi, *ka, n.* the east. [*Imit.* ka mihngi—ka sepngi.]

Mihpli, *v.* to stand as a substitute for, to succeed.

Minot, *v.* to persevere, to devote, to take pains. [*Imit.* minot-ador.]

Mir, *v.* to throw a thing gently into a hole or throw it up to another to catch,—*a.* sallow,—*n.* myrrh.

Mlàn, Mlèn, } *ad.* robust, well-built; [as, "u briew uba khlaiñ *mlen.*"]

Mlein, *a.* shameless; impudent.

Mler, *a.* over-forward, careless in demeanour.

Mlien, *v.* to form a habit; to be accustomed to.

Mo ?=Is it not ?

Mo, Mu,=Synteng prefix for *máw* (stone), [as mulang for maw-lang].

†**Mokodduma,** *ka, n.* a law suit; a case.

---

* Hindi. † Bengali.

Mong, *v.* to be wounded, to be hurt.

Mohkhiew, *u, n.* hoe, a mattock.

†**Mohonmala**, *u, n.* a string of coral beads intermixed with round smooth lac-balls covered with gold.

†**Mohór**, *ka. n.* a mohur; a seal; a stamp.

Moi, *ka, n.* an instrument consisting of two pieces of split bamboo joined together for levelling a rice field which has been furrowed by the plough,—*v.* to level a ploughed field for the reception of seed.

Moi-moi, *ka, n.* the temples.

Moiñ, *ad.* to the brim [as, "thew ha ba'n da dap *moiñ* u shang"]; slightly (to smile).

Moina, *n.* a black bird belonging to the starling family.

Mom, *ka, n.* a mixture of fat, etc., for rubbing leather with; (*Hind.*=momragon).

***Momjama**, *ka, n.* a wax-cloth.

Mom-mom (jem-), *ad.* very (soft like cotton).

Mon, *ka, n.* a will; a maund.

Mopmop, *ad.* quiveringly; a drizzling.

***Moramot**, *v.* to repair.

†**Mormor**, *ka, n.* a thin cotton cloth of fine texture.

Morsha, *ka, n.* a ditch; an intrenchment.

Mot, *u, n.* monument; a tower; a pillar.

Mot-mot, *a.* easily broken; tender.

Mrád, *n.* a beast; an animal;—*a.* cruel, inhuman.

Mrán, *ad.* quite (healthy); [as, "I shait *mràn* mynta ba'n ia mynno mynno."]

Mráw, *n.* a slave. [*Imit.* u mráw—u dkhar.]

Mriang, *ad.* in readiness; [as, "u ap *mriang* ha lynti ba'n pom ia u."]

Mrit, *ka, n.* a migratory bird of a buff colour that comes in the winter.

Mrong, *ad.* watchfully, expectantly; (as a dog when sitting) [as, "balei phi ap *mrong* kumne ia u kumba u pang-eh?"]

Mtai, *ad.* in a large heap, (as, "ki la lah tih u 'dewiong *mtai*").

---

* Hindi. † Bengali.

mtong, *ad.* like a hillock; [as, "ei ba lùm ia une u khyndew *mtong* hangne?"]

Mu seh? *phr.* same as, mo seh?=Is'nt it?

§Muka, *ka*, *n.* a *muga* or Assam silk.

‡Mukjin, *ka*. *n.* a magazine.

Muk-mak, *ad.* quickly and roughly, (as, wat shu leh *muk mak* ia u khynnah).

†Mukor-kyndor, *ka*, *n.* a kind of ear-pendant.

*Muktiar, *u*, *n.* a muktar.

*Mukup, *v.* to abandon or leave off.

Mudki, *u*, *n.* a big earthen jar.

†Mudi, *n.* a retail shopkeeper.

Mudui, *v.* to lodge a complaint against. [*Imit.* mudui-phi-rat.]

*Múid, *n.* a buffalo.

*Muja, *ka*, *n.* stockings, socks.

†Mula, *ka*, *n.* a low stool made of plaited canes; a cane chair; a vegetable.

Mulla, *u*, *n.* an executioner (in folk-lore).

Mulot, *ka*, *n.* a worn-out and useless coin; a thing which has no sale value.

*Muluk, *ka*, *n.* a country; a kingdom.

Muri, *ka*, *n.* a drain, a culvert.

Mur-mur, (stem-), *ad.* very (yellow, like a well-ripened fruit).

*Musári, *ka*, *n.* a mosquito curtain.

Mushlia, *v.* to meddle with,—*a.* meddlesome.

*Musla, *u*, *n.* spices; (*Hindi*) mosáli. [*Imit.* musla—musli.]

Mustul, *u*, *n.* a chimney.

*Musúr, *ka*, *n.* an export duty; royalty. [*Imit.* ka dàn-ka musur.]

Mut, *v.* to think, to design;—*ka*, *n.* an ornamental carving.

Muta, *a.* rough, coarse.

*Mutia, *n.* a porter, a carrier.

Mut-ngiew, *v.* to hallucinate, to have a presentiment.

Mutlop, *a.* stubborn; stupid; obstinate; stiff-necked.

Myngkew, *ka*, *n.* husband's sister.

---

* Hindi. | † Bengali. | ‡ English. | § Assamese.

Myńgkoi u Jom, *ka*, *n.* hell; *lit.* the tank of Jom or king of death.

Myllái (used negatively with *ym*), *v.* not to be satisfied to any appreciable degree.

Myllen, *ad.* by way of diverting one's attention,—*v.* to while away time, [as, "ngi ia shongkái *myllen*, hangne; ngi ia sip soh ot tang ban *myllen*."]

Myllung, *a.* pathetic.

Myn=(1) Prefix in adverbs of Present and Past times; (as, *myn*-hynnin, *myn*-ta, *myn*-tan, etc.).
(2) it also sometimes denotes a doer, as, u *myn*-tuh=a thief.
(3) *Synteng*, an abbreviation of *um* (river), as *myn*-khen for um-khen, it is generally pronounced as *myng*.

Myn-aria, *ad.* some time ago.

Mynba, *conj.* when (referring to past time).

Mynbarim, *ad.* in olden times. [*Imit.* mynbarim-mynbajah.]

Myndér, *n.* an outsider, a stranger.

Myndong, Myndung, } (song-), *ad.* well (rolled up); well-packed; [as, "a-iu phi song *myndong* kumne?"]

Mynhakato, *ad.* on that (particular) occasion.

Mynhyndâi, *ad.* in ancient times. [*Imit.* mynhyndâi-mynhynthâi.]

Mynhynnê, *ad.* a short time ago (but on the same day).

Mynhynnin, *ad.* yesterday.

Mynja, *u*, *n.* a thread smeared over with a mixture of powdered glass and paste used in flying paper-kites.

Mynjli, *u*, *n.* a kind of necklace composed of coral beads and crescent-like gold cases.

*Mynjur, *v.* to agree; to consent.

Mynli-iur, *ad.* in summer, in the rainy season.

Mynmiet, *ad.* in the night time. [*Imit.* mynmiet-myniong.]

Mynno? *ad.* when?

Mynno-mynno, *ad.* formerly; usually.

Mynnor, *ad.* some time ago.

Mynnymwei, *ad.* last year. [*Imit.* myn-nymwei-myn-nym-ar.]

Mynráin khymat, *ka*, *n.* compensation for breach of an agreement (*esp.* a marriage-contract).

---

* Hindi.

Mynri, *n.* a tribe of the Mikirs whose habits are migratory and which lives by *jhum* cultivation.

Mynsáin, *ka, n.* a place cleared all round like a fire-line, and reserved for the growth of trees; a reserved forest.

Mynsâw, *v.* to be wounded, to have an accident. [*Imit.* mynsáw—mynsnám.]

Mynsaw-ia, *ad.* since four days.

Mynshem-taiew, *ad.* last week.

Mynsngi, *ad.* in the day time. [*Imit.* mynsngi-mynshái.]

Mynshisngi, *ad.* the day before yesterday.

Mynshuwa, *ad.* before; previously; formerly.

Mynsiem, *ka, n.* a spirit; the soul. [*Imit.* ka mynsiem—ka sngár.]

Mynsiem-Bakhúid, *u, n.* the Holy Ghost.

Mynstep, *ad.* in the morning.

Mynta, *ad.* at present; now. [*Imit.* mynta-mynnê.]

Mynta-mynnê, *ad.* up to the present day; still.

Myntait, *ka, n.* the bark of a certain tree which is chewed with *pan* or betel.

Myntan, *ad.* a little while ago (an hour or so); just now.

Mynthi, *ad.* ironically; sarcastically,—*a.* silent; sullen.

Mynthna, *n.* a mithan (*Bos frontalis*).

Myntlang, *ad.* in the winter.

Myntói, *a.* profitable,—*n*, gain; profit.

Myntór, *ka, n.* a *mantra* or magic.

†**Myntri**, *n.* a minister. [*Imit.* u myntri-u-korbari.]

Myntúh, same as *nongtuh.* [*Imit.* myntuh-mynthiem.]

Mynwei, *ad.* years ago. [*Imit.* mynwei-myn-ar.]

Myrsiang, *n.* a jackal; a fox.

Mythen, } **Mythùn**, } *a.* big and muscular (calf).

Mythian (shong-dem-), *ad.* quite (full or coiled up), [as, "u shong *mythian*; u dem u ksew ha ka shang *mythian.*"]

---

†.Bengali.

N.

N—The thirteenth letter in the Khasi Alphabet.

Na, *prep.* from, of.

Naba, *conj.* for, because.

Nabár, *ad.* from outside, externally, [as, "ka iing ka itynnad *nabár* hynrei ka jakhlia hapoh."]—*a.* outside.

Na-kêd, *a.* ragged, torn.

Nakra, *ka*, *n.* a big drum.

Nadang, } *prep.* since, from.
Nadúh, }

Nadien, *ad.* from behind.

Nadong-shadong, *ad.* altogether; from beginning to end, [as "dap da ka jingbakla suda *nadong-shadong.*"]

Nadúh-hadúh, *ad.* from beginning to end, [as, dei ma u uba lah ia nga *nadúh-hadúh.*"]

Naei? *ad.* whence? from what place?

Nang=a prefix denoting progression (as, *nang*roi=go on progressing).

Nang, *v.* to know, to be able.

Nang-ang, *a.* using low scurrilous language; having a bad tongue. [*Imit.* nang-ang-nangháp.]

Nangne, *ad.* hence, from this place.

Nangno? *ad.* from what place?

Nangno-nangno, *ad.* from any place, whatsoever.

Nangno-re-nangno, *ad.* from some place or other.

Nah, *n.* (voc.) a stepfather or stepmother; an aunt (mother's younger sister).

'nái, (*abbrev.* of *bnai*), *u*, *n.* a month; moon; (*abbrev.* of khnái); a mouse, a rat.

'nái-khadsáwsynñia; *u*, *n.* a full moon.

'nái-kyllalyngkot, *u*, *n.* January.

'nái-iaiong, *u*, *n.* April.

'nái-iing, *ka*, *n.* a house-rat.

'nái-jylliew, *u*, *n.* June.

'nái-jymmang, *u*, *n.* May.

'nái-lár, *u*, *n.* August.

'nái-lber, *u*, *n.* March.

'nai-lúr, *u*, *n*. September.

Nái-nái, *ad*. very (sickly or weak—used with *pang*).

'nái-nohprah, *u*, *n*. December.

'nái-pilang, *u*, *n*. a large hill rat which is eaten by some of the people of the Khasi Hills.

'nái-risáw, *u*, *n*. October.

'nái-rymphang, *u*, *n*. February.

'nái-sáw, *n*. a small hill mouse.

'nái-tung, *u*, *n*. July.

'nái-wieng, *u*, *n*. November.

Najan, *prep*. near, from or by the side of. [*Imit*. najan-napa.]

*Najir, *u*, *n*. a nazir.

Nalór, *adv*. from above, externally; besides.

Nám, *ka*, *n*. fame, reputation;—*v*. to portend (used with "ka tyngab"=a crow); to be spoken well of by the people (as, ki la *nám* baroh ia ka jingbha jong u); to request earnestly, to supplicate (as, u la *nám* u la ud ka bym lah ba'n ong ha nga haduh ba nga la sngewsynei ia u); *tangnám*, *phr*. nominally, [as, "ynda nga la kyrpad jindei, u ia ai, *tang ban nám*, shi suka."]

'nám (*abbrev*. of *snám*), *ka*, *n*. blood.

'nàm (*abbrev*. of *khnam*), *u*, *n*. an arrow.

Namar, *conj*. because, for.

Namarkata, *ad*. therefore, for that reason.

*Nám-katai, *v*. to be dismissed: to resign.

'nám-iong, *ka*, *n*. dark blood; an arrow with a distinguishing black mark on it.

'nàmlang, *u*, *n*. a kind of reed or *ekra*.

'námlymbong, *ka*, *n*. a large clot of blood.

'nàmphiah, *u*, *n*. a single feathered arrow, generally used by boys.

'nàmpliang, *u*, *n*. an arrow with a spear head, generally used in warfare and in hunting.

'nàmpúr, *u*, *n*. a feathered arrow.

'nàm-sop, *u*, *n*. an arrow having a tapering iron-head like a cone, generally used in archery contests.

'nàmtohrih, *u*, *n*. a kind of grass.

---

* Hindi.

'nám-tylli, *ka*, *n*. congealed blood, a clot of blood.

'nàm-tympem, *u*, *n*. one of the three arrows shot from the funeral pyre.

Nan, *ka*, *n*. a tank.

Naneng, *ad*. from above.

Nano-nano, *ad*. from anyone.

Na-no re-na-no, *phr*. from someone.

||Nanti, *ka*, *n*. an ear pendant.

Nap, *v*. to devote oneself entirely to doing a thing;—*ka*, *n*. tongs or pincers.

Nap-bania, *ka*, *n*. tongs used by a goldsmith; a niggard, a miser.

Naphang, *ad*. wholly, entirely; from one side, (as, puh ia ka kper *naphang*); without exception (as, u bám *naphang* kat kaba ai).

Naphrang, *ad*. from the beginning, in the front.

*Napit, *n*. a barber.

Napoh, *ad*. from beneath.

Nar, *u*, *n*. iron.

Nar (eit-), *ka*, *n*. slag.

Nara, *ka*, *n*. a kind of Assam silk generally worn by women.

||Narad, *v*. to object.

Nar-ka-bili, *ka*, *n*. fetters.

Nar-liang, *u*, *n*. a solid raw iron which has been cleft into two halves and sold in the market.

Nar-púh, *u*, *n*. a pickaxe.

Narsam-im, *u*, *n*. a sharp piece of iron for boring wood.

Narsáw, *u*, *n*. a red hot iron.

Narsúh, *u*, *n*. a piece of wire used for roasting flesh, fish, etc.

Narum, *ad*. from below.

Narwah, *u*, *n*, a lump of melted iron, one split in the middle which can be hung up. See *Narliang*.

Nat, *ka*, *n*. a bunch of plantains;—*u*, *n*. (an abbrev. of *pnat*) a branch of a tree (cut so as to resemble a prong).

Náw-náw, *ad*. hard and dry; (as, kane ka doh ka la eh *naw-naw*).

Nawei, *ad*. from another.

Náwei-na-ár, *ad*. from some other person or quarter.

Naw-rang, *ad*. harshly (speak); [as, u kren *naw-rang* ia kiba ha iing ha sem.]

---

* Hindi. | || Arabic.

Ne *conj.* or.

Nê (*an enclitic word*) = or thereabouts; (as, wallam kumba 20 sér *nê* u riwhadem)—*ka, n.* Something or some article understood between the speakers.

Neng, *ka, n.* elevation, north.

Neh, *v.* to remain, to stick to.

Nei, *u, n.* til. (*Bot. Perilla ocimoides*).

Nei-iong, *u, n.* sesame, gingelly or *til*-seed.

'nem, (*abbrev.* of snem); *ka, n.* a year; 2. (*abbrev.* of "tyrnem" a hammer) [as, '*nem*-bah, '*nem*-rit, etc.]

'nemsniew, *ka, n.* a famine.

Nep, *ka, n.* a bed covering, a razai. [*Imit.* ka nep ka tun g];—(*abbrev.* of "snep") a covering, skin, rind, bark; —*a.* sharp, pointed, intelligent.

'nepboh, *u, n.* the white outer covering of a lemon that remains after the pungent part has been pared off.

'nep-iang, *u, n.* the outermost part of the skin or rind, etc.

'nér (*abbrev.* of snér), *ka, n.* a feather.

'nér-liang, *ka, n.* the feather at the extreme end of the wings.

'nér-lung, *ka, n.* the down of a bird.

Net-net, *ad.* carelessly (as, kane ka khynnah ka trei *net-net* ia kaei kaei baroh), roughly.

Ni, *a.* smooth, fine.

Nia, *ka, n.* reason, argument. [*Imit.* ka nia-ka jutang.]

Ñia, *n.* wife of an uncle on the mother's side.

Ñiak, *ad.* much, greatly; (as, ki briew ki la ia khynwin *ñiak*= they are making a great commotion).

'ñiakha, *ka, n.* aunt (father's sister).

Ñiad, *v.* to wipe, paint.

Ñiadkalai, *v.* to tin, to enamel.

Ñiad-rong, *v.* to paint.

'niang, *n.* (*abbrev.* of "sniang)" a pig; 2. (*abbrev.* of "khñiang") an insect, a worm.

'ñiangbabung, *u, n.* a very large kind of fly.

'ñiangbading, *ka, n.* a glowworm.

'ñiangblen, *ka, n.* a blindworm.

'ñiangbliar, *ka, n.* a kind of small lizard.

'ñiangboit, *u*, *n*. a wood-worm.

'niangbri, *u*, *n*. a wild pig, a boar.

'ñiangbshiah, *ka*, *n*. a chamelion.

'ñiangbulot, *u*, *n*. a kind of fly.

'ñiangkalaw, *ka*, *n*. a cockroach.

'ñiangkhap-kór, *u*, *n*. an earwig.

'ñiangkhar, *u*, *n*. chicken-pox.

'ñiangkhnap, *ka*, *n*. a disease which attacks the hoofs of cattle; a foot-and-mouth disease.

'ñiang khriat, *u*. *n*. a small eruption on the body produced by cold.

'ñiang kongwieng, *ka*, *n*. a species of beetle which is very common in the lowlands, so called from its cry.

'ñiangkseh, *u*, *n*. a long insect covered with thick fur generally found in pine trees.

'ñiangksem, *ka*, *n*. an insect which emits a fluid very injurious to human eyes, and having a very bad smell.

'ñiangkulia, *u*, *n*. syphilis, gonorrhœa.

'niangkwang, *u*, *n*. a wild boar that has separated himself from a herd.

'ñiangkynjah, *ka*, *n*. any insect which chirps at dead of night.

'ñiangkynthah-um, *u*, *n*. a May-fly.

'ñiangkyntur-eit. *ka*, *n*. a lamelicorn beetle.

'ñiangdkhiat, *u*, *n*. the parasite causing itch, scabies.

'ñianglarthám, *ka*, *n*. a scorpion.

'ñianglong, *u*, *n*. chrysalis.

'ñianglyngkut, *u*, *n*. red leprosy.

'ñiangmat, *ka*, *n*. opthalmia.

'ñiang-miaw, *ka*, *n*. a tiger-beetle.

'ñiangmong, *u*, *n*. a discolouring of the face.

'ñiangphlang, *u*, *n*. an insect found everywhere among grass on the higher plateau of the Khasi Hills, and which is eaten by some of the people.

'ñiangpyrsit, *u*, *n*. measles.

'ñiangrah, *u*, *n*. a white-ant. *See 'Kruin'*.

'ñiangrait-hoh (shong), *a*. having a bad temper and envious spirit.

'ñiangraitliang, *u*, *n*. a tape-worm.

'ñiangraitwáit, *u*, *n*. worm generally found in stagnant water.

'ñiangrait-wei, *u*, *n*. a barren boar.

'ñiangriang, *ka*, *n*. a water beetle.

'ñiangricj, *u*, *n*. a wood-worm.

'ñiangsér, *u*, *n*. a very bad kind of sore caused by parasites.

'ñiangshit, *u*, *n*. prickly-heat.

'ñiangsohpet, *u*, *n*. an infantile disease which affects the navel.

'ñiangsynrang, *u*, *n*. leprosy (black).

'ñiangtari, *u*, *n*. a small kind of millepede.

'ñiangteng, *adj*. indolent, lazy.

'ñiangthangdoh, *ka*, *n*. a firefly, a moth.

'ñiangthylliej, *u*, *n*. thrush.

'ñiangthylliew, *u*, *n*. small-pox.

'ñiangting, *ad*. long and thin, slim; (as, u "briew uba raikhoh *ñiangting*").

'ñiangtrew, *ka*, *n*, a very bad sore caused by itch.

'ñiangtyngkhap, *ka*, *n*. a tick.

'ñiangtyrkhang, *u*, *n*. a millepede.

'ñiangtyrsim, (sa-), *kaba*, *n*. whitlow.

Ñiangwap, *ad*. very (weak); [as, "u briew uba tlot *ñiangwap* u ia pyn-eh."]

Ñiah, *v*. to drive (cattle), to herd.

Ñiai, *ka*, *n*. solder for tin utensils; lead.

†Niam, *ka*, *n*. religion, religious usages, customs.

Niam-ka-rukom, *ka*. *n*. religious customs and ceremonies.

Ñiamra, *ka*, *n*. an abyss, a hole; *khyndai pateng ñiamra*—hell.

Ñian, *v*. to stow, to dress in, to stuff, to cram.

Ñiar, *adj*. thin, having large interstices;—*ad*. scarcely, seldom.

Ñiat, *v*. to push forward;—*ad*. suddenly, [as, "tang shu ioh-i ia ka ïaje u khyunah u shu shim *ñiat*."]

'niat, *ka*, *n*. (*abbrev*. of bniat), a tooth.

'niat-ksew, *ka*, *n*. the canine tooth.

'niat-duh, *ka*, *n*. the wisdom tooth.

'niat-iawbei, *ka*, *n*. a milk tooth.

'niat-pyrshah, *ka*, *n*. a front tooth.

'niat-tyng-am, *ka*, *n*. a grinder, a molar.

---

† Bengali.

'nieh (*abbrev.* of snieh), *ka*, *n*. a skin, a hide.

'niehkdop, *ka*, *n*. a skin bag used by carpenters for carrying tools.

Ñiep-ñiep, (khih-), *ad*. like many insects which are moving or creeping away in different directions, [as, " nga ioh-i ba ia ka masi la bám da u ksain uba khih *ñiep-shi-ñiep*."]

'nier (*abbrev*. of snier), *ka*, *n*. entrails.

'nierbah, *ka*, *n*. the stomach.

'nierkhad-ár-syrtap, *ka*, *n*. a part of the intestines which has many folds.

'nier-lang, *ki*, *n*. the part of the intestines which twist together.

'nier-wait, *ka*, *n*. the small intestines.

Ñiew, *v*. to count, to reckon; to consider.

Ñiew-bciñ, *v*. to treat with contempt; to lower in estimation.

Ñiew-kór, *v*. to value highly; to prize; to appreciate.

Ñiewsting, *v*. to make light of.

Ñiewtang, *v*. to recount in detail, to relate.

Nir-nir, (stang-), *ad*. very (thin), [as, " kane ka kotsada kaba stang eh *nir-nir*".]

'ñiuh (*abbrev*. of shñiuh), *u*, *n*. hair.

'ñiuhkhlieh, *u*, *n*. the hair of the head. [*Imit*. ñiuhkhlieh-ñiuh-reng.]

'ñiuhkyndeh, *u*, *n*. fine hair.

'ñiuhliar, *u*, *n*. the end of the tuft of hair.

'ñiuhlieh, *u*, *n*. grey hair.

'ñiuhmat, *u*, *n*. the eyelashes or hair growing on the eyebrows.

'ñiuh-moh, *u*, *n*. a beard.

'ñiuh-tmáin, *u*, *n*. moustache.

ñiuh-trong, *u*, *n*. a tuft of hair on the top of the head, a pig-tail.

Ñiuma, *ad*. very well, alright.

Ñiún, *a*. to be out of sorts; to be indisposed. [*Imit*. ba ñiun-ba-ñiep.]

Ñiun-ñiun, *ad*. shakily, [as, une u maw jingkieng uba khieh *ñiun-ñiun* du.]

Ñiup-ñiup, (jem-), *ad*. hairy and soft, [as, "u shñiuh dngiem u long uba jem *ñiup-ñiup*."]

Ñiur-ñiur, *ka*, *n*. a bog, a quagmire;—*ad*. tremulously, [as, "une u lyngstong uba khih *ñiur-ñiur*"].

Ñiurei, *n.* a pheasant.

Ñiut, *u*, *n.* weeds. [*Imit.* u ñiut-u ñier.]

Ñiutmáw, *u*, *n.* moss.

—no = a suffix in Interrogative Pronouns and in Adverbs of time, place, condition, etc., as *uno*? who? *hangno*? where? *mynno*? when?

Nok (ia-), *n.* a game of cards.

†Nokod, *ad.* ready-money, in cash.

†Nokol, *ka*, *n.* a copy.

‡Nod, *u*, *n.* zero or nought;—*ka*, a nose-ring.

Nong, *ka*, *n.* wages, gain, profit: a hired man or woman; anything given out for hire. [*Imit.* ka nong-ka ni.]

Nong=a square measure=6 dieng×2 dieng (a dieng or pole =9½ feet.)

'nong (*abbrev.* of shnong), *ka*, *n.* a village, a town, a city; 2. (*abbrev.* of rnong), *ka*, *n.* brass or bronze.

Nong= a prefix denoting a doer or agent; (as, u *nong*tuh); a resident of a village (as, u *nong*-Mawkhar, u *nong*-Sohra, etc.)

Nongkhaii, *u* or *ka*, *n.* a merchant, a trader. [*Imit.* nongkhaii-nongpateng.]

Nongkhát, *ka*, *n.* rent (of land). See *Báiwái*.

Nongkheiñksúid, *u*, *n.* a man who cures diseases or propitiates evil spirits by means of sacrifices, a diviner. [*Imit.* nongkheiñksúid-nongkheiñkhrei.]

'nongkhynráw, *ka*, *n.* what one earns while unmarried. [*Imit.* 'nongkhynráw-'nongkhyndeiñ.]

Nongkitnong, *u* or *ka*, *n.* a coolie, a porter. [*Imit.* nongkitnong-nongkitni.]

Nongkylliang, *ka*, *n.* a compensation, retribution.

Nongkyndong, *n.* a person who lives in an out-of-the-way village, a villager. [*Imit.* nongkyndong-nongkynshrot.]

'nongkynti, *ka*, *n.* personal property.

Nongiapam, *n.* a fighting man; a soldier.

Nonglehpalat, *n.* a transgressor, an offender. [*Imit.* nonglehpalat-nonglehpaliang.]

'nonglieh, *ka*, *n.* a platinum-like metal. [*Imit.* 'nonglieh-'nong-'tem.]

Nongphira, *u*, *n.* a watchman.

---

† Bengali. | ‡ English.

Nongmuna, *ka, n.* a specimen, a pattern.

Nongphlang, *ki, n.* the Khasis living on the higher plateau of the Hills (as the Shella people call them).

Nongra, *ka, n.* any worn-out old brass vessel.

Nongrim, *ka, n.* foundation; site of an abandoned village.

Nongsám, *ka, n.* silver, gold or whatever is burnt in the funeral pyre with the dead body, and which those who look after the burning of the dead body divide among themselves. [*Imit.* nongsám-nongpiet.]

Nongsáid-thma, *u, n.* a politician; a babbler. [*Imit.* nongsáidthma-nongsáidktien.]

Nongsharái, *n.* a cowherd, a pastor.

'nong-tem, *ka, n.* a yellowish brass. [*Imit.* ka nonglieh-ka nongtem.]

Nongtymmen, *ka, n.* ancestral property; an heirloom. [*Imit.* nongtymmen-nongsan.]

Nongwei, *u, n.* a stranger. [*Imit.* nongwei-nong-ár.]

Noh, *v.* to throw into;—*ad.* away; (ia-) to add a little quantity or number in excess of that sold or bought.

Nohblei, *v.* to throw away the idols after the ceremonies of worship are over. [*Imit.* nohblei—noh-dken.]

Nohmynsiem, *v.* to be low-spirited; to sigh.

Noh-práh ('nái-), *u, n.* December.

Nohrem, *v.* to be a cause of offence to the gods or spirits.

Nohtasor, *ka, n.* a silk *dhoti*, a piece of cloth worn by males round the loins.

Nohtah, *ka, n.* a ladder made of a single piece of wood with steps cut into it, a temporary bridge.

Nohteh (*colloquial enclitic word*), *ad.* very much, [as, " ka krem kaba jylliew *nohteh.*"]

Noi, *u, n.* a small bamboo pipe, especially one for applying to the hole of a *hookah* when smoking.

Noi-sha, *u, n.* a pipe fixed to the cocoa-nut shell of a *hookah.*

*Nuksa, *ka, n.* a figure, a pattern, a picture, a plan.

Núd, *v.* to dare.

'núd (*abbrev.* of dohnúd), *u, n,* the liver; the heart.

'núid, *ka, n.* a piece of fruit cut in the shape of a prism.

*Nújor, *v.* to scrutinise, examine, compare.

---

* Hindi.

'nup (*abbrev.* of knup), *ka*, *n.* a Khasi leaf-umbrella, somewhat like a shell, (as, ka '*nup*-Mawiang=a *knup* made and brought from Mawiang).

Núp, *ka*, *n.* the seed of a certain creeper growing in a pod used by the Khasis in washing their heads.

Núp-khohsiew, *ka*, *n.* the knee-cap.

Núr, *ka*, *n.* a channel, a ditch, a drain.

†Nurok, *ka*, *n.* hell.

*Nusip, *ka*, *n.* luck.

*Nuti, *ka*, *n.* a prostitute.

Nyngkong, *a.* first, beginning. [*Imit.* nyngkong-nyngsháp.]

Nylla, *a.* pure, unalloyed.

Nyllong, *ka*, *n.* the rectum.

O.

O—The fourteenth letter in the Khasi Alphabet.

O! *Interj.* oh! ah!

Ong, *v.* to say, to tell;—*ong la*, *conj.* if in case, (as, "*ong la* dei ia nga, nga la shoh ia phi").

Oh, *v.* to cut, to notch.

Oh-kuna, *v.* to impose a fine. [*Imit.* oh-kuna-oh-káid.]

Oh-jri, *v.* to tap an Indian rubber-tree.

Oh-shrong, *v.* to cut or notch ornamentally; to carve. [*Imit.* oh-shrong-oh-shrub.]

Oh-tah, *v.* to cut slightly at short intervals, to tap.

Oi, (a verbal answer),—yes, here I am.

On, (leit-), *v.* to go along with, to reach at.

Onksúid, *v.* to throw away things for propitiating a devil.

On-kurim (leit-), *v.* to accompany a bridegroom to the house of a bride.

On-nong (leit-), *v.* to go and carry a load on hire to its destination. [*Imit.* on-nong-on-ni.]

On-rong, *v.* to present anything, especially liquor, to the spirit of the dead person at the time when sacrifices are made on his behalf. [*Imit.* on rong-on rup.]

-Op (a suffix)=by suffocation, (as in the words, iap-*op*, set-*op*, etc).

---

* Hindi. † Bengali.

Ór, Órpait, } *v.* to crack, to break into chinks.

Or-or (s'aid), *ad.* very (warm), [as, "nga sngew s'aid *or-or* hapoh ka nep."]

Ot, *v.* to cut, to mow, to reap.

Ot-balang, *v.* to excommunicate from church membership.

Ot-doh, *v.* (*lit.* to cut flesh—hence, to kill an animal for eating purposes.) [*Imit.* ot-doh ot-kah.]

Ot-sher, *v.* to circumcise.

P.

P—The fifteenth letter in the Khasi Alphabet.

Pa, *i, n.* father.

-Pa, — a repeating particle, as in the word leh *pa*-leh=to continue to do.

Paka, *ad.* complete, satisfactory, *pucca* ; —*iing-paka, n.* a stone-walled house.

Pakang, *v.* to flow in a jet ; to shoot forth.

Pakái, *ka, n.* a share, a part allotted, a turn ; — *ad.* as a reflective act, [as "nga kren ia kiwei, nang sngewrem *pakái* ma phi ?"]

'pakha, *u, n.* a male-relative (father's side).

Pakha, *ka, n.* a fan, a *punkah* ; a species of palm.

Pakhang, *v.* to hinder, to obstruct, to block.

Pakhár, *v.* to throw away to a distance.

Pakhing, *v.* to resist. Same as *iakhing.*

Pakhop, *v.* to strive against or resist when dragged.

Pakhúd, *v.* to pull or drag along the ground.

Pakhynnah, *i, n.* a paternal uncle (father's younger brother).

*Paki (iing-), *ka, n.* a house roofed and walled with bricks.

Pakór, *v.* to unite in sexual intercourse (applicable to beasts only), to cover.

Pád, *n.* a measurement from the tip of the middle right-hand finger right across the chest to the tip of the middle left-hand finger, both hands being extended horizontally.

Padai, *v.* to swing.

Padàn, *v.* to obstruct, to hinder, to interfere.

Padat, *v.* to throw to a distance (said of a heavy object).

---

* Hindi.

Padiah, *v.* to play on a small drum; to multiply words unnecessarily; to meddle.

Padok, Pdok, } *ka, n.* the bladder of a fish.

Padoi, *v.* to swing.

Padóm, *v.* to drag roughly.

*Padri, *n.* a clergyman, a missionary. Same as *Phajri.*

Padún, *a.* slightly curved or sloping.

Pang, *v.* to become ill.

P'ang, *v.* to straddle. Same as *Pyang.*

Pangah, *v.* to move the head from side to side; to jolt, to express dissent, to dissent. [*Imit.* pangah-pangaiñ.]

Pang-at-top, *v.* to have dropsy.

Pang-bhur, *v.* to have epilepsy.

Pang-khlieh, *v.* to have a cold. [*Imit.* pangkhlich-pangreng.]

Pangkhmat, *v.* to have pain in the eyes, to be opthalmic.

Pangkhrew, *ka, n.* a wasting or chronic disease. [*Imit.* pangkhrew-pangkhriap.]

Pangkuhek, *ka, n.* hysteria.

Pangdohnúd, *v.* to be heart-rending, to be painful at heart. [*Imit.* pangdohnúd-dohnám.]

Pang-iap-iong, *ka, n.* a mildew, blight.

Pang-iapshiliang, *v.* to have palsy, to be paralytic.

Pang-mat, Pang-sh'ing, } *v.* to have rheumatism. [*Imit.* pangmat-pangpung.]

Pangmet, *v.* to suffer from fatigue or pain all over the body as from over-exertion or beating; wounded in feelings; pain. [*Imit.* pangmet-pangphát.]

Pangiong, *ka, n.* *kalá-ázár.*

Pangshipai, *ka, n.* influenza.

Pah, *v.* to cry (as an animal or a bird); to allure; to bait; to feed.

Pah-ding, *v.* to set fire to.

Pah-shalyngngiang, *kaba, n.* the whistle-like sound often heard within the ear.

Pahám, *ka, n.* a valley.

*Pahara (ap), *v.* to guard as a sentinel.

---

* Hindi.

Paheb, *i*, *n*. a grandfather (*i.e.* father's father); a respectful appellation of an old man.

Pahúh, *a*. overflowing, abundant. [*Imit.* pahúh-pahai.]

Pái, *u*, *n*. sugarcane; *v*. to pare (a stick) as with a *daw*.

Pài, *ka*, *n*. a number = 20 kani = 8,000.

*Paia, *u*, *n*. a pillar.

Páid, *u*, *n*. crowd, *same as* "páit"; *ad*. chatteringly.

Páidbhòr, *u*, *n*. common ignorant people.

Páidkár, *u*, *n*. people of no position, the mob, the masses.

Paila, *u*, *n*. a coral bead.

Paila-sada, *u*, *n*. a string of coral beads without gold beads.

Pailen, *u*, *n*. water-fungus; —*a*. bald.

Pàiñ, *ka*, *n*. solder, cement, a joint.

Pàiñtali, *u*, *n*. a chisel.

Pairah (soh), *u*, *n*. a kind of fruit much used by the Khasis for washing clothes. [*Hind.* ritha.]

*Paisa, *ka*, *n*. a pice, ¼ anna. [*Imit.* paisa-pailaiñ.]

Pàit, *v*. to crack, to break.

Páit, *u*, *n*. a crowd;—*v*. to open by placing the finger on one side of an aperture.

Paitdohnúd, *a*. heart breaking. [*Imit.* paitdohnúd-paitdohnám.]

Paitpuraw, *n*. a small bird of blackish colour and having a crest and a little patch of red fur under the tail; a *bulbul*.

Pajait, *v*. to pull with a jerk.

*Pajama, *ka*, *n*. pyjama.

Pajih, *ad*. aloof, at some distance, [as, "ieng *pajih*, wat iatur eh hajan."]

Pajut, *v*. to pull up a heavy thing.

Pajuwa, *ka*, *n*. a kiln (also spelt "Pajwa").

Palat, *v*. to exceed, to trespass; passed (as, "u dang palat dang kumne myntan").

Palat-paliang, *a*. distantly related.

*Palki, *ka*, *n*. palanquin.

Palei, *a* innocent, simple, quiet, calm.

Palngang, *a*. having a round small head, [as, "u briew uba *palngang* ka khlieh."]

---

* Hindi.

Palngáw, *a.* round and small (head).

Palhiw, *a.* with sunken eyes, [as "u briew uba *palhiw* ki khmat kumba la khlong."]

Pali, *ka, n.* one's turn.

Palong, *ka, n.* a bedstead; a soap-bubble.

*Palwan, *u, n.* an athlete.

Pam, *v.* to cut, to win (in gambling).

Pamblang, *ka, n.* the Durga Poojah.

Pamthwat, *v.* to skirmish; to fell a number of trees in a place.

Pán, *v.* to ask, to demand.

Pàn—(a *prefix*)=what is tied round [as, in the words—*pan*poh, *pan*ti, *pan*khyllong, etc.]

Pànkhyllong, *ka, n.* a knot of hair on the head.

Pánkwah, *v.* to wish for what is wrong or bad [as, "lada phi *pánkwah* eh ban duk, phi'n jin da duk shisha"]; to court.

Pànjung, *ka, n.* a bladder.

Pánpoh, *ka, n.* a girdle, a belt.

Pánsngiat, *ka, n.* a crown.

Panshandi, *ka, n.* a very small tortoise.

Panshandi-dem-lór-khah, *phr.* a wife who is eagerly expecting the return of her profligate husband.

Panti, *ka, n.* a strip of cloth tied round the left wrist to protect against the impact of the bowstring when shooting arrows.

Pán-'tien-sâid, *kaba, n.*—in a battle array, before any of the parties commences to give battle, an address is generally made by either of the contending parties to justify their own cause; such a form of address is called *kaba pán-'tien-sâid.*

Pap, *ka, n.* sin, transgression, fault (same as *pop*).

Papun, *u, n.* an unfortunate fellow.

Pár, *v.* to creep, to crawl; —*ka, n.* a mine, a quarry.

Para, *u,* or *ka, n.* a younger brother or sister.

Para (*prefix*) = one associated in common interests, occupation, etc., with another, as in the words *para*-Khasi, *para*-nongshún, *para*-mrád, *para*-khynráw, etc.,

Para-ba-eh, *phr.* of equal strength, resources, etc., to match with an opponent.

---

* Hindi.

Para-briew, *u*, *n*. having no relationship either by blood or marriage; a fellow-man.

Para-kha, (shi-), *a*. a relationship between children of brothers.

Para-khér-paramér, *u*, *n*. a neighbour.

Para-ksiew, *u*, *n*. grandnephew or niece on the mother's side.

Para-kynsi, *ka*, *n*. wife's younger sister or husband's younger brother.

Paramynshong, *u*, *n*. a husband of one's wife's sister.

'parád, *i*, *n*. a maternal grandfather.

Para-shnong, *n*. a person of the same village; a co-villager. [*Imit.* parashnong-para-tháw.]

Para-shongkha, *u*, *n*. a man who marries in the same family. [*Imit.* u-para-shongkha-parashongmàn].

Para-trái, *ki*, *n*. persons who have a concern in the matter. [*Imit.* para trai-para dkhuh] *u*, or *ka*, brother or sister of the same parent.

Pariah-parai, *a*. having engaging manners.

Paring, *v*. to pull or tug.

Paro, *n*. a pigeon.

Paron, *ka*, *n*. a basket placed in the channel of a streamlet for catching fish.

Partúh, *n*. (see "pyrtuh").

Parum-pareh, *a*. many, in great numbers (of persons only.)

Pasa, *ka*, *n*. luck.

Pasan, *i*, *n*. an uncle (father's elder brother).

Pasngoh, *v*. to strike the head against anything repeatedly.

Pashat, *v*. to hand anything to a person by throwing it up gently.

Pashait, *v*. to splash up water by striking with the sole of the foot sideways against it, to spatter.

Pashing, *ad*. on the side, sideways.

Pashór, *v*. to drag, to handle roughly.

Pashór-kait, *ka*, *n*. plantain flower.

Pasiang, *a*. inclining or sloping; peaceful, flowing (speech), social.

Pasiaw, *v*. to whisper.

Pasied, *v*. to splutter.

Pasoh, *ka*, *n*. the fleshy part of the body, the muscles.

Paswia, Paswut, } *v.* to whiz.

Pat, *ad.* again,—*v.* to fall.

Pata, *ka, n.* a patta; a licensed liquor-shop.

Patán, *v.* to pull on both sides.

Patar, *v.* to tear to pieces as with the teeth.

Pateng, *n.* a joint or link;—*ad.* indirectly, through another source (as, nga *ioh-pateng* ia kane ka shithi na kiwei pat ki briew).

Patengbynriew, *ka, n.* a generation.

Pateng-pateng, *ad.* at every interval or stage.

Pateng-la-pateng, *ad.* from generation to generation.

Pathár, *ka, n.* the width or stretch of a ford or stream.—*a.* thoughtless, heedless.

Pathat, *v.* to snap (a thread).

Patháw, *n.* a squash gourd. (*Hind.* kádu).

Pathi, *u, n.* betel, *pán* (as, called by the Nongkrem, Mylliem and the Synteng people).

Patiaw, *v.* (used in negative expressions, with *ym*), to give ear to, to care.

Patied, *v.* to strike or knock against, *e.g.*, to bully; to spatter.

Patiew, *n.* the purlin.

*Patloi, *u, n.* a thick brass cooking vessel. (*Hind.* batloi.)

‡Patlun, *ka, n.* pantaloons, trousers.

Patoh, *v.* to hit with a stone or ball that has touched the ground on its way; to ricochet.

Patóm, *v.* to drag by the hair.

Patór, *u, n.* an officer in the Synteng district next in position to a Daloi, a minister.

Patrong, *v.* to pull or clutch by the hair.

*Patsha, *n.* an Emperor.

Páw, *v.* to seem, to appear, to be evident.

*Pawa, *ka, n.* a powa, $\frac{1}{4}$ of a seer.

Pawang, *v.* to swing, to swagger.

Pawái, *ad.* unsteadily (to walk, to stagger).

Páwbynriew, *v.* to be in a tolerably good position.

Páwkhmat, *v.* to be prominent, to be present.

---

* Hindi. ‡ English.

Páw-pen-ryngkew, *v.* to have the real state of things brought to light.

Páw-ráiñ, *v.* to be exposed to shame.

Pda, *v.* to throw to the farthest distance possible.

Pda-khár-ei, *kaba, n.* an arrow shooting competition in which he who shoots the farthest obtains all the arrows shot.

Pdang, *v.* to crack.

Pdam, *v.* to come to an end, to be over; to cease; to be disappointed.

Pdeng, *ka, n.* the middle.

Pdem, *v.* to steep, to incubate.

Pdiang, *v.* to receive, to accept.

Pdiang-Balang, *v.* to receive into the church membership (Christian).

Pdiet, *v.* to open by placing the finger on one side of an aperture.

Pdok, *ka, n.* the bladder of a fish.

Pdot, *u, n.* the throat, Adam's apple.

Pdung, *ka, n.* a circular sieve or winnowing circular flat basket. —*v.* to blister.

Pduh, *v.* to strike with a stout or heavy stick on the head, to thwack.

Peh, *v.* to winnow;—*a.* not going in a straight line when shot, like a bad winged arrow.

'péh (*abbrev.* of *spéh*), *u, n.* a spike, a stake (as, "u *péh* sylli").

'péh-dyngkhiet, *u, n.* a porcupine quill.

'péh-sylli, *u, n.* a very sharp spike made from a species of bamboo called u *sylli*; a ready-witted man.

Pei, *a.* having a hole;—*v.* to penetrate.

Peibylla, *v.* to be pierced right through, to pass clean through.

Peidohsáw, *v.* to be cut to the quick or to the sensitive flesh.

Peiñ (ia-), *v.* to barter, to exchange.

Peit, *v.* to look at, to gaze; to be awake.

Peitkynriang, *v.* to squint.

Peitngór, *v.* to stay up at night.

Peitmat, *v.* to be awake or conscious; to be healthy;—*a.* good looking (person). [*Imit.* peitmat-peit-mut.]

Peit'mat-dong, *v.* to look through the corner of the eye, to look suspiciously.

Peit'matlieh, *v.* to show the white of the eye.

Peitmiet, *v.* to stay up at night. [*Imit.* peitmiet-peit-iong.]

Peit-seh, *v.* to stare vacantly.

Peitshin, *v.* to observe or mark the form or manner of a person.

Peitshongshán, *v.* to look with a suspicious eye.

Pem-pem, *ad.* lukewarm ; not tasty.

Pen, *n.* a number=80 (of fruits, red pepper, etc.)

'pen (*abbrev.* of soh-pen), *u, n.* a wild earthnut.

Pep, *v.* to desist from going or from doing a thing.

Pér, *v.* to float;—*a.* light, careless.

Pet, *v.* to buy rice or any kind of cereals.

'pet (*abbrev.* of soh-pet), *u, n.* the navel.

'pet-káw, *u, n.* an umbilical hernia.

Pha, *pers. pro. fem.* thou, —*v.* to risk, to jeopardize, to hazard.

Phang, *ka, n.* quarter, side, allotted part.

'phang-ér, *ka, n.* a periodical continuous wind which blows towards the end of the cold season.

Phah, *v.* to send, to despatch; to order for.

Phahkhot, *v.* to send for.

Phahkylli, *v.* to propose to (a girl). [*Imit.* phahkylli-phahpyrthew.]

Phái, *v.* to turn.

Phaik poh-u-Blei, *phr.* to favour, to take a favourable consideration (*lit.* to face).

Phái-khmat, *v.* to face.

Phái-dien, *v.* to turn backwards.

Phak, *ad.* violently, [as, " nga ioh-i ba u saheb u tháp *phak* ia u mali."]

Phalang, *v.* to reflect, to rebound.

Phaliep, *a.* slightly inclined or cut.

Phaloh, *v.* to splash over, to spurt, to spill.

Phalór, *ka, n.* a gate.

Phalúp, *v.* to beat with a big stick; to hew out roughly.

Phan, *u, n.* a potato; a household god. [*Imit* u phan-u-kyrpád.]

Phanang, *v.* to fling as a piece of stick by holding it from one end.

Phan-karo, *u, n.* sweet potato (white rind).

Phan-ew, *u, n.* a person who has no fixed opinion of his own.

Phan-longsyiem, *u, n.* the household deity of a Siem.

Phan-longspah, *u, n.* a household god who brings in wealth to the family. [*Imit.* u phan-longspah-phanlongphew.]

Phan-mlúh, *u, n.* a kind of sweet potato with dark and prickly rind.

Phan-mongor, *u, n.* a common round potato.

Phan-sái, *u, n.* potatoes which grow in a garden out of the small useless tubers after the crop has been gathered.

Phan-sawlia, *u, n.* sweet potato (red-rind).

Phan-shynreh, *u, n.* yam.

Phan-súid-iap, *u, n.* one of the ancestral spirits selected and invoked for giving blessings to the living and to the dead.

Phar, *ad.* entirely, wholly; it is also used as an intensifying particle, as, "u la jhih *phar* rynjaiñ";—*ka phar, n.* a ploughshare.

Phara, *ka, n.* a heap of metals (generally = 10 c. ft.)

Pharait, *v.* to spatter, to squirt.

Phareng, *n.* a European.

Pharep, *v.* to make a false charge or complaint against a person.

Pharia, *v.* to split into small pieces.

Pharshi, *ka, n.* a parable, a proverb.

Pharuh-phareh, *ad.* in a careless manner (to work), [as, "u briew u la shu tháw *pharuh-phareh* ia kane ka ruh."]

***Phasi**, *v.* to hang.

Phat—an intensifying particle (same as *phár*), [as, "u la jhieh *phat* rynjaiñ."]

Phawár, *ka, n.* a set of rhymes generally in couplets, as,
(*a*) "u sohlang u sohphie u risang u shakyntir," "ko para shynrang dangkhie kynjih pynnang te jir."
(*b*) Haba lam u thyrnia u ksái u shu búd.

Phawer, *v.* to hint, insinuate.

Phawur-phawer, *ad.* faintly, as a rumour, [as, "nga shu sngew *phawur-phawer* kumba ka sor-Shillong kan leit noh."]

* Hindi.

Pheit! *Int.* fie! *-la*, (*colloq.*), *expr.* of anger or disapproval (a, "*pheit la* iap").

Phér, *v.* to differ; *ymphér*, it matters not.

Phèr, *ad.* brilliantly, very (as, "ka bneng ka la shai bha *phèr* b'ym don shuh u l'oh.")

Phet, *v.* to run.

***Phetkiri**, *u, n.* alum.

Phet-iap, *v.* to fly for life or headlong. [*Imit.* phet iap-phet-im.]

Phet-lyndet, *v.* to go away without taking leave. [*Imit.* phet lyndet-phet-tuh.]

Phet-thong, *v.* to run a race.

Phew = ten, as shiphew 10, arphew 20.

Phewse, *ad.* to my surprise, (as, "nga tharai ba u lah ba'n ryngkang, *phewse* u háp pynban").

Phngáiñ, *a.* clear, not misty.

Phngár, *ad.* extremely, (as, "uba la sian *phngar* u mrad").

Phngit, *u, n.* flying cinders or other particles, atoms.

Phngóit, *v.* to peep so that the head only can be seen.

Phngúid, *v.* to eat gluttonously.

Phi, (*per. pro.* 2nd person), you.

Phiak, *ad.* at the centre or part aimed at.

Phiang, *ka, n.* a brass plate.

Phiang-phiang, *u, n.* a bird of greenish colour with a crest on the head.

Phiang-phlang, *v.* to arrange and tie grass into bundles for roofing purposes.

Phiangsbâi, *ka, n.* a porcelain plate.

Phiah, *v.* to split.

Phikir, *v.* to be in earnest, to take pains to do a thing.

Phieng, *a.* awe-inspiring; sublime, majestic.

Phi'm (*pers. pron.*), you will not.

Phi'n (*pers. pron.*), you will.

Phir-phir, *ad.* very (clean and white).

Phira, *v.* to guard, to watch;— *n. u phira* = a sentry.

* Hindi.

Phita, } *u*, *n*. tape.
Pita, }

Phla, *v*. to confess; to admit.

Phlang, *u*, *n*. grass. [*Imit.* u phlang-u kynbat.]

Phlait, *v*. to slip, to miss;—*ad*. right through (pierced), [as, "u sàm pynpei *phlait* ia ka lyntang."]

Phlán, *v*. to flatter, to cheat, to pretend.

Phlán-dumán, *v*. to humbug.

Phlàr, (pei-), *ad*. right through (to pass).

Phlei, *v*. to vomit, to disgorge, to flood, to blow profusely.

Phlér, *v*. to get an abrasion, to come off (as skin).

Phliat, *v*. to turn (the intestines) inside out.

Phlin phlin, } *ad*. very (slippery), [as, "une u maw uba btuid
Phlóiñ-phlóiñ, } *phlin phlin*."]

Phloit, *v*. to come off, as a ring from the handle of a hatchet.

Phlór, *v*. to become loose and fall off (said of a ring).

Phluit, *ad*. suddenly (come out), [as, "u kak u mih kynsan *phluit* na u bitor."]

Phna, *v*. to fasten a door with two cross-bolts, thus ×.

Phniang, *u*, *n*. a small seed.

Phñian, *v*. to stow; to stuff, to cram.

Phñaiñ-phñaiñ, (rit-), *ad*. very (fine), [as, "don ki shara kiba rit *phñaiñ-phñaiñ*."]

Phnieng, *v*. to raise the bolt of a trap so as to make it ready to entrap animals or birds; to set a trap.

Phong, *v*. to put on (as a coat or shoe);—*u*, *n*. a kind of reed, the inside of which is as soft as a cork.

Phohsniew, *v*. to dream.

Phohsniew kynsha, *v*. to have bad dreams.

Phoi, *v*. to be offended, to find fault with; to be captious.

Phoikynsha, *v*. unreasonably captious.

Phoidari, *ka*, *n*. a criminal case.

Phóiñ, *ad*. entirely (finish); [as, "u lah ba'n bám *phoin* ar pliang ka doh."]

Phon, *v*. to cook for a long time, (as bones, etc); to entrap, entice. [*Imit.* phon-pah.]

Phorshi (same as *pharshi*).

Phot, *a.* cutting, sharp;—*v.* to get an intertrigo.

Phra, *a.* eight.

Phrak-phrak, (kren-), *ad.* straight-forwardly, [as, "u K u long u briew uba kren *phrak phrak.*"]

Phrang, *ka, n.* the front;—*v.* to temper an iron; to test.

Phrangsngi, *ka, n.* the beginning, the first.

Phrah, *ka, n.* plaited bamboo work; — *v.* to obstruct the doorway etc., by planting cross-sticks.

Phreit, *n.* a small migratory bird (very depredatory to paddy and Italian maize).

Phret, *v.* to be broken to pieces, to be crushed into powder or small pieces.

Phrew, *v.* to play with a small bundle of sticks; — *ad.* in all directions (scatter).

Phria, *u, n.* hailstone.

Phriang, *v.* to spread out, to scatter.

Phrieh, *v.* to feel nervous or feverish.

Phròd, *a.* foppish.

Phrong *ka, n.* fat left after the oil has been extracted by frying.

Phroh, *v.* to feed (as a mother-bird does her young ones).

Phroh-jyndem, *u, n.* a hoopoe.

Phroi, *v.* to crush a thing into powder and to sprinkle it.

Phrung, *v.* to push in, enter, insert.

Phúd, *ka, n.* the bed of a stream, a mountain gorge; —*u, n.* a gannet.

Phuh, *v.* to blossom; to appear cheerful.

Phuhmat, *v.* to be cheerful in appearance. [*Imit.* phuhmat-phuhmut.]

Phuhsámrkhie, *v.* to smile.

Phui, *v.* (*Imperative*) Let bad luck attend you; let it be otherwise.

Phu-iong, *u, n.* soot (*esp.* in cooking vessels).

Phui-phui, *u, n.* dust floating in the air.

Phúid, *v.* to clear or make a drain with a hoe.

Phúiñ-phúiñ, *ad.* very (clean in appearance), [as, "une u khynnah uba bha-briew *phuiñ-phuiñ.*"]

Phùit, *ka, n.* number of times won in any competition or match; score.

*Phûj-u-pyrton, *u, n.* an army. (*Hind.* Fauj).

Phulid, *a.* playful, cunning, jocular.

Phùm-phùm, *ad.* soft like cotton, [as, "une u phan u la ih bha *phùm-phùm.*"]

Phup-phup, *ad.* very (bushy), like snowflakes, [as, "u shñiuh jong phi u la lieh *phup-phup.*"]

Phúr, *v.* to hold a ceremonial dance on the occasion of the cremation, *esp.* of a grandmother or grandfather (father's mother or father).

Phùt, *v.* to uproot.

Phutoi, *ka, n.* a waistcoat.

Phylla, *a.* wonderful, strange.

Phyllâd, *n.* a kind of mongoose.

Phylla-soi, *ad.* unusually, as an exceptional instance, [as, "mynno mynno phi'm ju wan kai, mynta phiwan *phylla-soi* a-iu ka? "]

Phyllâw, *ka, n.* the front court of the house.

Phylliah-ding *u, n.* a flying cinder or spark.

Phylliew, *v.* to pour water from one vessel to another small-mouthed vessel.

Phyllùd, *u, n.* a kind of mucilaginous plant.

Phyllúng, (at-), *v.* to have waves.

Phyrbew, *u, n.* a solitary jackal with a peculiar howl.

Phyrdap-lyngkór, *ka, n.* a piece of bamboo or wood attached to the two-split pieces of bamboo for levelling an irrigated rice-field and also to the horizontal post which rests on the neck of bullocks.

Phyrngâp, *ad.* early (in the morning); [as, "khie lashai dang step *phyrngap*, ho."]

Phyrngup, } Phyrngap, } *a.* with drooping hair or branches; [as, " ka dieng kaba noh *phyrngup* ki tnat harud wah."]

Phyrmân, *ad.* with plenty of whiskers; [as, " u tngáw u long u shrieh uba don 'mainkér *phyrmán.*"]

Phyrnâi, *a.* glittering, shining.

Phyrnep, } Phyrnop, } *v.* to dip or plunge; to duck.

---

* Hindi.

Pi, *v.* to draw water by dipping a small vessel in it.

Pia, *ad.* heavily, more than enough (to eat or carry) ; as, " u kit ha ba'n da khia *pia* ka dieng."]

Piada, *n.* a peon.

*Piala, *ka, n.* a porcelain cup, a tea cup.

Piam, *v.* to embrace, to clasp.

Pi-an, *a.* short and stout.

P'ian, *ad.* firmly (sit) ; [as, " u shong *p'ian* ha ka shuki."]

P'iar, *v.* to stretch out : to extend. Also spelt *pyiar*.

Piat, *u, n.* an onion ;—*ad.* firmly ; (as, " u la shong *piat* ba'n bam.")

Piaw, *v.* to be peevish or sulky.

Pi-ê, *a.* full or swollen (as an overfull stomach).

Pied, *v.* to split with the hands ; to tear off.

'pieng, 1. (*abbrev.* of kpieng), *u, n.* a bead.

2. (*abbrev.* of sohpieng), *u, n.* a mango.

'piengsohphi, *u, n.* a string of coral beads which have been strung alternately with gold beads resembling *u sohphi.*

Pien, *v.* to wrap a piece of cloth round the waist.

'pien (*abbrev.* of *jympien*), *ka, n.* undergarment worn by women.

'pien-arna, and 'pien-lasubon, are the two variety of waistcloths (jympien).

'ping (*abbrev.* of sping) *u, n.* a handle ; as u '*ping*-sdie.

Pihia, } *ad.* short and fat, [as, " i briew iba lyngkot *piho.*"]
Piho, }

Pihuin, *a.* envious.

Pilang (nái-), *n.* a kind of large rat.

*Pipa, *ka, n.* a cask.

Piréit, *ad.* with a distended abdomen, [as, " ka dohkha kaba pun pylleng ka heh kpoh *pireit.*"]

*Pirit, *ka, n.* a small porcelain plate ; a saucer,—*v.* (coloq.) on terms of very close intimacy.

Pirú, *n.* a turkey.

Pisa, *v.* to feel uneasy, to fidget, to be restless.

*Piskot, *u, n.* a screwdriver.

*Pita, *u, n.* a tape, a ribbon.

---

* Hindi.

Pjah, *a.* cold.

Pjar, *v.* to drain.

Pjiah, *v.* to feed carefully; to nurse.

Pjóng-pjóng, *ad.* like the leap of a deer, [as, "nga ioh-i hynne ia ka skei ba ka hér *pjóng-pjóng.*"]

Pla, *ka, n.* a bag, a pocket.

Plak, *ad.* utterly, totally (in a bad sense), [as, "nga nang kren bha, u pat u krensih *plak.*"]

Plaiñ-plaiñ, *ad.* jet (black), [as, "u briew uba iong *plaiñ-plaiñ.*"]

Pláit, *v.* to open out, to clear a way.

Plan, *ad.* completely, [as, "u bám ha ban da lut *plan* shi-pliang pynshong."]

Plar, *v.* to vomit (only of infants) ;—*ad.* lying helplessly (many), [as, "tang shu rung hapoh Aspatal, nga ioh-i kiba pang ki thiah *plar.*"]

*Plastor, *ka, n.* a plaster.

Pléng, *ad.* after all; oh! I see now, [as, "*pléng* u Saheb-bishar uba jrong du."]

Pleiñ-pleiñ, *ad.* hard and unripe (fruit), [as, "u sohmon mynta u dang im *pleiñ-pleiñ.*"]

*Pleit, *ka, n.* porcelain plate.

Pli, *v.* to change.

Pliang, *ka, n.* a plate.

Pliah, *adj.* clear, pretty, [as, "ka khláw Mawpat mynta ka la *pliah*"; "ka briew kaba *pliah* khmat."]—*n. ka,* cash.

Plie, *v.* to open.

Plied, *v.* to open, unfold.

Plod, *ad.* fully, (as, "u la bám ha ba'n da kdang *plod.*")

Ploiñ, *ad.* entirely (as, la lut *ploin*).

Pluk, *ad.* unexpectedly (bad sense), [as, "u iathuh *pluk* ia kaba rih].

Plúh, *v.* to be on fire, to take fire.

Pnah, *a.* tenacious, eloquent.

Pnan, *ad.* quite stiff, (as, "u la iap *pnan.*")

Pnar, *ka, n.* a shell ;—*ki,* the Syntengs as distinguished from the Khasis.

---

* Hindi.

Pnat, *u*, *n.* a branch of a tree resembling a fork.

Pnek-pnek, *ad.* very (sticky) [as, "ka um kaba mih na ka kseh ka long kaba dambit *pnek-pnek.*"]

Pnóh, *ka*, *n.* one side of "ka jainsem"—a Khasi woman's outer-garment.

Pong, *v.* to bore, to make a hole.

Pongka (khún), *n.* a child whose father is unknown; a bastard.

Pongkdung, *ad.* bulging out like a balloon (as, "ka jáiñ ka at *pongkdung* ba beh ka l'er").

Pongkhuh, *ad.* like a big animal lying helpless (as, "nga tharai ba ym shym dei ba nga siat ia ka sier hynrei nga shem ka la kyllon *pongkhuh*").

Pongkiang (or pyngkiang), *ad.* crosswise:—*n. ka*, breadth.

Pongpet, *v.* to come to nothing, to fail.

Pongsháì, *ka*, *n.* a side-door of a Khasi house; an aperture for letting in the light.

'poh (*abbrev.* of kpoh), *ka*, *n.* the abdomen, the belly.

Poh, *a.* low; less, short of.

P'oh (or pyoh), *v.* to be exposed to smoke or fire; to smoke.

Pohbah, *v.* to be near delivery.

Poh-ia, *a.* low or mean (action);—*ka*, *n.* weekday.

Pohjaid, *a.* low-caste, low-born. [*Imit.* pohjait-pohrati.]

Pohjat, *ka*, *n.* the sole of the foot.

Poh-rati, *a.* low-born.

Pohsah, *ad.* inwardly or within one's own mind.

Poh-tit, *ka*, *n.* the armpit.

Poi, *v.* to reach, to arrive at.

Poi-poi (lwet), *ad.* easily (crumbling or mouldering [as, "kane ka jaiñ ka la lko *poi-poi*".]

Poi-bnái, *v.* to menstruate.

Poi-kha, *v.* to marry. [*Imit.* poikha-poiman.]

Poi-ktien, *v.* to get a word or reply. [*Imit.* poiktien-poithylliej.]

Pòit-pòit, (dih-), *ad.* with a successive little quantity of smoke or water puffing off, [as, "ki 'khar Mudi ki mlien ba'n dih duma *pòitpòit.*"]

Pom, *v.* to cut (with a *daw*), to sever.

Pomblang-u-dkhar, *ka*, *n.* the Durga Poojah.

Pomblang-u-Siem Nongkrem, *ka*, *n.* the annual festival of the Siem of Nongkrem.

Pom-pom, *ad.* to ashes (reduced); [as, "dung ha ba'n da lwet *pom-pom.*"]

Pompyrthat, *v.* to be struck with lightning.

Pomtah, *v.* to cut slightly (of trees), to tap.

Pomwait, *v.* to win in gambling.

Pop, *n.* sin. (same as *pap.*)

Pór, *ka, n.* time, period; a small bird.

Prang (see "prong").

Prah, *u, n.* a winnowing basket.

Prai, *ad.* small and in large numbers, (as, "ka pung ka dap da ki khun dohkha *prai.*")

Prâit, *v.* to give way or to be torn as an old garment, (as, "ka patlun ka la rim eh kumta ka la *prâit* haba shong.")

Pràn, *v.* to venture, to dare, to be presumptuous (as, "me *pràn* kóp iaei haba me'm lah ?").

Prat, *v.* to break through, (as, "ka masi ka la *prat* ia ka kpér"); —to cut (grass).

*Prek, *u, n.* a nail.

Prem, *ad.* like a sudden appearance of people standing in a group (as, "kyndit-kyndit la mih saw ngut *prem* ki nonglute"); prominently; like the appearance of a collection of sticks set on end.

Pret, *v.* to throw away.

Prew, *u, n.* small dry bamboo or reed; a torch.

Prie, *v.* to vomit.

Prie-umksang, *v.* to vomit bile.

Pring, *u, n.* soot;—*a.* black.

Prip, *ad.* like a collection of small objects, [as, "u jhur u la mih *prip* mynta."]

Prong, *v.* to break through a fence or wall, same as *prang.*

Proh, *u, n.* a fork, a prong.

Proh-jingmut, *a.* intelligent, sharp.

Proi, *ka, n.* tumour; an evil spirit who causes cancer, especially in very dangerous parts of the body, as in the sides, arm-pits, etc.

Prúh, *ka, n.* a cubit, 18 inches, used in measuring all lengths.

Prûid, *v.* to draw a line, to scratch.

---

* Hindi.

Prûm, *ka*, *n.* sore, ulcer.

Prup-prap, *ad.* simultaneously and hurriedly (as, "ki iabám lang *prup-prap*").

Prut, *u*, *n.* a species of grass much liked by cattle.

Ptéj-ptéj, *ad.* very (adhesive), [as, "tylliat ia ka ja haba ka'n da pnah *ptej-ptej.*"]

'pu, (*abbrev.* of kpu), *u*, *n.* a loaf; ground rice; cakes ['*pukhleiñ*, '*pumaloi*, '*putharo*, etc., are different kinds of cakes made from rice.]

Puka, *n.* a paddy bird, an egret.

*Pukir, *n.* a fakir. [*Imit.* u Pukir-u Pukra.]

Pukni, *n.* a vulture.

Pukri, *ka*, *n.* a well.

Pûd, *ka*, *n.* a boundary;—*v.* to omit.

Púd-púd, *a.* timid.

*Pudina, *u*, *n.* marsh mint.

Pung, *ka*, *n.* a pool; a joint.

Pung-kjat, *ka*, *n.* a leg.

Pung-kti, *ka*, *n.* an arm.

Púh, *v.* to dig, to peck, to bite.

Púh-kylla, *v.* to dig the garden with a hoe and turning the soil upside down.

Pui-pui, *u*, *n.* dust floating in the air; mist.

Pûid, *v.* to rip open, to lance, to dissect.

Púid-púid, *a.* coward.

Puit, *u*, *n.* grasshopper.

Puit-suwa, *u*, *n.* a locust.

Pujér, *u*, *n.* ground rice distributed at the christening of a child.

Pule, *v.* to read.

Pulit, *ka*, *n.* a lock-up, a private room; a policeman.

Pulo, *ka*, *n.* a hen-coop.

Pulom, *v.* to come to nothing, to be fruitless.

Pum-pum, *u*, *n.* a mist; dust floating in the air.

Pún, *v.* to pave, to bridge over.

Pun, *v.* to gestate, to conceive, to be with child.

---

* Hindi.

Pún-jingkieng, *v.* to throw a bridge across.

Pûr, *v.* to creep, to spread.

*Pura, *a.* complete, full. [*Imit.* pura-puri.]

Puramit, *v.* to league with ; to hold secret consultations.

Puraw, *v.* to give in substitution or compensation ; to recoup.

'purew, *u, n.* dry pounded rice.

Púr-khnam, *v.* to feather an arrow.

Puri, *n.* a fairy.

Puria, *u, n.* a small dried fish. [*Imit.* puria-purap.]

Puriskâm, *ka, n.* a fable, a fiction.

Puron, *ka, n.* one of the female deities of the Khasis representing. the first maternal ancestress.

*Pushara, *ka, n.* a whitewash, *v.*—to whitewash.

*Pur-a-na, *ka, n.* a parwana or notice.

*Puson, *v.* to ponder, to muse ; to appreciate.

Put, *v.* to sound a wind instrument ;—*ad.* yet, (used with negative verbs in the past tense).

Pute, *v.* to be thwarted in one's plan or project, to end in nothing.

Putet, *ad.* besides ; at the same time.

Pyngkat, *a.* not quite full or to the brim.—*Ka, n.* The name of the day on which Mynso hât is held, in the Jaintia Hills.

Pyngkhoh, *v.* to fold ; to wrestle with.

Pyngklit, (iaid) *v.* to go by a roundabout way so as to avoid meeting. [*Imit.* pyngklit-pyngklat.)

Pynkriang, *v.* to catch hold of one on the way.

Pyngngâd, *a.* cool, refreshing.

Pyngieng, *ad.* perpendicularly, upright (same as *pynieng*).

Pyiar, *v.* to stretch, open, extend.

Pyjah, *v.* cold, same as *pjah.*

Pyjar, *v.* to strain, to drain, (same as *pjar*).

Pylla, *ka, n.* the pan of a pair of scales.

Pyllaiñ (peit-), *ad.* with prominent small eyes, [as, "balei me peit *pyllaiñ* ia nga ?"] ; staringly.

Pyllait, *v.* to liberate, to set free.

Pyllait-ktien, *v.* to break off the match.

---

* Hindi.

Pyllait-ksûid, *v.* to let loose a fowl or any animal sacrificed to the evil-spirit ; to let a person free from any agreement.

Pyllait-lân, *v.* to let loose an animal to roam at large.

Pyllait-rih, *v.* to let loose a fowl sacrificed to *u rih* or the fever demon.

Pyllait-sansh'ing, *v.* to divorce. (Divorce among the Khasis is effected by exchanging 5 cowries between the husband and the wife in the presence of witnesses).

Pyllaw, *ad.* staring fixedly, [as, "u peit *pyllaw* kum ka dkhoh."]

Pylleng, *ka, n.* an egg.

Pylliaw, *ad.* with small sunken eyes, [as, "ine i khynnah i peit pylliaw."]

Pyllon, } *a.* round.
Pyllun, }

Pyllup, (dem-), *ad.* on the belly (lie).

Pyn=a prefix of many causative verbs.

Pyn-adke, *v.* to bring a thing to naught.

Pyn-am, *v.* to keep together by means of a V-shaped vice, to cause to bite.

Pyn-at-khu, *v.* to be envious.

Pyn-atshyntur, *v.* to pout, to sulk.

Pynbàn, *a.* still, nevertheless.

Pynban, *v.* to add to, to give more ;—*ad.* nevertheless, still but.

Pynbeit, *v.* to correct, to make straight.

Pynbúd, *v.* to let a thing follow, to be as a sequel to. [*Imit.* pynbúd-pynrap.]

Pynbyllan, *v.* to join or attach to.

Pynkhieklong, *v.* to make a sacrifice in order to ratify an oath or agreement.

Pynkhúid-dâr, *v.* to be free from blame or imputation, (*lit.* to clear a passage for a boat to pass).

Pynkhyllew, *v.* to flatter.

Pyndûh, *v.* to destroy.

Pyn-ngat, *v.* to let a thing be caught in a spoon or net ;—to fell a tree.

Pynhiar, *v.* to let down ; to have diarrhoea ; to export.

Pynhiar-kput, *v.* to avenge.

Pynhiar-mynsiem, *v.* to breathe.

Pynhiar-synjat, *v.* to make a formal betrothal.

Pyniáid, *v.* to manage (*lit.* to let a thing walk).

Pyn-iar, *v.* to extend, to stretch ;—*u*, *n.* a batten.

Pynieng, *v.* to make a thing stand up ;—*ad.* perpendicularly (followed by *da*), [as, " buh *da pynieng* ia ka suloi."]

Pynjhieh, *v.* to wet, to moist ; to urinate.

Pynlah, *v.* not to give in or yield in argument, to be headstrong ; to be obstinate,—*v.* to finish up.

Pynlat, *v.* to delay, to procrastinate.

Pyn-ong, *v.* to inform, to deliver a verbal message.

Pynphuh, *v.* to beautify or make grand ; (*lit.* to make a thing blossom).

Pynpiar, Panpiar, } *v.* to girdle or wrap a piece of cloth round the bust.

Pynryngkang-pár, *v.* to banish, to send into exile ; to deport.

Pynshád-kháw-ïang, *v.* to speak or behave as if intoxicated with liquor.

Pynshâdkhûn, *v.* to dandle.

Pynshâdsuloi, *v.* to have parade exercises, to drill.

*Pynshait, *v.* to be forward ;—*ka*, *n.* an arbitration or *panchayet* ; *u*—an arbitrator.

Pynshok, *ka*, *n.* in Khasi States, contributions for State purposes.

Pynshong, *v.* to make a reasonable settlement ;—to give full measure.

Pynshoi, *v.* to tempt, to entice, to allure. [*Imit.* pynshoi-pynshâd.]

Pyntha, *ka*, *n.* a level country.

Pynthame, *v.* to mesmerise, to dazzle, to enchant.

Pyntian, *v.* to put into the mouth.

Pyntip, *v.* to make known.

Pyrkhat, *v.* to consider, to think. [*Imit.* pyrkhat-pyrdaiñ.]

Pyrkhing, *ad.* tightly, strictly.

* Hindi.

Pyrkhung, } v. to bend, to arch.
Pyrkhun, }

Pyrda, *ka*, *n*. hangings, a curtain.

Pyrdet, *ad*. behind, (as, "ki la khúm ia u nongpyniap-briew da *pyrdet*").

Pyrdóng, (niam-), *ka*, *n*. a ceremony which is performed at the time when reconciliation is brought about between two contending parties.

Pyrdung (at-), *ad*. well-arched, [as, "ka jaiñ ka at-*pyrdung* ba beh ka lyer."]

Pyr-em, *ka*, *n*. the spring season.

Pyr-en, *ad*. with a swollen belly.

Pyrha, *ka*, *n*. a basket for measuring rice, containing from 4 to 7½ seers.

Pyrhut, *a*. breezy, windy ; hungry.

Pyrjah, *v*. to smack the lips as a sign of anger or appreciation of food.

Pyrmán (khmih-), *ad*. from a distance or as a spectator (as, "nga shu ia khmih *pyrmán* ia u Khasi mynta").

Pyrsa, *n*. a nephew or niece ; (*voc.*) a son or daughter-in-law.

Pyrsa-ksiew, *n*. a grand-niece or nephew (mother's side).

Pyrsát, *v*. to breathe, to blow, to hiss.

Pyrshang, *v*. to attempt, to try.

Pyrshah, *prep*. against, opposite to.

Pyrshen, *u*, *n*. a pimple, a stye.

Pyrshong (soh), *u*, *n*. a kind of sour fruit, Assamese *kamranga*.

Pyrsia, *v*: retail buying and selling. [*Imit*. pyrsia-pyrkat.]

Pyrsit, *u*, *n*. fine particles of broken rice or pulses.

Pyrsut, *ka*, *n*. a pair of bellows—*v*. to blow, to set air in current.

Pyrta, *v*. to cry out, to call aloud.

Pyrta shnong, *v*. to cry round the village.

Pyrthat, *u*, *n*. thunder ;—*kaba tied u pyrthat*, a clap of thunder.

Pyrthei, *n*. the world, [*phr*. ym don *pyrthei*=very, exceedingly.]

Pyrthiew, *v*. to come out (as an eruptive disease) ; to burst (of roasted grain).

Pyrthuh, *v*. to imitate.

Pyrto, *v*. to cherish a grateful remembrance of.

*Pyrton, *ka, n.* a regiment.

Pyrtung, *ad.* bulgingly (as, " ka doh ka at *pyrtung* ba dait u dkhew ").

Pyrtuh, *ka, n.* a domestic-poojah of a S'iem (same as " partuh ").

Pyrwa, *v.* to care, to be mindful of.

R.

R—The sixteenth letter in the Khasi Alphabet.

Rakâid, *a.* young, stunted, [as, " u khynnah uba dang *rakáid* u shlan ba'n dih duma."]

Rakep (bah-), *ad.* awkwardly (carrying a big person on the back, or sticking to another's back), [as, " u khynnah uba la san ruh u phah bah *rakep* ha i kmie."]

Rakêd, *ad.* in ragged or torn clothes, [as, " ynda shang khláw eh, ki jaiñ ki jot *rakéd.*"]

Rakên, *ad.* waddlingly, (as, " u iaid *rakén* ba sa tohjáw").

Rakhe, *v.* to observe.

Rakho, *u, n.* one who tends cattle, a cowherd.

*Rakot, *ka, n.* a *rakshasas,—a.* voracious, greedy.

Raktui, } *ad.* shabbily, [as, " ki nongkyndong ki leh *raktui* ia lade
Raktai, } wat lada ki long ki ba ioh-ba-kot eh ruh."]

'rád, (*abbrev.* of *mrad*), *n.* an animal; *abbrev. of* " *kynrád* " (q.v.).

'rad-bah, *u, n.* a giant.

*Radha, *n.* a goose.

Rang, *v.* to cease to rain, to be fine (said of weather).

'rang, (*abbrev.* of shynrang), a male.

'rangbah, *u, n.* a man, an elder;—*a.* grown up. [*Imit.* rangbah-rangsan.]

R'ang, *ad.* with feet entangled in a raised position in such things as a creeper or barbed wire, same as *ryang.*

Rangai, } *ad.* with long dishevelled hair, [as, " u shñiuh katai ka
Rangei, } briew u long uba *rangai* kum u jong ka dngiem; kane
Rangiep, } ka dieng kaba heh *rangai.*"]

Rang-'iar-khád, *u, n.* a sacrificial cock.

Rangli, *ka, n.* a poor lonely woman. [*Imit.* ka rangli-ka juki.]

Rah, *v.* to lift, to carry.

---

* Hindi.

Rah-rong, *v.* to carry about as a show; to expose other's faults, to calumniate. [*Imit.* rah-rong rah-nám.]

Rái, *v.* to decide, to pass orders.

'rái (*abbrev.* of krái), *u, n.* millet, as u *rái*shan, *rái*soh, *rái*truh.

Raibi, *ka, n.* hereditary taint.

Raikhoh, *a.* lean, thin, reduced.

Raiaiñ, *a.* big and having much foliage (said of a tree).

Rai-eh, *ka, n.* a waste land covered with thick jungle; virgin soil. [*Imit.* rai-eh-rai-dàm.]

Raiep, *ad.* like a fool clad in shabby clothes (as, "balei me ieng *raiep* hangne?")

Ráid, *a.* stunted, dwarfish, degenerated.

Ráiñ, *ka, n.* self-respect, honour.

Raimâw-raidieng, (her-, phet-), *ad.* wildly, anywhere and everywhere (run), [as, "ki kynthei tang shu ioh-i ia ki Sik ki hér *raimáw-raidieng.*"]

*Raiot, *n.* a subject, a *rayat.*

'raishán, *u, n.* (*Bot. Paspalum Sanguinale*) a species of millet resembling grass.

Rái shilliang, *v.* to be partial in the decision of a case;—*n.* ex parte judgment.

'raisoh, *u, n.* Italian millet; (*Bot. Setreria Italica*).

Raitong, *n.* a poor lonely man. [*Imit.* raitong rainot.]

'raitruh, *u, n.* (*Bot. Eleusine Coracana*); (Bengali) মাড়ুয়া। a species of millet.

Raiup, *ad.* reaching down to the ankle (as, "u phong ka sopti kaba jynsur *raiup*").

*Ráj, *ka, n.* jurisdiction, a State—*u ráj*, the people, the constituency.

*Rajai, *ka, n.* a razai.

*Rájinama, *n.* deed or instrument of compromise.

*Rajon, *ka, n.* resin (Hind. *dhoob*).

Ràm, *ka, n.* a debt.

Rám, *ka, n.* a jungle which has been cleared for *jhum* cultivation.

Ramân, *ad.* fiercely (like a tiger), [as, "nga ioh-i ia u khla uba heh *ramân.*"]

---

* Hindi.

Ram-ew, *ka*, *n.* the goddess of earth, the ground ; *terra firma.*

Ramhah, *u*, *n.* a giant.

Ràm-ia, *ka*, *n.* dream, illusion ; hallucination, —*kren ràm-ia*, to speak as in a dream ; to be under a hallucination.

Ram-shangki, *ka*, *n.* an old fashioned gun used by the Khasis long ago ; a jingal.

Ram-shandi, *ka*, *n.* the goddess who inspires the people when engaging in any dangerous undertaking as in a battle.

Ran, *v.* to contract, to shrivel, to shrink.

Randa, *ka*, *n.* a plane.

Rañaiñ, *ad.* having plenty of foliage, [as, " ka don kawei ka dieng kaba *rañaiñ* harúd surok."]

Ranáp, *ka*, *n.* the slope of a hill.

Rani, *ka*, *n.* a reward given to the discoverer of a lost article.

'rap, 1. (*abbrev.* of iarap), *v.* to help ; 2. (*abbrev.* of " tráp ");—*ka*, *n.* a Khasi circular flat leaf umbrella.

Rapiej, *ad.* as if pressed with a heavy load on the back, [as, " nga iashem ia u ba u kit *rapiej* la u phan shi byrni."]

*Rashi, *ka*, *n.* a sickle.

Rashing, *ka*, *n.* a slope, a side of precipice.

Rasong, *ka*, *n.* great good fortune ; the goddess of good luck.

Rat, *v.* to up-root. [*Imit.* rat-thiew.]

Ratáp, *ka*, *n.* a piece of plaited bamboo work to protect the body from the impact of a load when carrying it ; a trap.

Rat-da, *phr.* used with *yn* or *ym* ; to denote conditional possibility ; as, " u'n *rat da* lei lada phi leit " ; " ym *rat da* lah batai ia kane."

Rati, *n.* a small seed used for weighing gold and silver ; a very small quantity.

Rdóng, *ad.* in an arched position, as a cat does before springing on a rat.

Red, *u*, *n.* a fabulous sea-monster, a brave or daring fellow.

R'ê, *ad.* full (as, " nga sngewdap ka kpoh *r'e* ba nga bám soh-phlang ") ; puffed up (belly) ; same as *ryê.*

R'eng, *ad.* raised by a prop on one side, (as, " ka kpoh ka long kum-no re *r'eng* ") ; same as *ryeng.*

Reng, *ka*, *n.* a horn, an antler.

Reng-ngáp, *ka*, *n.* the cheek-bone.

Reng-'mat, *ka*, *n.* the eyebrow.

---

* Hindi.

Rem, *v.* to be defeated, to be guilty ; to be expensive, to get offended ; highly priced,—*a.* dear.

Reit-shán, *u, n.* a very hard and durable wood used for posts.

Ren, *u, n.* a sea-monster.

Rep, *v.* to cultivate, to plant. [*Imit.* rep-riang.]

Rew, *ka, n.* honeycomb ;—*a.* brittle, weak—said of wood only.

Rnga, *u, n.* charcoal.

Rngat, *v.* to be dried up and evaporated.

Rngái (ha-), *n.* an illusion or dream, hallucination.

Rngaiñ, *ad.* holding fast (of a bite) ; [as, " u ksew u am *rngaiñ* na ka ryndang u masi."]

Rngaiñ-rngaiñ (iong-), *ad.* as black as coal.

Rngáw, *v.* to cease raining for a time.

Rngiew, *ka, n.* luck ; individuality ; essence of humanity ; spirit. [*Imit.* rngiew-rwiang.]

Rhang, } *ad.* disappointed, (as, " ki briew ki la lah ioh, phi phi
Rheng, } dang ap *rhang* hangne ! ").

Rhah, *v.* to be envious ; to meddle. [*Imit.* rhah-rhing.]

Rhem, *a.* glowing, burning.

Rhew, (duna-), *ad.* conspicuously or markedly (less or short of), [as, " ei ba bám ba duna *rhew* u kék kumne ? "]

Rhong, (ap-), *ad.* agape ;—(pei-), having a small aperture ; eagerly.

Rhing, *ad.* persistently, (as, " balei phi shún *rhing* ia nga ? ").

Rhúin-rhúin, *ad.* very (red or glowing), [as, " u sohphi uba sáw *rhúin-rhúin.*"]

Ri, *v.* to keep, to take care of ;—*ka, n.* a country, a province ;—*u, n.* a kidney bean, asparagus.

'ri (*abbrev.* of *thri*), *u, n.* a cane, a bamboo tie.

Riang, *ad.* in order, in a row, [as, " ki buh *riang* ki ben ba'n shong ki briew."]

Riaj, riej, *v.* to shrink from ; to recoil from fear, disgust, etc., forbear.

Riam, *v.* to dress ; to entrap ;—*ka, n.* a suit of clothes. [*Imit.* ka riam ka beit.]

Riampop, *v.* to entrap wild beats by pitfalls ; to mine.

Riat, *ka, n.* a precipice, a cliff. [*Imit.* ka riat-ka ram.]

Riaw (rap-), *ad.* in great numbers and simultaneously, [as, "ki tang shu pyrta, ki rap *riaw* baroh."]

*Rikap, *ka*, *n.* a stirrup.

Ri-kynti, *ka*, *n.* a private landed property.

Riew, *v.* to give out a sound, to produce a sound.

'riew, 1. (*abbrev.* of *briew*), *n.* a person ; 2. (*abbrev.* of *shriew*) an arum.

'riewbah, *n.* one who is not related, a stranger. [*Imit.* 'riewbah-'riewsan.]

'riewbha, *a.* rich, wealthy. [*Imit.* 'riewbha-'riewmiat.]

'riewbiej, *n.* a foolish or ignorant person. [*Imit.* 'riewbiej-'riewthem.]

'riewblei, *a.* godly.

'riewdakáit, *n.* a cruel person.

'riewdangkhie, *ki*, *n.* young people, the rising generation.

'riewdkhot, *n.* a member of a community or any organisation.

'riewngeit, *n.* a fellow-believer, a person who holds the same faith.

Riewhadem, *u*, *n.* maize, Indian corn.

'riewhok, *n.* a godly man, an honest person. [*Imit.* 'riewhok-'riewsot.]

'riew-iáid, *ka*, *n.* a woman of bad character, a harlot.

'riewlieng, *u*, *n.* a boatman, a sailor.

'riewnar, runar, *adj.* cruel, wicked. [*Imit.* u runar-u ruser.]

'riewpop, *n.* a sinner.

'riewradbah, *n.* a giant.

'riewsâid, *u*, *n.* a pleader.

'riewsaid-lah, *n.* a person who holds on in argument although he is beaten.

'riewsaidthma, *u*, *n.* a statesman, a clever man.

'riew-u-s'iar, (dang-), *phr.* at the crowing of a cock, early in the morning.

'riewspah, *a.* rich, wealthy. [*Imit.* 'riewspah-'riewphew.]

'riewstád, *n.* a wise person. [*Imit.* 'riewstád-'riewnang.]

'riewtymmen, *n.* an old person, an elder.—*ad.* like one who is in an advanced age, thoughtfully (as, "ine i-Babu i-kren *riewtymmen* shibun haba ia shongkái") [*Imit.* riewtymmen-riewsan].

---

* Hindi.

Ring, *v.* to pull, to tug.

Ring kongór, *v.* to compel formerly by force a man to marry a S'iem's female relative.

Ring-dong, *v.* to do a thing so as to suit one's interest or object.

Ri-ngér, *u, n.* a small kind of rattan cane, a species of *calamus*.

Ring-jingmut, *v.* to infer, to draw a conclusion.

Ringmáw, *v.* to bring a monolith from a distance.

Ring saiphla, *v.* to confirm a statement by referring to an eye-witness who would act as an arbiter.

Ringsamthiah, *v.* to be drowsy.

Ringsán, *v.* to catch fish by driving them along in water with a bamboo fence.

Ringsdot, } *v.* to pine away, to languish.
Ringswái, }

Ringsúr, *v.* to sing.

Ringtyllái, *kaba, n.* a tug-of-war.

Ringtyrkhong, *v.* deject, depress, pine away.

Rih, *v.* to hide ;—*u, n.* a fever demon ; ague.

Rijied, *u, n.* a post. [*Imit.* u rijied-u khnong.]

Rim, *a.* old.

'rimet, *u, n.* a large rattan cane (*Bot calamus*).

Rin, *ad.* in a row or line (as, "ki briew ki ieng, *rin*, harúd wah").

'riphin, *u, n.* a very small species of rattan cane.

'ri-ráj, *ka, n.* a raj or public land.

Risa, *v.* to shout exultingly.

Risang, *n.* a squirrel.

Risáw, *u, n.* October ; a small bamboo used for making arrows.

Rishot, *u, n.* the chief post, a pillar.

Rit, *a.* small.

Riti, *ka, n.* legal customs, established customs.

Rit-jingmut, *a.* narrowminded.

Ri-Wár, *ka, n.* the lowlands on the southern slopes of the Khasi and Jaintia Hills.

Rmen, *n.* the people living in the north of the Nongkhlaw elaka ; valleys.

Rmiang, *ka, n.* the margin, the rim ; border (cloth).

Rmiang shyntur, *ka, n.* the lip.

Rmiew (um-), *ka, n.* exudation on a wound or sore, serum.

Rniang, *u, n.* an anvil.

Rnong, *ka, n.* brass or bronze.

Rnúid, *a.* having groves as a peeled orange;—*n. ka, rnúid*=groves, furrow.

Rñai, *u, n.* a tough kind of bamboo, used in making string (same as *Riñai*).

Rô, *ka, n.* mercury.

Rong, *ka, n.* colour, paint; a show, a display [*Imit.* ka rong ka rup.]—*v.* to carry between the teeth, as a cat does a rat; to carry away.

Rongbthuh, *ka, n.* gray or mouldy colour.

Rong-ka-tamsa, *ka, n.* a show, a display; *tamasha.*

Rong-iong, *ka, n.* black colour; tar.

Rong-jngem, *ka, n.* a reddish black colour.

Rong-jyrngam, *ka, n.* green or blue colour.

Rong-jyrngum, *ka, n.* a blackish-green colour.

Rong-lieh, *ka, n.* white colour.

Rong-pád, *ka, n.* lead-foil, tinsel.

Rongphong, *a.* showy, gay; having something of sham or pretence, ostentatous.

Rong-pyllun, *ka, n.* the heart (in card playing).

Rong-sáw, *ka, n.* red colour.

Rong-sawdong, *ka, n.* the diamond (card playing).

Rong-shiria, *ka, n.* the club (card playing).

Rong-stem, *ka, n.* yellow colour.

Rong-thám, *ka, n.* a spade (card-playing).

Roi, *v.* to increase, to make progress.

Roiñ-roiñ, *ad.* full of holes; riddled with small holes, [as, "ba'n lait lyer, ki tap da ka tin kaba poi *roiñ-roiñ.*"]

Roit-roit, *ad.* with violence and in quick succession (as, "ki nongshohnoh ki la beh *roit-roit* ia u").

Ron, *ka, n.* the least of all the deities worshipped by the Syntengs.

Ronsing, *ka, n.* a blowing horn, a trumpet.

Rot, *v.* to desist, to shrink from; to object, see also *ihrot.*

Rshám, *ka, n.* all the necessary things spread on the ground at the time of making a sacrifice, (*e.g.* bottle-gourd, leaves, rice, a sieve, etc.).

Rshiang, *u, n.* a kind of sun-grass.

Rta, *ka, n.* ago (same as *ryta* or *yrta*).

Rtàn, } *ad.* fast (cling), [as, "ba'n leit shano shano ruh ym
Rten, } lait ba une u khún u bat *rten.*"]

Rtiang, *ka, n.* a tree bearing that name, (*Bot. Quercus serrata*).

Rtin, *ad.* tenaciously (as, "u 'sew-beh u bat *rtin* ia ka skei").

Ruái (same as rwái), *v.* to sing, [*Imit.* rwái-siaw.]

*Rubibar, *ka, n.* Sunday.

Rúd, *ka, n.* border, side ;—*leit rúd,* to relieve the bowels.

Rukom, *ka, n.* manner, custom, way.

Rukom-rukom, *ad.* of different kinds, [as, "ki don *rukom-rukom* ki briew ha ka pyrthei."]

Rung, *v.* to enter.

Rung-Balang, *v.* to enrol or be admitted as a member of a church.

Ruh, *ad.* also ;—*ka, n.* a cage, a snare.

*Rui, *u, n.* cotton.

Rúid-dak, *v.* to draw a line, to put a mark.

Ruid-núr, *v.* to cut a drain.

Rui-rui, *u, n.* dirt suspended in water.

Rum, *ka, n.* the lower or hinder part ; south.

Ruma, *v.* to be delirious, to speak or act incoherently. [*Imit.* ruma-rutit.]

Rumar, *ka, n.* a pocket handkerchief.

Rumpei, *ka, n.* the last room of a Khasi house next to the hearth, where odds and ends are kept.

Runar, *see* riewnar. [*Imit.* runar-ruser.]

Rup, *ka, n.* the side of a cloth not coloured or the colour of which does not come out distinctly ; the reverse side.

Rupa, *ka, n.* silver.

Rupatylli, *u, n.* the collar bone ; a silver necklace.

Rusni, *ka, n.* firework.

*Ruti, *u, n.* a loaf.

---

* Hindi.

Rwa, *v.* to be diminished ; to become less (in quantity).

Rwái, *v.* to sing. [*Imit.* rwái-siaw.]

Rwái-myllung, *v.* to sing a pathetic song.

Rwat, *v.* to be on the lookout ; to explore ;—*ka, n.* a trace (road).

Rwing, (wan-, leit-), *v.* to go and return the same day.

Rwiang, *ka, n.* luck. [*Imit.* ka bok-ka rwiang.]

Rwieng, *u, n.* the intestines of a bird.

Ryben, *a.* thick (same as *rben*).

Rykhiang, *a.* dry (same as *rkhiang*).

Rykhie, *v.* to laugh (same as *rkhie*).

Rynga (*see* "rnga"). ?

Ryngkang, *v.* to jump, to pass over ; to trespass, to ford. [*Imit.* ryngkang-ryngkoh.]

Ryngkap, *ka, n.* a quiver.—*ad.* with child on the back.

Ryngkat, *ad.* along with, together ;—*a.* equal.

Ryngkew *ka, n.* dry land (as opposed to water).

Ryngkew-u-Basa *u, n.* a village patron God.

Ryngngi, *ka, n.* the sunny side of a place, (the opposite of *dymmiew*).

Ryngkhái (ot), *ad.* closely, too near (cut), [as, "wat ot *ryngkhái* eh ia u dieng."]

Ryngkhat, *ad.* accidentally, by chance, [as, "nga shu iashem *ryngkhat* ia u."]

Ryngkhi, (bud-), *ad.* following very closely (of children's ages); —*ka, n,* the back (of a knife or sword).

Ryngkhiang, *a.* dry, parched.

Ryngkúh, *ad.* bending, but tall and big.

Rynghang, *ad.* widely open, ajar, (as, "wat ieh *rynghang* ia ka iing").

Ryngiew (*see* "rngiew").

Ryngmang-ryngmang, *ad.* quite unexpectedly, (as, "ei ba'n leit lah kren *ryngmang-ryngmang* ha u paitbah?")

Ryngwiang, *u, n.* a fishing rod; a small leafless bamboo.

Rymbái, *u, n.* a Khasi bean.

Rymbái-ktung, *u, n.* (*Bot. glycine soja*), a species of bean.

Rymbái-ja, *u, n.* (*Bot. Phaseolus calcaratus*), a species of bean.

Rymbáiñ (shri-), *ad.* with a wrinkled face.

Rymmòiñ, } *ad.* beautifully (smiling) [as, "ka jingwiat sam-
Rymmùiñ, } rkhie jong u kaba i-tynnad *rymmuiñ.*"]

Rymphang, *u*, *n.* February.

Rymphài (noh-), *ad.* like flowing hair, [as, "u shñiuh u noh *rymphài.*"]

Ryndang, *ka* or *u*, *n.* neck ; voice. [*Imit.* u ryndang-u tang ngúid.]

Ryndang-kjat, *ka*, *n.* the ankle.

Ryndang-kti, *ka*, *n.* the wrist.

Ryn-ieng, *ka*, *n.* stature. [*Imit.* ryn-ieng-ryn-iot.]

Ryndia-tlem, *ka*, *n.* *eri* silk cloth.

Rynjaiñ, *ad.* as if many things are adhering or clinging, [as, "nga'm lah ba'n leit kái ba bún ki kam *rynjaiñ.*"]

Rynjap (noh-), *ad.* with breasts hanging down, [as, "ka sniang kaba don khún ka raikhoh *rynjap.*"]

Rynñiaw, *n.* a black bird with a long tail which imitates the cries of other birds.

Rynsán, *ka*, *n.* a raised platform, a gallery.

Ryshám-kñia (*see* "rsham").

Rynsi, *u*, *n.* ground rice or maize mixed with molasses and rolled like a ball.

Rynsied, *v.* to jump, to caper, to spring upon.

Rynsong, *ka*, *n.* a kind of flute made of bamboo.

Rynsun, *u*, *n.* garlic.

Ryntan, *ad.* holding tight to the clothes (as a child does to its mother's).

Ryntih, *ad.* together, unanimously, in order.

Ryntieh, *ka*, *n.* a bow.

Ryta *see* ("rta").

S.

S—The 17th letter in the Khasi Alphabet.

Sa= (1) a prefix which means to contract a disease ; to be affected with, as, *sa*-prum, to be affected with sore ; other intances are, *sa*-mattah, *sa*-khñiang, etc.

(2) a suffix which means peevishly ; sulkily ; as, in leh*sa*, kren*sa*, etc.

(3) it is the sign of future tense, denoting contingency, as, "nga'n *sa* leit ynda lah bam ja."

(4) it is used as an *adverb* with verbs in the past tense, as, "ynda kumta u *sa* leit noh."

(5) In the absence of any other better alternative, as "nga shu pdiang katba u ai namar ba ngam ioh *sa*."

*Sáb, *a.* cleanly. [*Imit.* sáb-suba.]

Sabiah, *adv.* at all;—*n.* *u sabiah,* rice cropped during the rainy season.

Sabñiup, *ad.* hairy, bushy [as, "u shñiuh ka dngiem u heh *sabñuip.*"]

†Sabon, *ka, n.* soap.

Sabuit, *v.* to corrupt a thing by enchantment or witchery, (applicable to eatable things only); to have "an evil eye." [*Imit.* sabuit-sakâi.]

Sabut, *ka, n.* proof, clue.

Sak, *ad,* straightway, straight ahead (as, "ka lynti ka beit *sak* naugne haduh iing").

Sakár, *ad.* not closely, apart from one another (as, "ieng *sakár* wat ia ieng syndah eh").

Sa-ka-sâid, } (lait-), *ad.* very narrowly (escaped), [as, "*sa-i-sâid*
Sa-i-sâid, } ba u máw ba kawang u briew u'n dei ia nga."]

Sakhap, *a.* lean and stunted.

*Sakhi, *n.* witness ; evidence. [*Imit.* sakhi-satar.]

Sakhúh, *v.* to knock the head against, to butt.

Sakhóit, *u, n.* itch caused by a parasite.

Sakhrái, *v.* to feel tired or stiff.

Sak'iah, *ka, n.* hiccough, same as *sakyiah.*

Sakma, *v.* to go astray.

†Sakor, *ka, n.* wet sugar, unrefined sugar.

Sak-sak (iaid-), *ad.* straight on (walk), precariously (ill), (*ot-*) without any consideration or mercy.

Sakthe, } *ad.* reaching down to the knee like a clergyman's coat.
Sakthu, }

Saktiaw, *ad.* like a poor little girl, [as, "ine i khynnah i leh *saktiaw* ialade, balei?"]

---

* Hindi. | † Bengali.

Saktup, *ad.* like a bull frog, [as, "nga ioh-i ia ka hynroh kaba heh *saktup*."]

Sakuda, *ka, n.* a notch or corn; hard swelling.

Sakudóm-rai-eh, *i, n.* a thick-set fellow.

Sakùi, *ad.* covered with long hair all over like a bear.

Sád, *ka, n,* a ceiling; the goddess who takes care of the Siem's clan, —*v.* to comb;—*iingsád*, the house where the Siem performs his poojah, *i.e.*, the house of the S'iem's youngest sister or niece. [*Imit.* ka sâd-ka sunon.]

*Sada, *a.* blank, plain.

Sadai, *ka, n.* earnest money.

Sadhái, *ad.* at pleasure, at random, (as, iaid *sadhái*).

Sadóm, *v.* to drag or beat.

Sador, *ka, n.* tin.

Sang, *a.* incestuous, sacrilegious, forbidden; taboo;—*n. sangia* and *sangkla* are certain religious observances of the Wár people. [*Imit.* ka sang-ka ma.]

S'ang, *v.* to roast, to toast, same as *syang*.

Sangam, *ka, n.* the part of the jungle thick with trees and wet. [*Imit.* ka sangam-ka sajah.]

Sangeh, *v.* to pause, to stop.

Sangem, *ad.* inwardly, secretly (as, "ka met baroh shirynñeng ka shu pang *sangem*").

Sangoh, *v.* to butt (the head).

Sangot, *u, n.* a town crier, a village policeman or petty official.

Sangrang, *ad.* dear, (as, "kane ka jain ka la rem *sangrang* eh");—*a.* hard, unrelenting.

Sangsot, *a.* forbidden, piteous, [as, "kaba sngew*sangsot* ba'n lehbeiñ ia kiba pli ki khunswet."]

Sah, *v.* to remain, to lag or stay (behind); to elbow, to strike, to ram; (*suffix*) over and over the same thing, continually, [as, leh*sah*, shong*sah*, thiah*sah*, ieng*sah*.]

Sahám, *v.* to yawn; to warn, to hint at.

Sahkut, *v.* to be confined or kept in a place.

Sah-daiñmur, *ka, n.* a form of punishment in the Khasi Penal Code by which a criminal is confined for life

*Saheb, *u, n.* a European. [*Imit.* u saheb-u suba.]

---

* Hindi.

Sahiaw, *u*, *n*. asthma ; a bronchial wheezing sound.

Sahit, *ka*, *n*. firmament, sky.

Sah-jit, *v*. to remain unnoticed or rejected by all.

Sah-nang-ang, *v*. to be known as a tell-tale. [*Imit*. sahnang ang. sahnanghâp.]

Sah-pûd, *v*. to be omitted.

Sah-teng, *kaba*, *n*. what still remains to be done or completed.

Sah'ti, } *ka*, *n*. a ring.
Sati, }

Sahuh, (leh-), *ad*. lavishly, prodigally.

'sái, (*abbrev*. of *ksái*), *u*, *n*. thread.

'sái-kait, *u*, *n*. a fibre of a plantain tree.

'sáikhúm, *u*, *n*. a rope for binding a criminal. [*Imit*. sáikhúm saiteh] ; bonds.

†'sáikun, *u*, *n*. a rope attached to a boat for drawing it along shallow water.

'sáid, } *v*. to plead, to argue.
'sáit, }

S'áid, *a*. warm, same as *syáid*.

Sáid-ksan, *v*. to hold on in argument in spite of failure with a view to carry the point.

S'aid-ding, *v*. to warm near the fire.

Sáid-lah, *v*. to keep on arguing in spite of failure ; obstinately stupid.

Sáid-lwet, *v*. to gossip.

S'aid-sngi, *v*. to bask in the sun. Same as *syaid-sngi*.

Sáid-thma, *v*. (*originally* to debate) ; to deliver a speech in a Khasi Darbar ; to babble, [*Imit*. sáidthma-sáidktien.]

'sáihon, *u*, *n*. sun-hemp.

'sáilung, *ka*, *n*. a jhumed piece of land recently allowed to run waste.

'sáilum, *u*, *n*. a raw cotton thread.

'sáimuka, *u*, *n*. a *muga* silk-thread.

Saiñ, *v*. to melt, to smelt.

Sâiñ, *v*. to burn a part of grass so as to clear a fire-line ; to please.

'sái-nalia, *u*, *n*. jute ; *riha* (Assamese).

'sái-nàr, *u*, *n*. a wire ; telegraph wire.

---

† Hindi.

Sáiñ-lung, *ka, n.* a place that has been recently reserved for the growth of trees.

'sáipâd, *ka, n.* a finer kind of *muga* cloth.

'sáipan, *u, n.* a long purse worn round the waist; a waist-thread.

'sáiphareng, *u, n.* rolled English cotton-thread.

'sáiphla, *u* or *ka, n.* a witness; a third person to whom the case is referred for confirmation.

'sái-ryndia, *u, n. eri*-silk thread.

'sái-s'iang, *u, n.* a fiddle-string having the highest pitch.

'sái-siej, *u, n.* a bow string.

'sáispur, *u, n.* cottonyarn.

'sái-steiñ, *u, n.* a thread obtained from a fibrous plant called *Villebrunia integrifolia.*

Sàit, *v.* to wash.

Saitmet (used with *sngew*—, *i*—), *a.* offensive.

'sái-tár, *u, n.* a telegraph-wire.

'sái-tluh, *u, n.* a very tough fibre obtained from the bark of a tree called "ka tluh."

'sái-tylláі, *u, n.* a rope.

'sái-woh, *u, n.* a skein.

'‡sâi-wul, *u, n.* wool.

*Saja, *ka, n.* punishment,—*v.* to punish.

Sala, *ka, n.* cotton cloth.

Salia, *a.* disgusted, tired of, bothered. [*Imit.* salia-saláit.]

Salit, *ad.* not in the body but from the side, (as, "u kuli u shu dei *salit* nadong u maw"),—*ka, n.* chip. [*Imit.* salit-samong.]

Salu, *ka, n.* a red cotton cloth.

Sâm, *v.* to divide, to share.

Sàm, *v.* to bore, to pierce; (*prefix*) to feel inclined, to feel a desire (as, in *sàm*-thiah, *sàm*-khyndew).

S'am, *v.* to be peevish, to be sulky (same as *syam*).

Sameh-blang, *ka, n.* a kind of shrub having tough bark and milky juice.

Samep, *a.* woolly, thick with hair, [as, "u ñiuhtmoh jong u uba *samep.*"]

Samla, *n.* a youth. [*Imit.* samla-samhoi.]

---

* Hindi. | ‡ English.

Sammut, *a.* funny, fanciful, exciting mirth (as, "phi khie *sammut* aiu ? u wan leh *sammut.*")

Samoi, *ka, n.* season, time.

Samparat, *ka, n.* a kind of palm-tree with plicated leaves which generally grows on precipices.

Sàmsàm, *ad,* bitter (cold), [as, " ka um ka la daitthah *sàmsàm.*"]

Samsia, *a.* terrible-looking.

Samtari, *u, n.* a sentinel.

Samtawi (shád-), *v.* to have giddiness.

Samúh, *ad.* with a long beard, [as, "u dkhar uba jrong u ñiuhtmoh *samuh.*"]

San, *n.* five ;—*v.* to grow up.

Sanad, *ka, n.* a sanad or appointment letter (same as *sunod*).

Santér, *v.* to grow up prematurely (of person).

Sani, *v.* to remand a case for retrial.

Sañium, *ka, n.* a place overgrown with grass.

Sañiur, *a.* like a heap of tall grass, [as, " balei phi iehnoh *sañiur* la ka kper."]

Sap, *ka, n.* inherent quality, instinct ; alloy ; genius ;—*bamsap,* to take bribes.

Sapa, *a.* enough, sufficient (generally used with *ym,* as, " phi ai khyndiat eh ym sngew *sapa* ei ei ").

Saphriang, *v.* to spread, to extend.

Saphret, *a.* scattered ;—*ki, n.* crumbs. [*Imit.* saphret-saphrong.]

Sapiet, *ka, n.* a splinter, a chip. [*Imit.* ka sapiet ka sapâi.]

Sapoh, *ka, n.* rice mixed with yeast and fermented for making liquor, a malt.

Sapra, *v.* to scatter.

Sâr, *v.* to sweep ;—*ka, n.* serge, a Kashmiri chadar.

Sara, *v.* to raise seedlings for transplantation.

Sarang, *v.* to become rusty ;—*ka, n.* rust.

Saraw, *ka, n.* an earthen saucer or plate.

Sarew (prúm), *ka, n.* scab of a sore, scales.

Saro, *ka, n.* a bird of the starling family.

Sarong, *a.* proud ;—*ka, n.* a kind of violin.

Sat, *a.* hot, acrid, pungent ;—*ad.* sorely ;—*ka, n.* trouble, calamity. [*Imit.* ka sat-ka jew.]

S'at, *a.* addicted to, much given to. Same as *syat.*

Satap, *ka, n.* space between strata of rocks; a crevice.

Satar, *a.* tough; *ka doh satar-, n.* tough flesh.

Sat-byrsia, *a.* pungent, acrid.

Sa-tdam, *ad.* short and stout, [as, "I D i long i briew iba lyngkot *sa-tdam.*"]

Satep, *ka, n.* thatch at the ridges of the roof of a house.

Sathê, *ad.* with a big and long coat, [as, "ki Bhutia ki phong ka sopti kaba heh *sathê.*"]

Sati, *ka, n.* a ring.

Satia, *ad.* at all; *sngew satia, v.* to feel annoyed at; *leh satia,* to annoy, to tease.

Sati-synjat, *ka, n.* a wedding ring.

Sati-yngkúid, *ka, n.* a magic ring in Khasi folklore, supposed to have the same virtue as the "Wonderful Lamp" of the Arabian Nights.

Satlak, *ad.* all over (as, "*satlak* ka pyrthei ki kmie ki ieit ia la ki khún").

Satlip, *ad.* with swollen eyelids.

Sator, *a.* weak, unsteady. [*Imit.* sator-sajap.]

Sat-syllang, *a.* very hot or painful.

Satrew, *ka, n.* sore caused by itch.

Sáw, *a.* four; red.

S'áw, Syaw, } *v.* to put near the fire, to expose to the action of smoke.

Sawa, *v.* to sound, to echo.

Sawang, *a.* light; portentous.

Sawar, *u, n.* a plummet.

Sáw-ka-sian, *ka, phr.* excitement; heat of passion.

Sawdong, *a.* four-cornered;—*ad.* all-round.—*ka, n.* a square.

Sawiah-bsein, *u, n.* a species of wild arum very common in the Khasi and Jaintia Hills.

Sawlia, *a.* very tender and reddish.

Sáwphew, *a.* forty.

Sawrang, *a.* red (sunburnt).

Sawreng, *a.* brown (as if from smoke).

Sawriang, *a.* red (like the dawn).

Sawriej, } *a.* bloodshot.
Sawtriej, }

Sàw-sàw-mynsiem, *a.* hot-tempered, irritable.

Sáwsyng-iang, *a.* bright red, crimson.

Sawtriang, *a.* red (as from anger).

Sbak, *ad.* with a thud (falling).

Sbâi, *u, n.* a cowry ; shell ; money.

Sbiak, } *ad.* exactly (fit), [as, " ka jingtap ka biang bha *sbiak*
Sbok, } ha u suspon."]

Sboh, *ka, n.* manure ;—*a,* thick (as rice-water),—*lèh sboh,* to pretend to be kind.

Sbu, *u, n.* a plant yielding a black colour used in dyeing cloths (*Bot. Strobilanthes flacidifolius*).

Sbuh, *v.* to affect to be kind.

Sbun, *a.* kind, good-hearted, generous.

Sbur, *a.* rich (soil).

Skak, *ad.* tightly (fasten), [as, " ki nonglute ki la syrwiah *skak* ia u trái-iing na ka ryndang."]

Skah, *a.* thick, adhesive (said of boiled rice or lime mortar).

Skâi, *v.* to corrupt food out of envy by *mantras* ;– *ka, a.* an evil spirit who causes flatulence.

Skáiñ, *u, n.* a fly ; *kaba kynjoh khaskáiñ,* housewarming.

Skap, *u, n.* husk.

Skáw, *u, n.* a small bottle-gourd for holding liquor or water, especially at the time of pujah.

Skei, *n.* a barking red deer, a muntjac.

Skhak, *ad.* tightly (bind) (as, " teh ha ba'n da skhem *skhak*").

Skhem, *a.* firm ;—*ad.* firmly, securely.

Skhep, *ka, n.* the hip.

Skit, *ka, n.* kinds, sorts.

Skong, *u, n.* a species of large bamboo.

Skop, *u, n.* the cover, husk.

Skop-khñiang, *u, n.* the cocoon.

Skùiñ, *v.* to itch ; to desire strongly.

Skum, *u, n.* a nest, a heap of grass, a butt ; the core of a boil.

Skul, *ka, n.* a school ; a chapel.

Skút, *v.* to trace a line round a plot of land; to mark out.

Sdád um, *ka, n.* the junction of rivers.

Sdang, *v.* to commence, to begin.

Sden, *v.* to dam a stream.

Sdér, *u. n.* long grass used in thatching.

Sdiah, *v.* to squeeze or press with the thumb-nail, as one would do a flea.

Sdie, *u, n.* an axe.

Sdieh, *v.* to fry.

Sdien, *v.* to hang, to suspend.

Sdot, *v.* to dwindle, to be reduced in strength, to pine away.

Sdung, *a.* good-sized (fish).

Seng, *v.* to lay as a foundation;—*ka, n.* an organization; a community; meeting of a family or clan.

Sẹngkhún, *v.* to be pregnant.

'seh, (*abbrev.* of kseh), *u, n.* pine-wood.

Seh,—a word used to complete a statement or to soften an expression; as, "kam long kumta mo *seh* ? ai *seh* kato ka tari."

'seh-blei, *ka, n.* (*Bot. Taxus baccata*), a species of tree.

'seh-khleiñ, *u, n.* a resinous pine-wood.

Sei, *v.* to produce; to pull out; to bring forth.

Sei lapeh, *a.* to have plenty of leaves, but without grain or fruit.

Sei-lung, *v.* to sprout, to shoot forth.

'seiñ (*abbrev.* of *bseiñ*), *u, n.* a snake; *-iong*, a cobra [*-her*, *-tyrnem*, *-thli*, *-tameh*, *-tyrsia*, *-star*, etc., are names of different kinds of snakes.]

Seisoh, *a.* productive, fruitful.

Sem, *ka, n.* a shed, a pen;—*v.* to wear a cloth (apron) called "ka *jaiñsem*."

Sep, *v.* to go down (sun), to set;—*a.* having no grain inside a pod.

S'ep, *n.* perspiration, sweat, same as *syep*.

Sep'ngi, *ka, n.* the west.

Sér, *ka, n.* a seer=80 tolas.

Set, *v.* to shut, to confine, to close.

'sew (*abbrev.* of ksew), *n.* a dog.

'sew-bna-lat, *u, n.* (*phrase*) one who attends at every entertainment held in the village, whether invited or not.

Sngâid, *a.* fat, plump.

Sngâid-diengthang, *a.* very fat (applicable to a baby; the belief is that when a baby is unusually fat, it is likely to die).

Sngap, *v.* to listen, to hear.

Sngâp, *ka, n.* a gill, a barb.

Sngàr, *ad.* severely, very, [as, "u la thâp *sngàr* ia u nà ka ngâp."]

Sngem, *a.* moist, wet.

Sngew, } *v.* to feel, to hear.
Sngow, }

Sngewbha *v.* to be pleased. [*Imit.* sngewbha-sngewmiat.]

Sngewbieij, *v.* to feel awkward, to feel out of sorts. [*Imit.* sngewbieit-sngew anna.]

Sngewblâw, *v.* to feel lonely.

Sngewbynriew, *v.* to feel better.

Sngewkmen, *v.* to be joyful.

Sngew-diaw, *v.* to have a melancholy temperament, to be low spirited.

Sngewngiew, *v.* to have a presentiment.

Sngewngûh, *v.* to be thankful, to be grateful.

Sngewhun, *v.* to be satisfied, to be contented.

Sngewjlep, *v.* to feel faint.

Sngewjli, *v.* to have nausea, to be sick.

Sngewjuh, *v.* to feel quite at home, to be tamed.

Sngewlem, *v.* to have sympathy for.

Sngewmyllen, *v.* to be absorbed in, to divert one's attention.

Sngewmyllung, *v.* to be pathetic.

Sngew-ñiun, *v.* to be unwell, to be out of sorts.

Sngewpeitmat, *v.* to feel better; to be wakeful.

Sngewsaitmet, *v.* to feel disgusted.

Sngewsih, *v.* to feel sorry for, to grieve. [*Imit.* sngewsih-sngew diaw.]

Sngewsyn-ei, *v.* to have pity for.

Sngewtngieng, *v.* to be squeamish.

Sngewthuh, *v.* to understand. [*Imit.* sngewthuh-sngewthâw.]

Sngop, *a*. growing between high trees so as to be entirely overshadowed by them.

Sngi, *ka*, *n*. sun ; day.

Sngi-Balang, *ka*, *n*. Wednesday ; a day when the Church meeting is held.

Sngi-palci, *ka*, *n*. Thursday.

Sngi-poh-ia, *ka*, *n*. week-day.

Sngi-saitjáiñ, *ka*, *n*. Saturday.

Sngi-thohdieng, *ka*, *n*. Friday.

Sngi-u-Blei, *ka*, *n*. Sunday (among the Christians only). See "*Rubibar*."

Sngúr, *a*. clear, transparent.

Sha, *prep*. to, towards ;—*u*, *n*. tea.

'sha ? (*abbrev*. of *shisha*)=really ? is it so ?

Shaba, *u*, *n*. chewed mixture of *pan* and betelnut ; the red layers and flesh inside the gill of fish.

Shaba kurat, *u*, *n*. sawdust.

Shabeiñ, *ad*. big and distorted (mouth) ; [as, "ki Negro ki don ka shyntur kaba heh *shabeiñ*."]

Shabár, *ad*. outside, externally.

Shabi, *u*, *n*. a key.

Shak (mar-), *a*. exactly equal ;—*n*. a bundle of dried fish.

Shakhàit, *v*. to handle or deal severely ; to gnaw.

Shakhat, *ka*, *n*. a small bird.

Shakiar, *ka*, *n*. the side of a house, the eaves. [*Imit*. ka shakiar-sharah.]

*Shakri, *u*. a servant. [*Imit*. shakri-shakor.]

Shaku, *ka*, *n*. a knife.

Shakuriaw, *ka*, *n*. a jingling small bell ; a tinkling *cymbal*.

Shakyntir, *ka*, *n*. a small bird of mouldy colour.

Shád, *v*. to dance. [*Imit*. shád-kmen.]

Shád-khalek, *v*. to dance round a group of girls dancing (by men only).

Shadem, *ka*, *n*. the chest ; the breast. [*Imit*. ka shadem-sharúh.]

Shadien, *ad*. behind.

* Hindi.

Shád-mastieh, *ka. n.* a sword-dance.

Shád-nohkjat, *ka, n.* a dance performed by the members of the family who organise the occasion before the general dance.

Shado, } *a.* old.
Shadod, }

*Shador, *ka, n.* a *chadar*; a thin white cotton *chadar*.

Shado-ki-shadia, *ki, n.* old persons.

*Shád-sawangki, *v.* to dance like *nautch* girls.

Shad-sohtyngkér, *v.* to dance round and round by joining hands together.

Shadúh, *ad.* up to, as far as.

Shang, *ka, n.* a basket;—*v.* to roam, to associate with.

Shah, *v.* to suffer, to endure, to permit; to side with; to be due from.

Sh'ah, *ka, n.* a cactus, same as *shyah.*

Shahksew, *ka, n.* a sill.

Shahaw, *ad.* having defective teeth (as, " ka tymmen kaba la lop bniat *shahaw*").

Shah-jing-it, *v.* to fast.

Shahshkór, *v.* to listen, to be attentive.

Shâi, *v.* to become clear, to become light.

Shaia, *ad.* late at night (as, wat iaid *shaia*).

Shái-byrngut, *v.* to become twilight.

Shaiñ, *v.* to chop.

Shaiong, *v.* to become dizzy, to be puzzled, to be dazed.

Shait, *v.* to be active, to be healthy; to be accustomed to; to be impudent.

Shaitmet, *v.* to become healthy or strong.

Shala, *a.* twisted, warped (said of a plank);—*n.* the inhabitant of Shella-poonjee.

*Shalak, *a.* clever active, tactful.

*Shalai, *v.* to manage.

*Shalami, *a.* inclined, sloping.

*Shalan, *v.* to export; to send up.

*Shalani, *ka, n.* a small round winnowing-basket; a sieve.

---

* Hindi.

Shaláp, *ka*, *n.* a chip, a small piece of wood split out of a big one. Same as *Thálàp.*

Shalór, *ad.* upwards.

Shaltóiñ, Shaltúiñ, } *a.* long and thick, oviform.

Shalyngka, *u*, *n.* a lever, a jumper.

Shalyng-or, *i*, *n.* a spinning top.

Shalyng-ur, *u*, *n.* a kind of wasp.

Shalymmén, *ka*, *n.* a small insect which chirps ; a cymbal.

Shalynnâi, *ka*, *n.* a small fish common in hill streams.

Shalyntem, *ka*, *n.* a wheel.

Shám-shám, *a.* very precipitous, [as, " ki pynnoh ia u 'men Langñiuh na ka riat kaba *shám-shám.*"]

Shamok, *v.* to produce fire from a flint, to strike (fire).

*Shamoit, *ka*, *n.* a small spoon.

Shán, *v.* to support, to prop, hold on.

*Shana, *u*, *n.* gram.

Shanam, *ka*, *n.* a small metal lime-case.

Shán-khung, *u*, *n.* rafter.

Shán-'dang, *u*, *n.* a gold or silver necklace.

Shánduh, *v.* to take or use a walking-stick.

Shanduwa, *ka*, *n.* a high canopy made of cloth placed above the funeral pyre; (a *shamianah*).

Shanc, *ad.* hither, this side.

Shaneng, *ad.* upwards; northward;—*n.* north.

Shaniah, *v.* to trust, to lean on, to confide in. [*Imit.* shaniah-shakhien.]

Shán-mohor, *ka*, *n.* an obsolete silver coin of the Jaintia Rajas.

Shano? *ad.* where?

Shano-shano, *ad.* anywhere, wherever.

Shano-re-shano, *ad.* somewhere.

Shán'ti, *v.* to support or rest on the hand.

Sháp, *ka*, *n.* a seal, an impression. [*Imit.* ka sháp-ka mohor.]—*v.* to impress.

---

* Hindi.

Shaphang, *prep.* towards, in the direction of; with reference to.

Shaphrang, *ad.* forward, to the front.

*Shaphrat, *ka, n.* a piece of iron or copper-plate worn by servants as a badge, a *chaprass.*

Shapia, *v.* to press, to sqeeze.

Shapoh, *ad.* inside, inwardly, internally.

Shapuloit, *ka, n.* a lark.

*Sha-pushi, *u, n.* a tea-pot.

Shár, *v.* to choke;—*ka, n.* a funnel.

Shara, *u, n.* small shot.

*Sharak, *ka, n.* a lamp.

Sharâi, *v.* to watch, to guard, to tend.

Sharâj, *ka, n.* an insect of a greenish colour sometimes used as a bait for fish; a kind of insect cocoon found among grass.

Sharati, *ka, n.* a flute used on funeral occasions.

Sharé, *ad.* dim-eyed ; squinting.

Sharing, *ka, n.* a slope, a declivity.

Sharúd, *ad.* outside, out o. the way;—*leit rud,* to answer a call of nature. [*Imit.* sharúd-shariang; sharúd-shakiar.]

Sharum, *ad.* downwards, southward—*n.* south.

Sharyntoh, *ka, n.* a mantis.

Shat, *v.* to throw, to cast.

Shata, *ad.* there (out of sight);—*ka, n.* an umbrella.

Shata-batabak, *ka, n.* a circular leaf umbrella with a bamboo-handle.

Shat-khmat, *v.* to cast one's eyes upon, to have a fancy for.

Shatei, *ad.* up there, northward;—*n.* north.

Shathie, *ad.* down there, southward;—*n.* south.

Shato, *ad.* towards that known direction, there.

Shaton, *ka, n.* a cap made of plaited cane and leaf for protection against the heat of the sun.

Shatri-jaiñ, *ka, n.* a cloth-umbrella.

Sháw, *v.* to fetch, to meet on the way.

*Shawkád, *ka, n.* a lintel, a frame of doors and windows.

Shawei, *ad.* to some other quarters, elsewhere.

---

* Hindi.

Shawei-sha-ár, *ad.* somewhere else.

Shawei-shawei, *ad,* towards some other parts, elsewhere.

Shawrod, *ka, n.* a plinth.

Shka, *ka, n.* a junction of rivers. See *ka sdád.*

Shkàit, *ad.* well (dressed) [as, "u riam saheb pyrton *shkàit* ha ka Dorbar."]

Shkáw, *n.* a husband or wife (Synteng).

Shken, *u, n.* a small species of bamboo.

Shkiah, *v.* to throttle, to press on the throat.

Shkór, *ka, n.* ear.

Shdài, Shdéi, } (rkhie-), *ad.* by showing the teeth; to grin; [as, "Haba nga kylli ia u, u rkhie pynban *shdài.*"]

Shéng-shéng, (jrong-), *ad.* very high (precipice); [as, "ka riat kaba jrong *shéng-shéng.*"]

Shem, *v.* to find, to meet, to discover.

Shem-duk, *v.* to be in trouble; to suffer calamity.

Shem-pap, *v.* to be visited with calamity.

Shemphang, *v.* to understand, to be clever. [*Imit.* shemphang-shemlád.]

Shemsang, *v.* to come across an evil omen; to come across a very rare thing. [*Imit.* shemsang-shem-má.]

Shem-sat. *v.* to meet with trouble or calamity. [*Imit.* shemsat-shemjew.]

Shen-shen, *ad.* soon, presently;—*ad.* staggering.

Shep, (i-), *v.* to suit, to fit.

Shep-da (ym-), *phr.* denoting improbability, would not; [as, "la u ialeh ruh u'm *shep-da* lah."]

Sheptieng, *v.* to be afraid of, to fear.

Shér, *v.* to plant in, to ram;—*u, n.* a small fish in the hill streams called by that name.

Shêrkhang, *v.* to plant sticks crosswise in the way so as to obstruct it; to set a barrier.

Shet, *v.* to cook, to boil; to deceive; to plot, to conspire.

Shet-kylla, *v.* to prepare a spiced curry; to deal treacherously.

Shet-jakái, *v.* to make a sham cooking as children do.

Shet-thái, *v.* to parboil.

Shet-ka-um-ka-ding, *phr.* to cook plainly (*i.e.*, with water, salt, and chillies).

Shngáiñ, *v.* to feel safe, to feel quite at home.

Shngiam, *a.* very tasty or palatable.

Shi-=*prefix*, which means *one*.

Shi! *int.* fie!

Shiah, *u, n.* a thistle, a thorn.

Shiah-búit, *u, n.* a briar.

Sh'iap, *u, n.* sand. Same as *shyiap.*

Shibhár, *n.* a number containing 32 fruits (at Cherra) (used in selling oranges.)

Shibit, *ad,* in a short time;—*a.* lasting for a short time. [*Imit.* shibit-arbit.]—*la shibit*, after a short time.

Shibriew, *ka, n.* one share, one vote.

Shibún, *a.* much, many;—*ad.* very much.

Shibyllai, *ad.* in large quantity or number, [as, "u la lum lpa ka dieng *shibyllai.*"]

Shibyllien, *ad.* in large number (of persons walking); [as, "nga ioh-i *shibyllien* u briew u leit sha iing Kashari."]

Shibynta, *ka, n.* one portion.

Shi-kaddei, *ad.* very much; [as, "nga sngewbha *shikaddei* ba phi la jop ha ka Eksamin."]—exceedingly.

*Shikár, *a.* profligate, licentious.

Shi-katta, *ad.* all the while.

Shikáw, *n.* a number containing 1280 or 16 *pens* (used with ties, cowries, and chillies).

Shikham, *ka, n.* a handful.

Shikha-shi-man, (iadei-), *n.* to be related by marriage.

Shikhem, *ka, n.* a ball of rice or earth, as much as could be grasped between the fingers and palm of the hand.

*Shikhep, *ka, n.* one occasion.

Shikhmat, *ka, n.* life-time.

Shikhrum-ka-bneng, *phr.* the whole world, the whole lot.

Shikhub, *ka, n.* a measurement equal to the breadth of four fingers.

†Shikia, *ka, n.* a circular frame of cane or bamboo-tie suspended for putting in or carrying things.

---

* Hindi. † Bengali.

Shiklah, *ka*, *n*. an arm's length.

Shiktien, *ka*, *n*. a mouthful.

Shi-kur, *ka*, *n*. one clan. [*Imit.* shikur-shikmie.]

Shi-kuri, *ka*, *n*. a number containing 20, a score.

Shi-kuro, *ka*, *n*. a faction.

Shikyntien, *ka*, *n*. a morsel; a single word.

Shida, *a*. innocent, simple, unsophisticated.

Shi-dana, *ka* *n*. a bit, a little quantity.

Shi-dur, *a*. of the same form or shape; peculiar.

Shi-rukom, *a*. *sui generis*, peculiar.

Sh'ing, *ka*, *n*. a bone. [*Imit.* ka sh'ing-ka shruh.]—a cowrie a pice (when used after cardinal numbers);—*u*, *n*. a seed. Same as *shyieng*.

Sh'ing-búdlúm, *u*, *n*. the spine.

Shi-hali, *ka*, *n*. a number containing four.

Shi-hara, *ka*, *n*. a set, a group of the same kind of things.

Shi-húd, *ka*, *n*. one portion;—*ad*. in one way; [as, "ki dak jong u ba u thoh ki shu i-tynnad *shihúd*."]

Shi-iing-shisem, *ka*, *n*. one family, one house.

Shi-jháp, *ka*, *n*. a number containing 16 (applicable only to the number of children born); a quiverful.

Shiliang, *a*. half, opposite, one side, (as in the words—*shiliang*-mamla, *shiliang*-shnong, *shiliang*-wah, etc.).

Shiliang-khmat, *ad*. partially, dishonestly.

Shiliang-shiliang, *n*. each side, each party.

Shilot, *ka*, *n*. Sylhet.

Shi-lngér, *ka*, *n*. one whole length;—*ad*. throughout the whole length; uninterruptedly; [as, "baroh *shilngér* ka jingim jong nga dap tang ka khuslai suda."]

Shi-lymbher, *ka*, *n*. one large heap.

Shi-lynter, *ka*, *n*. the whole length, one piece (cut off from a whole length).

Shim, *v*. to take, to receive.

Shim-bteng, *v*. to take the place of; to continue; to succeed to.

Shim-khyndew, *v*. to wane (said of the moon).

Shi-mat, *ka*, *n*. one joint, a portion between two joints.

Shi-met, *ad*. personally, [as, "u briew ialade hi *shimet* u lah ba'n ioh bám kumno kumno ruh.]"

Shimi, *ka, n.* a chemise.

Shim-shah, *v.* to buy a thing on credit. [*Imit.* shim-shah-shim sham.]

Shim-siew, *v.* to take a thing by paying its cost price.

Shi-mynsiem, *ad.* dearly, intimately, ["as, ki ia ieit *shi-mynsiem* bad u."]

Shin, (peit-), *ad.* scrutinously, searchingly, [as, "u briew hynne u *peit-shin* ia uwei u khynnah.]

*Shini, *ka, n.* sugar.

Shipa, *ka, n.* need, want, trouble. [*Imit.* shipa-shipi.]

Shipád, *ka, n.* a length as much as can be clasped or embraced with both outstretched arms.

Shipài, *u, n.* a sepoy, a soldier;—*pang-shipài*, influenza.

Shiphang, *ad.* for a short time, for the time being, [as, "phi sngewbha ba'n ap hangne *shiphang*."]

Shiphah, *ka, n.* a measure=1 spoonful of iron-ore=$\frac{1}{2}$ of a lump sold in the market.

Shi-piam, *ka, n.* a length—as much as can be passed round with both the arms; a clasp.

Shi-piam-star, *ka, n.* a length—as much as can be passed round with a head-strap or "*star*."

Shipung, *ka, n.* a length—from one joint to another.

Shir, *ka, n.* an open handful of things, as much as will fill up the hollow of a hand.

*Shira, *u, n.* parched rice.

Shir-wat,
Shyrwat, } *u, n.* a small black bird having a long forked-tail.

Shi-ryn-ieng, *ad.* from head to foot.

Shisien, *ad.* once, at one time.

Shish! *Interj.* fie!

Shisha, *a.* true, real,—*ad.* indeed, of course.

Shisyndon, *ad.* at once.

Shit, *a.* hot, warm, close. [*Imit.* ka shit-ka syang.]

Sh'it, *v.* to pinch, to nip. Same as *shyit*.

Shi-tda, *ka, n.* a length measured from the tip of the thumb to that of the middle finger when both are stretched out.

---

* Hindi.

Shit-dang, *v.* to feel very hot (applicable to persons only).

Shiteng, *a.* half—*n.* once. [*Imit.* shiteng-shiliang.]

Shiteng-ar-teng, *ka, n.* more than one occasion, often.

Shiteng-synñia, *kaba, n.* midnight. [*Imit.* shiteng-synñia shiteng-dummoh.]

*Shithi, *ka, n.* a letter, an epistle.

Shithoh, *ka, n.* a very small quantity, (*lit.* as much quantity as can be taken with the tip of the finger); [as, "ym don mlúh ha iing *shithoh* ruh."]

Shitir, *ad.* devotedly, much (given to), [as, "u khla ba u'n da lah ba'n ioh te *shitir* keiñ ia ka miaw,"]

Shit-lhep, } *v.* to be close (atmosphere); to become oppressively
Shit-lhop, } hot.

Shitom, *ka, n.* trouble, pain, difficulty. [*Imit.* shitom-shijot.]

†Shitor, (kha-), *ka, n.* a large flat fish.

Shit-rhem, *v.* to become glowingly hot, to become zealous or enthusiastic.

Shi-tyllup, *ad.* all over, [as, "baroh *shi-tyllup* ka pyrthei ki tip ba don u nongtháw ia ka pyrthei."]

Shiwait, *ka, n.* one sweep of the sword; one score or throwing of the dice in gambling.

Shiwat, *ad.* once, on one occasion,—*n.* a single string of a necklace or string.

Shla, *v.* to be angry, to be indignant.

Shlàn, *v.* to dare, to venture.

Shlán, *ka, n.* a plant whose leaves resemble those of a pineapple plant. (*Bot. Pandanus.*)

Shlei, *v.* to overflow.

Shleiñ-shleiñ, (nep-), *ad.* pointed, [as, "ki rah la ki dieng kiba nep *shleiñ-shleiñ*"];—*a.* forward; impudent.

Shlem, *ka, n.* a smelting-house, an iron-workshop.

Shler, (nep-), *ad.* very (long and pointed), [as, "u sûm uba nep *shler.*"]

*Shlim, *ka, n.* a small earthen cup fitted to a *hookah* for smoking (*Beng.* kholki).

Shlir, (nep-), *ad.* very (pointed), taperingly.

---

* Hindi. | † Bengali.

Shloiñ, (mih-), *ad.* prominently (appear); [as, "u prek u tam *shloiñ* shabar."]

Shlòr, *a.* brave, courageous, daring.

Shmoh, *u, n.* (*Bot.*) *Plectocomia*; a species of cane.

Shmoiñ, } (dap-), *ad.* up to the brim (full), [as, "wat theh eh ka
Smoiñ, } um ha ba'n da dap *shmoiñ.*"]

Shmuiñ, *ad.* visibly (appear), [as, "ki reng ki la páw *shmuiñ.*"]

Shna, *v.* to make, to construct, to build.

Shnat, *ka, n.* quarters, division of a country. [*Imit.* ka shnat-ka kuna.]

Shnet, *ka, n.* a fin.

Shniah, *u, n.* a mason's chisel;—*v.* to chisel out.

Shñiuh, *u, n.* hair, fur.

Shnong, *ka, n.* a village, a town. [*Imit.* ka shnong-ka tháw.]

Shong, *v.* to sit, to settle. [*Imit.* shong-sah.]

Shong-basa, *v.* to live as a lodger or stranger. [*Imit.* shong-basa-shongbasuiñ.]

Shongkái, *v.* to sit for pleasure or for gossip; to be on a visit. [*Imit.* shongkái-shong-iáid.]

Shong-kha, *v.* to marry. [*Imit.* shongkha-shongman.]

Shongksâw, *v.* to be lucky, to be experienced.

Shongksûid, *v.* to have evil spirits; to be possessed. [*Imit.* shong-ksúid-shongkhrei.]

Shongkulái, *v.* to ride a horse.

Shongkùn, *v.* to have a fascinating or dignified appearance.

Shongkur, *v.* to marry a member of the same clan, which is considered incestuous. [*Imit.* shongkur-shongsang.]

Shongkurim, *v.* to marry, [*Imit.* shongkurim-shongkupái.]

Shongkyllaiñ-mungor, *v.* to sit cross-legged, to sit like a native tailor.]

Shongkyrnái, *v.* to sit, (without moving) on the same place.

Shongkyrni, *v.* addicted to.

Shongkyrthái, *v.* to squat in the same place, to be firmly seated.

Shonkynrong, *v.* to sit on the heels, to squat.

Shong-dór, *v.* to be worth. [*Imit.* shong-dór-shongmur]; to sit with body bent.

Shong-dùr, *a.* becoming, proper.

Shong-lyng-ngeit, *v.* to sit with the whole weight of the body.

Shong-mangkariang, *a.* bad tempered, envious.

Shong-nia, *a.* reasonable, right.

Shong-niang-raitliang, *a.* having an envious spirit, (*lit.* to be affected with tapeworm).

Shong-ñiangrait-hoh, *a.* having an ill temper.

Shong-pér, *a.* to become light-minded, to be flippant.

Shongprah-shongshang, *ad.* to a very old age. [It is a custom among some of the Khasis to place very old people in a basket, hence the meaning of the word.]

Shong-rait-hoh, *a.* stingy, niggard.

Shongsang, *v.* to contract an incestuous marriage.

Shongsah, *v.* to sit in the same place, to remain permanently, to abide.

Shong-sngi, *v.* to be off one's work, to rest.

Shongshán, *v.* to have an unpleasant or sinister appearance.

Shong-shiliangkhmat, *a.* having second sight.

Shongsynrán, *v.* to act as a bride's man or bride's maid.

Shongsynri, *v.* to be visited with the sin of any one who acts treacherously against any member of his clan.

Shongsynrop, *v.* to sit close together.

Shong-thàp, *v.* to settle temporarily in any place and not as a citizen; to sojourn. [*Imit.* shongthàp-shongbiang.]

Shoh, *v.* to beat; [*Imit.* shoh-dat.]—*a.* pleasing, touching, affecting.

Shoh-dáp, *v.* to castrate (a bull).

Shoh-doh, *v.* to kill an animal for food. [*Imit.* shohdoh-shohkah.]

Shoh-dohkha, *v.* to poison fish. [*Imit.* shoh-dohkha-shohdohthli.]

Shoh-'niangkur, *v.* to sacrifice a pig and to summon all the members of the same clan to come together in one house to partake of it.

Shoh-noh, *v.* to commit murder for the propitiation of "*u Thlen.*" [*Imit.* shoh-noh-shoh-túh.]

Shoh-samthiah, *v.* to drowse.

Shoh-tháh, *ka, n.* a robin-red breast;—*a.* smitten with frost.

Shoh-tháw, *v.* to work in iron, to work as a blacksmith.

Shoh tyndep, *v.* to confound, to mislead, to bewitch.

Shohshkor, *ka*, *n*. an earring.

Shoiñ, *ad*. to the brim (full);—*i*, *n*. a very small bird.

Shon, *v*. to press, to impress, to print.

Shop, *v*. to thrust out, to oust; to thresh (rice, millet, etc.), to husk a second time.

Shrak, } (ieng-), *ad*. in order, in a row, [as, "ki shipai ki ieng
Shriak, } *shrak* ha kyrkit."]

Shrang, *a*. dry, parched (earth or weather).

Shrah, *ka*, *n*. arable land, fallow land.

Shrat, *v*. to clear off the scales of a fish by means of a *daw* or other sharp instrument.

Shreng, *u*, *n*. the fin on the back of a fish; the rind of a jackfruit or of such like-fruit; spine, prickle.

Shrei, *ad*. appearing in great numbers, as eggs or teeth, [as, "dap da ki pylleng ksi *shrei* ha ka khlieh jong u"; "u rkhie *shrei* ia nga kumba rkhie u bieij"];—abundantly.

Shrem, *ad*. many (standing prominently), [as, "u ong ba ki mih kynsan 5 ngut *shrem* ki nongshohnoh ha lynti."]

Shri, *v*. to show the teeth, to grin.

Shriak, (ieng-), *ad*. well (arranged), in order, [as, "u pynieng *shriak* ia ki pliang ki luta ha ka almari."]

Shrieh, *n*. a monkey, an ape.

Shriew, *ka*, *n*. an arum-root.

Shrip, *ka*, *n*. a basket put in the stream for catching fish.

Shrong, *ka*, *n*. a carved-margin, ornamental work. [*Imit*. ka shrong-ka shrub.]

Shroiñ, *a*. brittle.

Shrop, *ad*. all at once, (applicable to money—being a form of onomatopæa), [as, "u siew baroh 20 tyngka *shrop* na ka bynta ka ram ki briew."]

Shrut, *v*. to seize with the teeth; to gnaw,—*u*, *n*. a cigar.

Shtah, *v*. to dress a stone with a masons chisel or a piece of wood with an adze or *dao*. Same as *stah*.

Shu, *ad*. just, only;—*v*. (*Imper*.) to set a dog upon.

Shuki, *ka*, *n*. a chair.

Shukor, *v*. to deceive, to cheat,—*a*. treacherous.

Shúh, *ad*. again, further more;—*v*. (*Imper*.) get away, get aside; wait! (menacing), I will see you!

Shúhshuwa, *phr.* wait for the present.

Shuin, *v.* to touch, to come in contact with; to press upon.

Shúm! *Interj.* there you are!

Shún, *v.* to hate, to be inimical with. [*Imit.* shún-pen.]

*Shùn, *ka, n.* lime.

Shùn-kot, *ka, n.* catechu.

Shùn-kpu, *ka, n.* slaked lime.

Shùn-dewiong, *ka, n.* lime burnt with coal.

Shùn-dieng, *ka, n.* lime burnt with wood.

Shùn-máw, *ka, n.* unslaked lime, quick lime.

Shûn-thlongmlúh-thlongsying, *phr.* to cherish a bitter inimical spirit, to be at dagger's drawn.

Shùn ym pat pei, la páw pen ryngkew, *phr.* to have the real nature of a person exposed prematurely.

Shùr, *v.* to press forward.

*Shuri, *ka, n.* a long knife, a dagger.

Shut, *v.* to sharpen, to whet; to hotly discuss.

*Shutak, *ka, n.* a chatak or $\frac{1}{16}$ of a seer.

*Shuti, *ka, n.* a dirty thing, a base thing, [*Imit.* shuti-shuwai]; a holiday; any underhand work.

Shuwa, *ad.* first, before, previously, beforehand.

Shwàr, *ka, n.* an evil spirit known by that name and believed to possess certain clans in the Khasi Hills; she is supposed to attack people by convulsive fits. [*Imit.* ka shwár-ka tyngkieng.]

Shyngkhan or (shyngkhen), *v.* to be in a fix or dilemma; to be between Scylla and Charybdis.

Shyngkúp, *ka, n.* the first room of a Khasi house; an enclosed porch.

Shyng-iar, *ka, n.* a jet of water, a stream of water, a fountain.

Shyng-óid, *ka, n.* a manger.

Shyllangmat, *ka, n.* the brow.

Shylliah, *ka, n.* a mat. [*Imit.* ka shylliah-ka tlieng.]

Shyllip-núd, *ka, n.* the pit of the stomach.

Shylluit, *v.* to bloom.

---

* Hindi.

Shym, = a particle used with negative verbs in the past tense, as "úm *shym* lah ba'n kren."

Shympet, *ka, n.* a carbuncle.

Shympriah'ti, *ka, n.* a finger.

Shympriah'jat, *ka, n.* a toe.

Shymprong, *u, n.* a prawn, a shrimp.

Shyndúd, (leh-), *ad.* poutingly, sulkily.

Shynna, *adv.* conspicuously, clearly.

Shynnái, *ka, n.* the afterbirth or placenta.

Shynrang, *u, n.* a male; a pipe.

Shynrang-kjat, *ka, n.* the shins.

Shynrái, *u, n.* turmeric.

Shynráiñ, (-i), noble, grand, dignified.

Shynràiñ, *ka, n.* a dried small twig. [*Imit.* shynraiñ-shynriah]—*v.* to cut jokes, to flirt. [*Imit.* shynraiñ—tyng-in.]

Shynreh, *n.* a buffalo.

Shynriah'ti, (same as shympriah'ti), finger

Shynrong, *ka, n.* a skull, an egg-shell; the timber frame of a roof.

Shynroiñ, *a.* beautifully set (teeth).

Shynroin-riap, *a.* possessing winning manners; sociable. [*Imit* shynroiñ-shynriap.]

Shyntur, *ka, n.* a mouth, a word.

Shyrkait, *ka, n.* the groin.

Shyrkhei, *v.* to set the teeth on edge; to be dreadful.

Shyrpet, *ka, n.* the fat oily part of a fish.

Shyrti, *v.* to clear the jungle for cultivation; to *jhum.*

Shyrtong, *u, n.* a crest (of a fowl or bird).

Shyrwat, *u, n.* (see *shirwat*).

'si, *n.* (1) *abbrev.* of "masi"= a cow or bull; (2) *abbrev.* of "ksi" =head vermin.

***Sia,** *ka, n.* ink;—*ad.* devotedly.

Siak, (beit-), *ad.* straight on, [as, "ka lynti ka beit *siak* nangne haduh shnong."]

* Hindi.

Siang, *ka*, *n*. a spoon;—*v*. to spread a cloth or a mat; to pave; (as, *siang* máw); to fall down from the sky, like a paper-kite; to offer an oblation to the spirit of the dead.

S'iang, *a*. high (pitch). Same as *syiang*.

Siang-tyrpeng, *ka*, *n*. the shoulder-blade.

Siah, *v*. to pare, to cut.

Sian, *a*. clever, intelligent.

Sianti, *a*. cunning, precocious, clever.

S'ian, (dap-), *ad*. full, [as, "u sein-iong u leit kyllaiñ *syian* ha lycit u rishot."] Same as *syian*.

Siap, *v*. to insert.

Siar, *v*. to sharpen a *daw* or knife with a small hone;—*ka*, *n* treachery between the members of the same clan or house.

'siar, (*abbrev*. of "ksiar"), *ka*, *n*. gold. (as, ka *siar* sla, ka *siar* tylli.)

S'iar, *n*. a cock, a hen, a fowl, (same as *syiar*).

Siarkait, *ka*, *n*. a plantain-flower; a work like a plantain-flower.

'siarkha, *ka*, *n*. a wristlet (ornamental and hollow ones).

'siarkhang, *ka*, *n*. an earring resembling the shape of a fan.

Siar-long-kha, *u*, *n*. any treacherous act affecting the father or his relatives.

Siar-shrong, *ka*, *n*. a kind of earring worn by males.

'siar-sla, *ka*, *n*. gold leaf.

'siar-tylli, *ka*, *n*. solid gold; a solid gold earring.

Sia-sia, *ad*. in anger and in a threatening attitude.

Sia-shi-sia, *ad*. unceasingly, constantly, [as, "u bám *sia-shi-sia* ia ka ja ha ba'n da lut shi khiew."]

Siat, *v*. to shoot, to infect.

Siat-jingmut, *v*. to strike one's mind.

Siat-shon-shiw, *v*. to tread on the corns of another.

Siat-thong, (ia-), *v*. to have a shooting match.

Siaw, *v*. to whistle.

Siáw-máw-iang, *v*. to teach one a hard lesson.

Siaw-siaw, *ad*. in a whisper. [*Imit*. siaw-siaw-soit-soit.]

'si-khar, *ka*, *n*. a small cow imported from the plains and considered to be of inferior kind.

'si-khynna, *ka, n.* a hill cow, a cow bred in the Khasi Hills considered to be of superior quality to that of the plains.

Sied, *v.* to pounce upon, to spring upon.

Sieng, *a.* smelling like snuff or chillies.

Sieh, *v.* to plant, to drive in;—*ka, n.* the afterbirth, the placenta.

Siej, *u.* or *ka, n.* bamboo. [*Imit.* u siej-u skong.]

S'iem, *n.* a king, a chief, any member of a Siem family. [*Imit.* u S'iem-u kmie.] same as *syiem.*

S'iem-iong, *u, n.* a term applied to the S'iem of Nongspung.

S'iem-lieh, *u, n.* a term applied to the S'iem of Nongkhláw.

S'iem-sád, *ka, n.* the eldest or the youngest female member of the S'iem's family, who has the charge of sacrificial ceremonies.

S'iem-Shillong, *n.* the original name by which the Siems of Khyrim (Nongkrem and Mylliem) were called, it is still used by the country people.

Sien, *v.* to adorn, to deck, to put on as a flower.

—Sien, (suffix)= time; as, shi*sien*=once, ar*sien*, etc.

Siep, *v.* to swell, to bulge out.

Sier, *n.* a deer, a *sambur*;—*v.* to turn the insides of entrails out and clean them.

Siew, *v.* to pay. [*Imit.* siew-tda.]

'siew, (*abbrev.* of "ksiew"), *n.* a grandchild.

Siew-baibat, *v.* to buy in ready money, to buy in cash.

Siewspah, *v.* to redeem, to compensate. [*Imit.* siewspah-siewphew.]

'siew-tun, *n.* a greatgrandchild. [*Imit.* u 'siewtun-u siewjiap.]

†Sing, *u, n.* a lion.

S'ing, *n.* ginger, (same as *sying*).

'sing, (*abbrev.* of "ksing"), *ka, n.* a drum.

'sing-dum-dum, 'sing-lynghai, 'sing mareh, = the different ways of drum-beatings in a Khasi female dance.

'sing-dymphong, *ka, n.* a small musical instrument made with soft split reeds and played as a drum.

†Sing-mana, *ka, n.* boundary.

'sing-mastieh, 'sing-shadwait, = the different ways of beating a drum in a sword dance of males.

† Bengali.

'sing-nakra, *ka*, *n*. a big drum.

'sing-nalai, *ka*, *n*. a long conical drum like a tom-tom.

'sing-padiah, *ka*, *n*. a small drum.

—Sih (suffix)=foul, indecent, bad, unpleasant, [as, kren-*sih*, leh-*sih*, sngew-*sih*, etc.]

'si-lúd, *n*. a young cow or bull.

'si-lyngrâw, *n*. a young-bull.

Sim, *n*. a bird. [*Imit*. ka sim-ka doh.]

'si-mád, *ka*, *n*. a bed-bug.

'si-met, *ka*, *n*. an insect-mite (*gama-sidae*), vermin which infests fowls.

Sim-krái, *i*, *n*. a small bird resembling a lark.

Sim-kyllai-dohdit, *i*, *n*. a wag-tail.

Sim-lái-dieng, *i*, *n*. a meddlesome and talkative fellow.

Sim-puhdieng, *n*. a creeper (bird).

Sim-puhwieh, }
Sim-ktieh, } *ka*, *n*. a snipe, a woodcock.

Sim-pyllieng, *u*, *n*. the rainbow.

Sim-sohphoh, *u*, *n*. a hoopoe, a fop.

Sim-tung, *u*, *n*. a blackbird.

Sim-tyngwieng, *u*, *n*. water-ouzel; a man who makes much show of his turban, a fop.

Sin, *v*. to nickname. [*Imit*. sin-rngop.]

Sip, *v*. to break a thing, as an acorn, between the front teeth.

Sip-sip-sap-sap, *ad*. in an underhand way, not openly.

S'ir, *a*. to feel giddy; to be afraid of. Same as *syier*.

Sisa, *ka*, *n*. lead.

Sisia, *ka*, *n*. wild cinnamon, cassia.

S'it, (used with "la-"), *ad*. evening, night-time. Same as *syit*.

Siw-siw, (khriat-) *ad*. very (cold).

Siw-siw-siaw-siaw, *ad*. whisperingly.

Slá, *ka*, *n*. a leaf, a surface, a page.

Slak, (dait-), *ad*. firmly, [as, "kane ka lyntang ka leit *slak* hang-ne."]

Slang, *ka*, *n*. a small bird.

Slait, *ad.* tightly, well (fit), [as, "kine ki juti ki biang *slait* ha nga."]

Sla'jat, *ka*, *n.* the sole.

Slap, *u*, *n.* rain.

Sla'ti, *ka*, *n.* the palm.

Sleh, *v.* to anoint, to wash (the head). [*Imit.* sum-sleh.]

‡Sleit, *ka*, *n.* a slate.

Slem, *a.* long, late.

Slew, *ka*, *n.* kind of palm-tree whose leaves are generally used in making leaf-umbrellas. (*Bot. Licuala.*)

Sliang, *v.* to thirst.

Sliah, *v.* to detach, to take off (as a spear head from its handle); to denude.

Slieng, *v.* to put on the loin cloth.

Sliew, *v.* to blow wind into, to kindle a fire.

Sloit, *v.* to detach off, to come off as a knife from its handle.

Slòr, *v.* to come off, as hair.

Slung, *ka*, *n.* a lock-up in which lunatics are confined in the Khasi Hills.

Sma, *v.* to have a bad smell, to smell.

Smak, *ad.* smartly, (beat), [as, "u tháp *smak* na ka khlieh."]

Smái, *v.* to swear, to take an oath. [*Imit.* smái-spot.]

Smaintien, *v.* to wash the lips.

Smàt, *a.* active, smart.

Smep, *ad.* in a large bundle (as herbs), [as, "u wallam u jhur shi *smep.*"]

Smiar, (dap-), *ad.* to the brim, [as, "ka pipa ka dap da ka um *smiar.*"]

Smiej, *v.* to feel ticklish, to feel dreadful.

Smoiñ, (dap-), *ad.* to the brim, [as, "dap *smoiñ* ka um ha ka pipa."]

Smom-smom, } *ad.* very (soft as wool), [as, "nga kum ktah ia
Smop-smop, } kaei kata kaba jem *smom-smom.*"]

Smur, } *a.* rich in soil, full of manure.
Sbur, }

Snád, *ka*, *n.* a comb, (same as snát).

‡ English.

Snah, *a.* to be expert in climbing up or sitting on a tree, a rock, a horse, etc., [as, "uba *snah* kiew dieng; uba *snah* shongkulái."]

Snái, *a.* tired, irksome.

Snaiap, *n.* a spirit, a ghost, a wraith;—*ban snaiap*, incubus.

Snait, *ka*, *n.* a strainer.

Snám, *ka*, *n.* blood. [*Imit.* ka snám-ka ksuit.]

Snap, *ka*, *n.* a relic, remaining articles.

Snàr, *u. n.* a wedge; a hard and seasoned wood, the heart (of a tree).

Sneng, *v.* to reprove, to correct, to advise. [*Imit.* sneng-kráw.]

Snem, *ka*, *n.* a year, an evil-spirit who brings on headache and other diseases; cholera.

Snep, *ka*, *n.* a bark, a rind, a cover.

Snep-kór, *ka*, *n.* a cocoanut.

Snér, *ka*, *n.* a feather.

Sni, *ka*, *n.* a sting;—*v.* to cherish a revengeful spirit.

Sning, *ka* or *u*, *n.* a tree of the oak family.

Sniang, *n.* a pig.

Snieh, *ka*, *n.* a skin, a hide, a leather.

Snieh-doh, *ka*, *n.* complexion, appearance.

Snier, *ka*, *n.* entrails, bowels. [*Imit.* ka snier-ka snàp.]

Sniew, *a.* bad, evil, wicked. [*Imit.* sniew-smeh.]

Sniew-bok, *a.* unlucky.

Sniew-jew, *a.* very ugly.

Sni-riang-ksiar, } *u*, *n.* a god of the Synteng people located in a
Soni-riang-ksiar, } plantain tree or shrub near a dwelling house.

Snoh, *v.* to cling to, to adhere, to hang on.

Snúid, *ka*, *n.* a grove; corrugation.

Snúr, *ka*, *n.* a cleavage, a crack, a seam.

Snúr-thapbawa, *ka*, *n.* a spider's web.

Sok, *a.* equal to the occasion, faithful.

Song, *v.* to pack, to tie up;—*ka*, *n.* the horn (trumpet), a bundle.

Soh, *v.* to cling, to adhere, to bear fruit;—*u*, *n.* a fruit. [*Imit.* u soh-u pái, u soh-u syntiew.]

Soh-amirphór, *u*, *n.* a fabulous fairy fruit.

*Soh-baingon, *u*, *n*. brinjal.

Soh-ben, *u*, *n*. a very palatable fruit eaten after being cooked, and resembling in shape the core of a mangoe-fruit stone.

Sohblei, *u*, *n*. a sacrificer or Puja maker, who is held sacred for the time being.

Soh-brái, *u*, *n*. a small sour fruit with a hard seed.

Sohbrap, *u*, *n*. a wild edible fruit having a thick rind and a reddish pulpy substance inside.

Soh-brap-phareng, *u*, *n*. passion flower, passiflora.

Soh-broi, *u*, *n*. an Indian jujube, a Chinese date-plum.

Soh-byrthit, *u*, *n*. a shrub, the flower or fruit of which sticks to the clothes coming in contact with it.

Sohkhalit, *ad*. by a lucky turn of events, per chance, [as, "*soh-khalit* lashái la jop ki Jap ia ki Rus."]

Sohkháw, *u*, *n*. a grain of rice;—*ka ba'm sohkháw* (*phr*.) useless.

Sohkháw-ryndang, *u*, *n*. the throat.

Soh-kháw-iong, *u*, *n*. blackberry.

Sohkhia, *u*, *n*. a cucumber; the dewlap of a cow.

Sohkhliang, *ka*, *n*. a scar.

Sohkhlúr, *u*, *n*. a small sour fruit about the size of a pea.

Sohkhroh, Sohkhruh, } *a*. pitted, having pockmarks.

Sohkhruh-sohkhràm, *a*. rugged, rough.

Sohkhrut-sohkhret, *a*. not smooth, rough.

Sohkhyllùm, *u*, *n*. a sour fruit resembling a guava.

Sohkjup, *u*, *n*. the flower of a hedge shrub containing honey-juice.

Sohkpu, *u*, *n*. bread fruit.

Soh-kynphor, *u*, *n*. a papaya.

Soh-kyrsiew, *u*, *n*. a tuber of a certain creeper about the size of a plum which is cooked and eaten; a kind of wild potato.

Soh-kwit, *u*, *n*. a citron.

Soh-kyrbam, *u*, *n*. chalita.

Soh-ngang, *u*, *n*. a small bitter brinjal, (*Bot. solanum indicum*).

Soh-iong, *u*, *n*. the Khasi cherry. (*Bot. prunus ferruginea*).

Soh-jew, *u*, *n*. sour fruit, lime. [*Imit*. sohjew-sohsat.]

---

* Hindi.

Soh-jhalia,
Soh-jalia, } *u, n.* a small lime.

Soh-jyllih, *u, n.* a lime fruit of very good quality obtained from Jowai.

Soh-jymbuiñ, *u, n.* teat, nipple.

Soh-lang, *u, n.* small wild fruit growing in bunches and much liked by children and birds.

Soh-lah, *u, n.* a kind of black potato, potato.

Soh-lapér, *u, n.* the fruit of a small palm.

Soh-lew, *u, n.* a fruit used in poisoning fish.

Soh-liang, *u, n.* a wild poisonous fruit about the size of a lemon, the stones of which are washed, cut and eaten. (*Bot. Guno Gardia odorata*).

Soh-li-ia, *u, n.* a small sour fruit with a rough outside, the bark of the tree of which yields a black colour used in dyeing earthenware. (*Bot. Myrica Nagi.*)

Sohlong, *u, n.* a lemon.

Soh-lyngdkhur, *u, n.* a mulberry.

Soh-lyngkait, *u, n.* a plaintain-like fruit of a certain wild creeper.

Sohma, *u, n.* small grain-like fruits growing in bunches, the outside of which is covered with a sour white substance resembling hoar frost, (it is used as a medicine in dysentery).

Soh-mád, *u, n.* a kind of citron, the leaves and rind of which have a very agreeable sweet smell.

Soh-manir, *u, n.* litchee.

Sohmlúh, *u, n.* Indian plum.

Sohmrit, *u, n.* black pepper.

Sohmyngken, *u, n.* chilli, red pepper.

Soh-myngngór, *u, n.* a shaddock or pomel.

Soh-mylleng, *u, n.* a sour wild fruit very common in the Bhoi country, after eating which water tastes very sweet.

Soh-myndong, *u, n.* a common lime.

Soh-myntait, *u, n.* a wild fruit as big as a bread fruit.

Soh-nepbah, *u, n.* the fruit of a certain shrub used as a bait for fish (very common by the roadside).

Sohñiangriang, *u, n.* a fruit of the lemon kind and of a sweetish taste.

Sohñiamtra, *u*, *n*. an orange. (Same as *soh myntra.*)

Soh-ot, *u*, *n*. an acorn which is eaten by the people.

Sohpyrdah, *v*. to cling to a thing as a hulook does to a branch of a tree; to hold the hands at the back of the head.

Soh-padoi, *v*. to rock, to swing.

Soh-pái, *u*, *n*. a fruit which looks like lime, but which has a sweetish taste.

Soh-pailen, *u*, *n*. water-fungus.

Soh-pairah, *u*, *n*. a fruit used for washing clothes. *Hind.* Ritha; (*Bot. Sapindus Mukorrosi*).

Soh-pdok, *u*, *n*. a small berry; tomato.

Soh-pdung, *ka*, *n*. the big tubercular root of a certain plant used as a target in archery matches; a butt.

Soh-pen, *u*, *n*. a wild earth-nut.

Soh-pet, *u*, *n*. the navel; the ends of a twisted string.

Soh-phán, *u*, *n*. a jack-fruit.

Sohphi, *u*, *n*. a sour fruit about the size of a plum having a rough outside.

Sohphlang, *u*, *n*. an edible root, (*Bot. Flemingia vestita*).

Sohphoh, *u*, *n*. a wild apple, a crab, (*Bot. Pyrus granulata*).

Sohphoh-Nongkhláw, *u*, *n*. pear.

Soh-pieng, *u*, *n*. a mango.

Soh-pong, *u*, *n*. species of fig.

Soh-prew, *u*, *n*. a species of fruit of a creeper, the cultivated variety of which is used as a vegetable; (*Bot. Luffa Œgyptiaca*).

Soh-pri-am, *u*, *n*. a guava.

Soh-pyrshit, *u*, *n*. a small black fruit, used by some as a fish-bait, and also for making ink.

Soh-pyrshong, *u*, *n*. a kind of fruit,—Assamese *kamranga*; (*Bot. Averrhoa carambola*).

Sohra, *ka*, *n*. Cherra punji;—*a*. bearing scanty fruits.

Soh-ramdieng, *u*, *n*. a small fruit; (*Bot. Baccauria sapida*) (*Beng.* latka).

Soh-ryngkhám, *u*, *n*. a very small eatable fruit of a shrub.

Sohsat,
Suhsat, } *v*. to be entangled, to be in trouble.

Soh-shang, *u*, *n*. a sour red fruit about the size of an apricot.

Soh-shanglew, *u*, *n*. the fruit of a shrub resembling an areca nut. The shrub is found all over the Bhoi country.

Sohshán, *u*, *n*. a strawberry.

Sohshnong, *u*, *n*. one who is not a citizen of a State or village, a stranger, an alien. [*Imit.* soh shnong-sohtháw.]

Sohshur, *u*, *n*. a wild pear.

Sohs'iem, *u*, *n*. an alien, a foreigner. [*Imit.* u sohsyiem-u sohtang.] a small species of orange but not so sweet.

Soh-sning, } *u*, *n*. an acorn.
Soh-stap, }

Soh-trun, *u*, *n*. a pine-apple.

Soh-tyngkoh, *v*. to limp.

Soh-tyntoi, *u*, *n*. a tamarind.

Soi, *v*. to sign a name; to pare with an adze or hoe;—*a*. lasting, durable;—*u*, *n*. a long pole used in propelling boats.

Sóiñ, (iaid-) *ad*. straight on, without difficulty, [as, "ka lieng ka iaid beit *soiñ* ynda la pyllait na ka lyngkór."]

Soit, (leit-), *ad*. away, [as, "ynda kumta u sa leit noh *soit* sha la iing."]

Soitán, *u*, *n*. Satan. [*Imit.* u soitán-u bhut.] same as *suidtán*.

Sop, *v*. to cover, to thatch;—*ad*. completely, as, "bsuh *sop* hapoh u phlang."

Sop-bajar, *v*. to thatch a house by putting another layer of grass over the old one; a form of putting thatching-grass on the roof.

Sop-jat, *ka*, *n*. a legging.

Sop-sarang, *v*. to become rusty.

Sop-sieh, *v*. to repair an old thatching by spreading grass where neccessary.

Sopti, *ka*, *n*. a coat. [*Imit.* sopti-sopjat.]

Sòr, *ka*, *n*. a station, an enlightened town;—*ad*. noiselessly, stealthily, (as, "ka miaw ka pár *sòr* ba'n thap kem ia ka khnái.")

Sorkár, *ka*, *n*. a Government.

Sorki, *ka*, *n*. mortar.

Sordár, *n*. a sirdar, a village headman.

S'or, *v*. to crack. Same as *syor*.

Sorjamin, *n*. local enquiry.

Sorshisor, *ad*. slowly but surely, (as, "u ia pah ia u *sorshi-sor* ba'n leit ia khalái.")

Sot, *v.* to catch, as with the tips of the fingers, to pick out.

†**Sotti**, *a.* pure, chaste.

Sotsakular, *ka*, *n.* a solemn promise. (Same as "soskular.")

Spah, *ka*, *n.* wealth, riches. [*Imit.* ka spah-ka phew.]

Spaiñ, *v.* to bandage, to swathe.

Spar, *u*, *n.* a prickly bamboo;—*ka spár*, a trap which a wild animal on touching a string is pierced by an arrow or spike.

Speh, *u*, *n.* a prick, a spike.

Spel, *v.* to commit to memory, to spell.

Sping, *ka*, *n.* a handle.

Spit, *u*, *n.* a very small species of bamboo very good for making ties.

Spong, *v.* to put on a turban.

Spúd-san, *a.* to be on the way to maturity, to be in the stage of growing (said of persons only).

Spur, *ka*, *n.* a coarse country cotton cloth.

Spúd, *v.* reduced in size, applicable to persons only.

Stád, *a.* wise, clever, learned. [*Imit.* stád-nang,]—*u*, *n.* a learned man. [*Imit.* u stád-u jhád.]

Stang, *a.* thin.

Stái, (iap-), *v.* to wither.

Stài, (shi-) *n.* a heap.

Stait, *u*, *n.* chaff, husk;—*v.* to be reduced.

Star, *u*, *n.* a head strap made of cane.

Steiñ, *u*, *n.* the fibre obtained from a bark of a tree used for making thread and rope. (*Bot. Villebrunia integrifolia*).

Stem, *a.* yellow.

Step, *ka*, *n.* morning.

Step-phyrngáp, *ad.* early in the morning.

Stet, *ad.* fast, quickly, (as, "ka rel ka iáid *stet* shibún.")

Stew, *u*, *n.* a short reed or ekra.

Sti, *v.* to become dry or wrinkle, to shrivel.

Stieh, *ka*, *n.* a shield. [*Imit.* ka stieh-ka wait.]

Sting, *a.* light, not heavy.

---

† Bengali.

Stir, *u*, *n.* a mud partition in a paddy field which separates one bed from another; isle.

Stong, *u*, *n.* a sod, turf.

Stoi, } *ad.* well (heaped up), (as, "u ci ba lum *stung* ia u khyndew kumne?")
Stung, }

Suba, *v.* to suspect;—*adj.* clean, (of persons only). [*Imit.* sáb-suba.)

Suba-ni, *ad.* fastidiously clean.

Suk, *a.* happy, contented. [*Imit.* suk-saiñ.]

Suka, *ka*, *n.* a four-anna piece, a *siki*, one-fourth of a rupee.

Suki, *a.* slow, gradual. [*Imit.* suki-suloi.]

Súd, *v.* to take off, to pull out (as grain from a bunch.)

†Sudu, *u*, *n.* a fool, a simpleton.

Suda, *a.* empty, vacant;—*ad.* entirely, wholly, only (as, "nga shem tang ka shitom *suda*.")

Sudakor, } *u*, *n.* a merchant.
Sydakor, }

Súh, *v.* to sew, to thrust; [*Imit.* súh-thaiñ]; to suffer from colic or throes. [*Imit.* súh-thàr]; to deal in an underhand way.

Súhbudkhia, *kaba*, *n.* a back-stitching.

Súh-buit, *v.* to incite, to plot.

Súh-khún, *v.* to be in labour.

Súh-khylliap, *kaba*, *n.* hemming.

Sûh-kyndang, *v.* to pass a string or thread or stick through the body of a thing; to string pieces of meat together.

Súh-dong, *v.* to stretch far inland or into another's kingdom.

Súh-jút, *v.* to have false pains.

Súh-jylläi, *v.* to have intermittent or neuralgic pains.

Súh-jyndong, *v.* to have dysury; *ka*, *n.* difficult urination.

Súh-mar-iap, *v.* to make the last effort, to plunge into any enterprise as the last resource; to hazard.

Súh-ot, *ka*, *n.* dysentery.

Súh-pynpúr, *kaba*, *n.* a running-stitch.

Súh-sat, *v.* to be entangled, to suffer trouble,—*n.* *ka*, calamity.

Súh-sieng, *a.* very pungent (smell).

---

† Hindi.

Súh-synri, *kaba*, *n.* the pain caused by the contraction of the womb after childbirth.

Súh-tak, *kaba*, *n.* a long temporary stitch, a tack.

Súh-thied, *v.* to take root.

Súh-tok, *v.* to throw gently (as in playing with cowries).

Súh-tyngka, *v.* to bribe.

'sûid, (*abbrev.* of "ksúid"), *n.* an evil-spirit, a devil.

Suid-khái, *v.* to care, to take heed (used with *ym*).

'súid-kynta-maram, *u*, *n.* the evil spirit who brings on headache.

'súid-ngon, 'súid-briew, } *u*, *n.* the evil spirit who attacks people in their evening or morning walk characterised by a stabbing pain in the sides or by hoarseness.

'súid-lam-iap, *u*, *n.* the executor of God's decree to carry away the souls of men ; he is represented as a gigantic being and wearing long dishevelled hair, each of whose teeth is as big as an axe.

'súid-nia, *u*, *n.* the spirit of the first grand maternal uncle of the clan.

Suid-ñiew, *v.* to care (used negatively with *ym*).

'súid-tynjang, *u*, *n.* a lame demon who lives in the jungle and is known by his call of "kâw-hoit—kâw-hoit"; it is believed that any one who calls out in response to his call is attacked by him and tickled to death.

'súid-um, *u*, *n.* the evil spirit who attacks women and causes miscarriage or sterility.

Suiñ, *ka*, *n.* the sky, an atmosphere.

Suit, *v.* to pour as a libation; to gild. [*Imit.* suit-shór.]

'suit, (*abbrev.* of "ksuit"), *ka*, *n.* matter from a sore or wound; pus.

Suit, *v.* to pour some water into the fire in order to put it out.

'suit-nám, *ka*, *n.* matter mixed with blood.

'suitán, *see* "Soitán."

Sule, *v.* to be useful; to be fit.

Suloi, *ka*, *n.* a gun. [*Imit.* ka suloi-ka mán.]

Suloi-shamok, *ka*, *n.* a matchlock.

Sulom, *u*, *n.* dandriff on the face.

Sum, *v.* to bathe. [*Imit.* sum-sleh.]

Súm, *v.* to spear, to lance, to hurl.

Sumar, *v.* to take care of, to be careful. [*Imit.* sumar-sukhér.]

Sunod, *ka, n.* a *sanad* or appointment parwana.

Sup, *u, n.* a big basket for putting in grain; etc.

Supdok, *ad.* short and stout, (as, "i briew iba lyngkot *supdok*").

Suphu, (heh-), *ad.* bulky, (as, "u briew uba heh *suphu*.")

Supiw, *ad.* with fat and sunken eyes, (as, "u briew uba dam *supiw* ki khmat.")

*Sur, *ka, n.* tune, voice, sound,—*sùr, v.* to blow the nose.

Súr, *v.* to stitch the mouth of a sack.

Súr-ang, *v.* to cover the mouth of an overfull sack with leaves, and then to stitch it, leaving it partially open.

Súr-dàm, *v.* to stitch so as to close an opening or rent.

Súr-eitmat, *v.* to have the eye glued with eye-pus.

Sur-eitmut, *v.* to blow the nose.

Suri, *n.* a wolf.

Surik, *v.* to conspire or secretly consult with.

Surok, *ka, n.* a road.

Súr-thapbawa, *v.* to be covered with spider's web.

Sut, *ka, n.* interest.

Sút, *v.* to pull gently; to drag.

Suwai, *u, v.* particles of dust or sand.

Suwan, *a.* satisfied, complete.

Suwaga, *u, n.* borax.

Suwara, *u, n.* saltpetre.

Suware, *ad.* perfunctorily.

Swái, *a.* frail, weak, infirm.

Swait, *v.* to fly about, to hover, to prowl; watching for opportunities, to be on the look-out.

Swar, *v.* to cross-examine.

Sybak, (*see* sbak), *ad.* with a thud (as, "nga tháp *sbak* na ka ngáp.")

Syboh, (same as sboh), *ka, n.* manure, adhesive froth. [*Imit.* ka sboh-ka sbùr.]

Sydang, *v.* to begin, to commence, (same as *sdang*).

Syngkái, *ka, n.* the waist; the loins.

---

* Hindi.

Syngkái-bamon, *u, n.* a god who causes people to die by a violent death, as in battle, by a tiger, etc.

Syngken, *ka, n.* an uncle's (maternal) wife.

Syngken-kurim, *ka, n.* mother-in-law.

Syngket, *ka, n.* a precipice.

Syngkha, *ka, n.* an armlet.

Syngkhien, *v.* to prop—*ka, n.* a pillow.

*Syngkhin, *ka, n.* a bayonet.

Syngkhlieh, *ka, n.* a pillow.

Syngkhor, *v.* to snore.

Syngngeit, *v.* to throw down to the ground with force.

Syng-iang, *ad.* bright (red).

Syng-it, *a.* tight, choking.

Syng-it-lúm, *ka, n.* the place or saddle where two hills meet.

Synglàn, } Synglen, } *ad.* bare headed, (as, "kă khlieh kaba khúid *synglàn*").

Sylla, *v.* to consult, to conspire, to plot, to instigate. [*Imit.* sylla-syllok.]

Syllang, (sat-), *ad.* very (hot or pungent), as from the effect of blisters.

Syllâi, *ka, n.* a cultivated land which has very recently been abandoned.

Sylli, *u, n.* a small species of bamboo found on the Cherrà side.

Syllih, *n.* a flying squirrel.

Syllok, *v.* to insinuate, to take counsel together; to have fellowship.

Syllut, (pei-), *ad.* from one side to another, right through, clean through (pierced).

Symbái, *u, n.* a seed.

Symboh, *u, n.* a grain, a piece of the inside of a fruit.

Symboh-kpieng, *u, n.* a single bead.

Sympa, *ka, n.* a natural hive, as in crevices of rocks or hollow trees.

Sympain, *v.* to wrap, to dress, to caress.

Symparat, *ka, n.* a species of palm which generally grows on precipitous places.

---

* Hindi.

Symparbret, *u*, *n*. nettle-rash.

Sympat, *v*. to whip, to thrash.

Sympei, *ka*, *n*. a heap of earth in front of the hole of a mouse.

Symphiah, *u*, *n*. a whisk.

Symphleiñ, *ad*. bloodlessly (white), as, "u briew uba lich *symphleiñ*."

Symphlen, *a*. destitute of hair.

Syndah, *ad*. close by, against;—*v*. to protect or put a thing between two things, (as in the sentence "haba kit eit masi da *syndah* da ka tráp ioh jakhlia ka met.")

Syndam, *a*. flat, low, depressed, well beaten.

Syndem, *a*. flat-nosed.

Syndim, *ad*. crouchingly, stealthily, (ás, "u nongtúh u rih *syndim* ha khap u máw.")

Syndong, *v*. to roll up the clothes as when wading a stream.

Syndon, *ad*. finally, once for all.

Syndot-myrsiang, (iw-), *a*. having the peculiar unpleasant smell as of a jaokal, smelling of musk.

*__Synduk__, *ka*, *n*. a box.

Syiang, *a*. high pitched.

Synjap, *a*. slack, not tight.

Synjat, *n*. a pledge, an earnest.

Synjor, *a*. loose, not tight, lax.

Synjuk, *v*. to be unanimous, to agree, to come to an understanding.

Synlâr, *a*. plain, simple (food).

Synñia, *ka*, *n*. night, darkness.

Synñiang, *u*, *n*. a collection, a contribution, subscription;—*v*. to contribute, to subscribe. [*Imit*. u synñiang—u bynhei.]

Synrang, *ka*, *n*. a coping of a rock or cave.

Synrâi, *ka*, *n*. autumn.

Synrân, *n*. a disciple, a follower.

Synrap, *v*. to join, to coalesce.

Synrei, *u*, *n*. a pestle generally made of wood.

Synreit, *v*. to sprinkle.

---

* Hindi.

Synrem, *u*, *n*. a kind of stinging nettle.

Synri, *u*, *n*. the womb.

Synriah, *v*. to sneeze.

Synrop, *a*. double, twin.

Synrúd, *v*. to sweep or scratch past a thing.

Synrum, *ka*, *n*. rubbish. [*Imit.* ka synrum-ka synrah.]

Synsár, *u*, *n*. a broom.

Synshár, *v*. to rule, to govern; [*Imit.* synshár-khadár];—*Ka*, *Synshár*, *n*. the highest goddess of the *Synteng* mythology.

Synshér, *v*. to ram, to drive in.

Syntái, *u*, *n*. a hunch, hump.

Syntán, *n*. a hardy or strong-minded fellow.

Synteng, *n*. people of the Jaintia Hills. [*Imit.* u Synteng-u Syngngór.]

Syntiat, *v*. to lay in ambush; to spy.

Syntiew, *u*, *n*. a flower. [*Imit.* u syntiew-u skúd.]

Syntiew-khmut, *i*, *n*. the tip of the nose.

Syntúid, *v*. to slip.

Syrbúd, *v*. to imitate, to follow.

Syrdeng, *ka*, *n*. a fence or wall made of bamboo or ekra, a partition wall made up of planks.

Syrdep, *v*. to patch up,—*n*. a piece of rag. [*Imit.* ka syrdep-ka syrphong.]

Syrngiew, *ka*, *n*. a shadow. [*Imit.* ka syrngiew-ka syrnget.]

Syriem, *a*. similar, like; (same as sriem).

Syrdoh, *v*. to make a knot, to tie in a knot.

Syrpái, }
Syrpúd, } *v*. to rub gently;—*ad*. to the brim, by flushing up.

Syrtap, *ka*, *n*. a fold, a layer; stratum.

Syrti, *ka*, *n*. a razor, a blade; an iron file.

Syrtok, *a*. up to the mark, complete; justified by result.

Syrwa, *a*. wasteful, squandering;—*ka*, *n*. a soup (*Hindi*).

Syrwet, *ka*, *n*. a trace, a mark, a form for the ratification of an agreement, clue.

Syrwiah, *v*. to fasten a rope round, to tie in a noose;—*u*, *n*. a noose.

T.

T, the eighteenth letter in the Khasi alphabet.

Tabah, *v.* to throw or hang across the shoulder.

Tabáiñ, *v.* to make the lips dirty.

*Tabit, *ka, n.* an amulet.

Tabla, *ka, n.* the shoulder-piece of an animal; a chine; a kind of Hindustani drum.

*Tabut, *ka, n.* a car used on the funeral occasion of great men; a *tazia.*

*Takda, *a,* urgent.

Takhaw, Takhew, } *a.* wretchedly poor; penurious; having scanty hair.

Takhúh, Tyngkhúh, } *v.* to knock the head against.

*Takma, *ka, n.* a medal.

Takór, Takraiñ, } *v.* to strike with the knuckles (when cursing).

Tad, *a.* cheap;—*ad.* as soon as, only. [As, "*tad* ioh u shu phet sha la shnong bak."]

Tád-tyrpeng, *ka, n.* an armlet.

Tad-ynda, *ad.* until, till, when.

Tang, *ad.* only; to make a finish of the plaiting of wicker-baskets or nets; to measure or heap up grain as much as a measuring basket can contain and holding one hand to support the grain.

'tang, (*abbrev.* of "ktang"), *ka, n.* a pipe.

Tang ba'n nám, *phr.* nominally, [as, "u ia ai kháw ia ki *tang ba'n nám*";] formally.

'tangkro, *u, n.* a windpipe.

Tangdep, *ad.* in a careless manner; done only to get rid of duty.

'tang-duma, *ka, n.* a hookah, a hubble-bubble.

'tangngúid, *n.* gullet, (same as tangsáw).

'tangmuri, *ka, n.* a pipe used in a Khasi dance.

Tangon, *v.* to club, to beat with big sticks on the head or body.

Tangon-u-lymban, *u, n.* a form of capital punishment amongst the ancient Khasis by beating a person to death with a club.

Tang-sáw, *u, n.* the gullet.

---

* Hindi.

Tangthari, *ka, n.* a weaver's shuttle.

'tang-um, *ka, n.* a bamboo pipe or *chunga* for carrying water.

Tah, *v.* to use anything as an external application or ointment; to smear; to use as sauce (*e.g.*, curry or salt);—*ka. n.* a snail.

Tahoh, Toh-hoh, } *adv.* wastefully; lavishly. [as, "wat ju leh *tahoh* eh ia ka jong ki briew."]

Tái, *v.* to winnow; to bring reasons to bear on an argument; to sift.

Tai-tai, *ad.* very (dirty); [as, "kane ka sopti ka la jakhlia *tai-tai.*"]

*Taiár, *v.* to get ready, to prepare.

Taiew, *ka, n.* a week.

Tàiñ, *a.* stunted, dwarfish.

Tàiñ-tàiñ, *ad.* loudly [as, "ia uba kyllut phi dei ba'n da kren eh *tàiñ-tàiñ.*"]

Táiñ-táiñ, *ad.* elastic.

Tait, (*abbrev.* of kyntait), *v.* to reject, to set aside.

Tait-kur, *v.* to be excommunicated from the clan. [*Imit.* tait-kur—tait-kmie.]

*Tala, *ka, n.* a lock.

Talad, *v.* to manage.

Taláiñ, *v.* to whirl; to wield.

*Talasi, *v.* to search.

Talba, *ka, n.* the shoulder-piece, same as *tabla.*

*Talbi, *v.* to manage; to conduct (*e.g.*, a case).

Talen, *a.* bald, destitute of hair;—*ka, n.* a talent.

Talép, *ad.* tall and foolish, [as, "u briew uba biej *talép.*"]

Talngeng, *ad.* big (head); [as, "nga ioh u dohthli uba heh *tal-ngeng.*"]

Talmah, *ad.* big, [as, "u khla uba heh ka khlieh *talmah.*"]

Talon, *v.* to belabour, to maul.

Talu, (pái), *u, n.* a sugarcane;

Talû, *a.* blunt.

*Talwar, *ka, n.* a sword.

Tám, *v.* to pick up, to gather.

---

* Hindi.

Tam, *ad.* more, in excess.

Tama, *ka, n.* copper.

*Tamsa, *ka, n.* a show, (*Hind.*) a *tamasha.*

Tamsneng, *a.* wayward, wilful; disobedient. [*Imit.* tamsa-tamhoi.]

Tamti, *v.* to have a stealing propensity, thievish. [*Imit.* tamti-tamjat.]

Tamtúiñ-tamtáiñ, *ad.* unevenly.

Tàn, *v.* to go and fetch a person, to go and meet a person on the way.

*Tán, *v.* to pull, to drag;—*ka, n.* straitened circumstances, emergency; crisis.

Tana-tani, *ad.* in a precarious manner, [as, "ngi shu ia im *tana-tani* mynta shi snem."]

Tania, *a.* frugal, economical.

Tañoiñ, *v.* to come and attack simultaneously (as a pack of hungry wolves).

Tap, *v.* to cover, to screen;—*ka, n.* a bundle of *pán.*

Táp, *v.* to overreach, to encroach upon.

Tap-khar-lyngngoh, *v.* to play blind man's buff.

Tap-kpoh, *v.* to perform a poojah ceremony for the safe delivery of a child.

Tap-Iawbei, *v.* to worship the spirit of the departed mother or maternal grandmother by means of sacrifices.

Tap-lubri, *v.* to perform the ceremony of naming a child.

Tàp lup, *v.* to cover completely;—*ad.* all over.

Tap-mohkhlieh, *ka, n.* a piece of cloth used by women to cover the head.

Tap-rngiew, *v.* to make sacrifices for one's own good luck. [*Imit.* taprngiew-taprwiang.]

Tap-Thawlang, *v.* to worship the original grandfather by means of sacrifices.

Tàr, *v.* to tear, to rend,—*ad.* scorchingly hot; [as, "tiew ia ka um ha ding ha ba'n da khluit *tàr.*"]

*Târ, *u, n.* a wire.

Tarajur, *ka, n.* scales, a balance.

Tarê, *v.* to grope.

---

* Hindi.

Tari, *ka*, *n*. a knife.

*Tarik, *ka*, *n*. date.

Taro, *ka*, *n*. the goddess of wealth among the Syntengs, of whom the people are in great dread. She resembles the evil spirit of the Khasis called "Ka Shuar." Those who are suspected of possessing her are shunned by all.

Tasa, *ka*, *n*. a kind of drum; a tambourine.

Tasàm, *ka*, *n*. a worn-out and useless tool or wares, [*Imit*. tasàm-takut], see also *thungtasàm*.

Tat, *conj*. if only, as soon as, [as, "*tat* shu lah kane, nga'n leit noh."]; —cheap.

Tâw, *v*. to put food into the mouth;—*ka*, *n*. a sheet of paper.

Tàw, *ad*. intensely (dark); [as, "ki ia sah ha lúm haduh ba'n da iongngit *tàw*"].

Tawah, *v*. to hang, to suspend, to throw across.

Tawain, }
Tawiar, } *v*. to go round and round.

‡Tawlia, *ka*, *n*. a towel.

Tawoin, [same as "tawain."]

Tba, *v*. to feel by touching.

Tbeng, *ad*. as if something is full in the mouth, or in a hollow vessel or pipe [as, "u dumasla u dang dap *tbeng* shi tyndong."]

Tbeh, *v*. to light.

Tbem, *ad*. as if biting some thing in the mouth, [as, "ka miaw ka dait *tbem* ia ka khnái ha ka shyntur."]; firmly (sticking).

Tbiak, *ad*. clean of, [as, "u dkhat *tbiak* ia u syntiew."]

Tbian, *ka*, *n*. floor.

Tbit, *a*. handy, skilful, tactful.

Tkai-tkai, *ad*. fat and plump, [as, "u kulái jong une uba sngáid *tkai-tkai*.]

Tkor-tkor, }
Tkur-tkur, } *ad*. fat and tender; [as, "une u khynnah uba sngáid *tkur-tkur*."]

Tda, *ka*, *n*. a span,—*v*. to creep like a leech.

Tdah, *ka*, *n*. the bottom: a running-stitch.

Tdaw-tdaw, *ad*. hard and tough, [as, "ka thaláp ka long kaba eh *tdaw-tdaw*."]

---

* Hindi. ‡ English.

Tdem, *ka a, n.* smoke.

Tden, *ad.* tenaciously, and firmly [as, "u khnam u neh *tden* ha u skum."]

Tdit-tdot, *ad.* at all, [as, "wat leit ai ei ei ia u *tdit-tdot.*"]

Tdong, *u, n.* tail. [*Imit.* ka tdong—ka shnet.]

Tdong-bohkhaila, *ka, n.* the fag-end of a *dhoti.*

Tdong-sier, *u, n.* a meadow barley.

Tdúh, *ka, n.* the end (of a thread) or anything.

Te, *conj.* then; it is also used at the end of a sentence to denote surprise, as "phi ong kumta *te*?" (you say so, do you?).

Teng, *ad.* at some time or other, once, [as, "u kren kum uba la shah ram *teng* ha nga"];—*n.* occasion, time; as shi*teng*, ár*teng*, lái-*teng*.

Teng-teng, *ad.* occasionally.

Teh, *v.* to bind, to fasten, [*Imit.* teh-khúm].—it is also used at the end of a sentence to emphasize the adjective before it, [as, "ew phi, u kulái u Jarnel u long uba heh noh *teh.*"]—and it is also used as a sort of digressive expression, [as, "la nga pyn-i ia kata *teh* u phoi pynban."]

Teh-kirmit, *v.* to be under a bond or agreement.

Teh-ktien, *v.* to be engaged in a marriage contract. [*Imit.* teh-ktien-teh thylliej.]

Teh-musorkár, *v.* to keep one under restraint or under the cognizance of the authorities.

Teh'sái-iong, *v.* to be engaged in a marriage contract (for young children only). [Probably from the ancient practice of binding a black thread to one of the toes of a girl as a pledge.]

Tei, *v.* to build, to erect.

Tei-pop, *v.* to charge with; to lay the blame upon.

Teiñ-thap, *u, n.* nettle rash.

Téj-téj, *ad.* adhesive, like gum, [as, "phi shet ka ja kaba jem *téj-téj* kum ia u mynpang."]

Tem, *v.* to play on a drum or stringed-musical instrument; to extinguish. [*Imit.* tem-put.]

Tém, *ad.* trailing like a tail, [as, "u khla u búd *tém* ia u briew."]

Ten-ten, *ad.* elastic, producing fibres, tough, [as, "ka doh kaba jwat *ten-ten.*"]

Tep, *v.* to bury, to inter.

Tep-eitmiaw, *v.* to affect to overlook a thing.

Ter, *ad.* in order, in a row.

Ter-lter, *ad.* one whole length, [as, "ka barrack ki shipai kaba jrong *ter-lter*."]

Ter-shi-ter, *ad.* in a series of objects ; one after another.

Ter-ter, *ad.* consecutively.

Tew-tew, (eh), *ad.* very hard, [as, " u tohjáw um pat ih, u dang eh *tew-tew*."]

Tnga, *n.* a husband or wife. [*Imit.* ka tnga-ka khún.]

Tngang, *ad.* violently (hit), [as, "u la kawang shimáw *tngang* na ka khlieh jong nga."]

Tngár, *a.* shady, cool.

Tngáw, *n.* a hanuman, a langur.

Tngen, *a.* comfortable, cool.

Tngit, *a.* dirty ;—*ka*, *n.* a dirt. [*Imit.* ka tngit-ka tngár.]

Thaba, *a.* glaring, brilliant, bright, dazzling.

Thakuraiñ, *ka*, *n.* a phenomenon which appears dazzling and brilliant like the sun, a mistress of the house.

Thád, *v.* to expose, to spread, to curse, to scold. [*Imit.* thád-bád]; —*ka*, *n.* an exposed flat country.

Thád-lád, *v.* to become shameless ; to put to shame.

Thád-rong, *v.* to use low or obscene words ; to tell tales.

Thang, *v.* to burn, to cremate.

Thang-khér, *v.* to be cremated by the State or by the public.

Thang-krei, *v.* to burn the body without gathering the bones or without performing any ceremony.

Thang-iong, *v.* to become sunburnt ; to become dark owing to exposure.

Thang-jngap, *v.* to have the discolouring of the face.

Thang-rang, *a.* to feel very thirsty.

Thang-rám, *v.* to burn a jungle for *jhum* cultivation,—*ad.* like a withered branch of a tree.

Thang-rong, *v.* to perform a cremating ceremony with great show.

Thang-sáw, *v.* to heat a thing till it is red-hot. [*Imit.* thangsáw-thangsian.]

Thah, *u*, *n.* ice, hoar-frost.

Tháiñ, *v.* to weave, to knit, to plait ;—*ka, n.* district, direction.

Thait, *v.* to cut asunder, to snap ;—*a.* weary, exhausted.

Thâit-thâit, *ad.* without intermission, incessantly, [as, "ki kynrup *tháit-tháit* ha doh ia u."]

Thala, *a.* vain ;—*ad.* vainly, uselessly.

Thaláb, *ka, n.* a chip of wood.

Thala-thaleiñ, (leh), *ad.* in a rough way, carelessly.

Thâm, *ka, n.* a crab.

Thamè, *v.* to loose the clear vision of things ; to befool.

Thamula, *a.* joking, funny, [*Imit.* thamula-thamuleiñ.]

Thàn, *ad.* too, excessively, unreasonably ;—*iaihàn, v.* not to do a thing when asked, simply because one looks to somebody else to do it.

*Thân, *ka, n.* one whole piece of cloth, a *thân* ;—*v.* to send for.

Thana, *n.* person having some relationship. [*Imit.* thana-thakhér.]

*Thanat, *ka, n.* a police station.

*Thanda, *a.* abated, cool, calm.

Thâp, *v.* to give a slap ; to brush past any object.

Thàp, *v.* to lay in wait, to ambuscade, to waylay, to be on the watch ;—*a.* poisonous (as, "une u tit uba *thàp*").

Thap-ba-ngem, *ka, n.* a ground spider.

Thap-ba-iong, *v.* to become dizzy.

Thap-balieh, *ka, n.* a butterfly.

Thap-balong, *ka, n.* a large black butterfly.

Thap-bawa, *ka, n.* a spider.

Thap-basim, *u, n.* a mole.

Thàp-biej, *a.* having some disordered state of mind ; demented.

Thap-bulong, *ka, n.* an evil spirit who brings insanity to the people.

Thàp-kór, *ka, n.* the back part of the ear.

Tháp-u-dáp, *u, n.* a common ignorant fellow.

Thàp-ngáp, *ad.* lonely, (sit), [as, "u shong marwei *thàp-ngáp* ha khláw."]—*ka, n.* swelling of the jaw gland.

Thàp-mrâd, *v.* to swoon, to be under the influence of evil spirits ; to stalk.

---

* Hindi.

Thàp-niang, *ka*, *n*. wing; side.

Tháp-shrich, *v*. to cob, to give a slap on the buttock.

Thàr, *v*. to be pierced with a thistle or prick; to feel hurt.

*Thár, *n*, *ka*. brass plate, a *thal*.

Tharai, *v*. to suppose, to think, to presume.

Thario, *ka*, *n*. a shallow and shingly bed of a stream.

Tharu-thare, *ad*. roughly, [as, "nga shu tháiñ *tharu-thare* ia kane ka rúh".]

Thatthari, *u*, *n*. one who works in brass.

That-that, (kyiuh-), *ad*. tremblingly, [as, "u kyiuh *that-that* ba'n leit mih Iing-kashari"],—shiveringly.

Tháw, *v*. to make, to create.

Tháwdur, (leh-, kren-), *ad*. in a queer or out-of-the-way manner, [as, "balei phi kren *tháwdur* kumta ?"]

Thawlang, *u*, *n*. the first maternal grandfather or the father himself. [*Imit*. u Thawlang-ka Iawbei.]

Thawlir, *a*. comical, joking.

Thawnang, *a*. comic, mimical.

Thawshia, *a*. confirmed, habituated.

Tháw-tháw, (jot-), *ad*. ragged or torn, in tatters, [as, "ki jáiñ jong u ki la jot *tháw-tháw*".]

Theh, *v*. to pour in, to spill.

Theh-sei, *v*. to pour out in abundance.

'thei, (*abbrev*. of kynthei), *n*. a woman.

'thei-kha-iapsáw, *a*. a woman who has once married and is hence experienced in the art of courting men.

'thei-iáid, *ka*, *n*. a woman of bad character.

'thei-iáw, *ka*, *n*. a woman of advanced age; an elderly woman.

'thei-sotti, *ka*, *n*. a virgin.

Them, *ka*, *n*. a hollow, a valley, a depression; — *v*. to subside; *ka iapthem*, *n*. cholera.

Thep, *v*. to stow, to put in.

Thep-máwbah, *v*. to deposit bones in a common ancestral tomb or cairn.

Thep-shyieng, *v*. to deposit bones in a tomb. [*Imit*. hopshying thepshrúh.]

---

* Hindi.

Thér, *v.* to beat (*esp.* the bush or jungle) ; to muster; to beat about the bush; to put up a bird.

Thèr-thèr, (iaid-), *ad.* with light springy steps and flowing garments, [as, "khmih ka mem ka iaid *thèrthèr* kumba ka kyr kieh eh".]

Thet, *v.* to wash the hands.

Thet-thet, *ad.* convulsively; writhingly.

Thew, *v.* to measure; to take aim at; to intend. [*Imit.* thew-woh.]

Thngâd, *v.* to promise or determine not to do the same thing over again, to repent. [*Imit.* thngád-thngaw.]

Thngan, *v.* to be hungry. [*Imit.* thngan-jing-it.]

Thngiat, *u, n.* a foreign particle in the eye, a mote.

Thiang, *a.* sweet.

Thiang-bluiñ, *a.* saltish sweet taste.

Thiang-byrjup, *a.* sourish sweet taste.

Thiang-jngap, *a.* honey-sweet.

Thiang-jlep, *a.* too sweet.

Thiah, *v.* to sleep; to lie down. [*Imit.* thiah-shong.]

Thiah-ang, *v.* to be asleep with the mouth open.

Thiah-basa, *v.* to sleep for the night or as a lodger. [*Imit.* thiah-basa-thiahbasuiñ.]

Thiah-kái, *v.* to lie down by way of taking rest; to take a short nap.

Thiah-jing-it, *v.* to go without food, to fast. [*Imit.* thiahjing-it -thiah thngan.]

Thiah-sngi, *v.* to sleep till late in the day. [*Imit.* thiah sngi -thiah them.]

Thiah-thái, *v.* to oversleep; to waste time doing nothing.

Thiar, *ka, n.* a barn; a large granary basket.

Thiat, *u, n.* yeast, leaven.

Thiaw, *ad.* away, completely, [as, "da kaba ialeh shitom u la jop *thiaw* ia ki jingeh baroh".]

Thik, *ad.* exactly, precisely.

***Thikna**, *a.* regular, certain, exact. [*Imit.* thikna-thikni.]

Thie, *v.* to give response or answer to a call.

* Hindi.

Thied, *u*, *n*. fibre, root, artery. [*Imit.* u thied-u jáw.]—*v*. to buy, to purchase.

Thied-baibat, *v*. to buy for ready money, to buy in cash.

Thied-ei, *v*. better to buy.

Thied-khutia, *v*. to buy retail. [*Imit.* thied khutia-thied khu-laiñ.]

Thied-laka, } *v*. to buy wholesale.
Thied-lang, }

Thied-shah, *v*. to buy on credit. [*Imit.* thied shah-thied shàm.]

Thied-snám, *u*, *n*. vein, artery.

Thiep, *ka*, *n*. an uphill; an ascent.

Thiet, same as *thied*.

Thiew, *v*. to weed.

Thir, *v*. to spin;— *ad*. away (fly, jump); [as, "u kulái u ryng-kang *thir* ia ka syrdeng."]

Thit, *ka*, *n*. birdlime.

Thlen, *u*, *n*. a devil in the shape of a serpent supposed to be kept by certain clans in the Khasi Hills. He is propitiated with human blood and the nails taken from fingers and toes, or failing which, with human hair and pieces of garments clipped by means of a pair of silver scissors. He is believed to bring wealth and prosperity to his keepers. The people of the Khasi and Jaintia Hills are in constant dread of being murder-ed by the keepers of this monster. A boa-constrictor.

Thlia, *v*. to bother, to tease. [*Imit.* thlia-thláit.]

Thlieh, *v*. to split, to strike.

Thliem, *u*, *n*. a small leech.

Thlien, *a*. nervous, painful.

Thliew, *ka*, *n*. a hole, a pit; depression. [*Imit.* ka thliew-ka syár.]

Thliew-ka iing, { *phr*. in every house; [as, "u Saheb Jerman
Thliew-iing, { Jones u ju leit rung man ka thliew iing.]

Thlip, *ad*. entirely (dark); [as, "phi pynran ia ka sharak ha ba'n da dùm *thlip*"?]

Thlong, *u*, *n*. a wooden mortar for husking paddy, etc., a *dhenki*. [*Imit.* u thlong-u synrei.]

Thlong-nar, *u*, *n*. an iron mortar.

Thlong-mluh-thlong-sying, *phr*. bitterly inimical; implacable.

Thlún, *a.* stammering, stuttering.

Thma, *ka, n.* war, battle, dispute [*Imit.* ka thma-ka ktien.]

Thma-ka-ktien, *ka, n.* law suit.

Thmit, *a.* too short, [as, "phi la suh *thmit* eh ia kane ka sopti".] —*n.* edge; margin.

Thmu, *v.* to purpose, to intend, to resolve.

Thnàm, *v.* to boil, to simmer.

Thnàm-sabon, *ka, n.* a lather.

Thnat, *a.* having a finger or a toe branched.

Thnat-syiàr, *ka, n.* the single horn-like claw of a cock.

Thnem, *a.* scarce and dear; in great demand;—*ka, n.* the compensation money paid by a woman or a man who marries within one year after the death of her husband or before his bones have been deposited in the ancestral tomb; compensation given to a husband or wife to procure a divorce.

Thning, *u, n.* a stalk (generally of a creeper), a plant destitute of leaves.

Thnom, } **Thnum**, } *v.* to mutter, to mumble.

***Thok**, *v.* to cheat, to deceive, to humbug. [*Imit.* thok-shukor.]

Thong, *v.* to bet; to offer money; (as, "u ioh kam sordár da kaba *thong* tyngka ia ki rangbah shnong".)

Thoh, *v.* to cut trees; to write, to make a mark; to take with the tip of a finger;— *a.* having a mark or spot. [*Imit.* thoh-tàr.] — *ka, n.* an ornamental edging or border of a garment; a mark, a spot.

Thoh-bráiñ, } **Thoh-brúiñ**, } **Thoh-brew**, } *a.* spotted, striped.

Thoh-khaláí-nusip, *v.* to play in a lottery.

Thoh-léng, *a.* having a white speck or a spot.

Thoh lung-thoh léng, *ad.* with stains here and there; perfunctorily.

Thoh mut-thoh mat, *a.* having dirty spots here and there;— *ad.* blotched.

Thoh-pan, } **Thoh-pen**, } *a.* striped (across).

---

* Hindi.

Thoh-pùid, } a. striped (lengthwise), having streaks.
Thoh-shùid, }

Thoiñ-thoiñ, *ad.* dearly, intensely (love); [as, "nga ieit *thoiñ-thoiñ* la ka ri"]—straight on, without any visible sign of difficulty; [as, "u khar bajikor u kiew *thoiñ-thoiñ* na u tylláі shalor u skong".]

Thom, *v.* to trample, to clear; to do in a high-handed manner.

*Thòr, *ka, n.* the plains.

Thor-thor, *ad.* flutteringly, tremblingly, [as, "balei ki leit k'iuh *thor-thor* ia u?"]; very (light).

Thra, (um), *ka, n.* the water or fluid which issues before the delivery of a child.

Thrang, *v.* to thirst, to pant.

Thràit, *ad.* suddenly and forcibly, [as, "u khla u la kynrup ia u kulái *thràit* na u pdot".]

Thràit-thràit, *ad.* at once or without hesitation or intermission (to attack); [as, "ki briew ki la tùr *thràit-thràit* kein sha ka met jong nga".]

Threw, *v.* to have a longing for, to have an ardent desire.

Thri, *u, n.* a cane, a bamboo string or tie.

Thu! } *Inter.* a bargain now! finished! [as, "*thu,* phi la lah
Thuthen! } ai-ei ho ia kane!".]

Thung, *v.* to plant, to cultivate. [*Imit.* thung-tep.]—to appoint, to elect; to get a carbuncle.

Thung baji, *v.* to fall head over heels; to stand on the head [*Imit.* thung baji-thung prah.]

Thung-shriew (*coloq.*) = to die.

Thung-shut, *u, n.* a species of sedge, a rush.

Thung-tasam, *v.* to swear solemnly. [When a Khasi solemnly repents and makes an oath of promise not to continue to do the same thing, he takes hold of any worn-out *dá* or other piece of iron and plants it in the hearth or fire-place]. [*Imit.* thung tasam-thung takut.]

Thuh-tang, *v.* to recount, to relate in detail, to slander. [*Imit.* thuh tang-thuh tháw.]

Thùi, (tdem-), *ad.* out (issue of smoke); [as, "nga ioh-i tad ynda la tdem *thùi* ka iing".]

---

* Hindi.

Thuia, *u*, *n*. a plume about 18 inches long worn by Khasis in their turbans when dancing.

Thuli, (dew-), *ka*, *n*. hard earth, clay.

Thúiñ, (ieng-, iaid-), *ad*. slowly up (walk away) ; [as, "ynda la kyntu eh, u sa ieng *thúiñ* ba'n leit sha iing".]

Thuit, (pluh-), *ad*. in smoke ; [as, "ka iing ka la pluh *thuit*".]

Thum, *v*. to take on one's lap ;—*u*, *n*. a mound, a boundary masonry pillar.

Thúp, *v*. to be reduced in size, to become lean.

Thup, *ka*, *n*. a regular heap of stones.

Thurmur, *ad*. inconsiderately, recklessly, [as, "wat ju leh *thurmur* ia kaei kaei ka jong ki briew".]

Thut, *v*. to be offended, to be sorry, to be aggrieved.

Thwei, *ka*, *a*. a deep pool of water (in a stream).

Thwat, *v*. to be on the lookout ; to clear jungle with a *dá*.

Thwet, *v*. to be on the scent of game.

Thwiat, (lait-), *ad*. to have a hairbreadth escape, [as, "nga la siat ia u mynthna hynrei lait *thwiat* na ka khlieh".]

Thyllah, *u*, *n*. a flea.

Thyllain, *ad*. very (heavy) ; [as, "une u dienngai uba khia *thyllain*".]

Thyllan, *v*. to get a shock.

Thylleng, *n*. very young fruit ;—*v*. bearing young fruits.

Thylli, *a*. empty ; without carrying anything.

Thylliang, *u*, *n*. the tree whose bark is improvised as a headstrap and string.

Thylliej, } Thyllieid, } *u*, *n*. tongue. [*Imit*. u thylliej-u sabieng.]

Thylliej-ding, *ka*, *n*. a tongue of fire, a flame.

Thyllieng. *u*, *n*. the soft part of the bamboo which remains after the hard tough cover has been peeled off (same as *khyllieng*).

Thyllieh, *u*, *n*. dandriff.

Thyllong, (soh-), *u*, *n*. a small fruit which a shrub growing on the riverside bears.

Thymmái, *a*. fresh, new.

Thymmei, *ka*, *n*. a scar, a mark.

Thynrang, *v*. to be athirst ; to feel thirsty.

Thynrám, *ka*, *n*. a tree whose leaves have fallen off, a dried twig.

Thynrei, *u*, *n*. an evil spirit who is supposed to make the disease worse;— *v*. to become aggravated, to become worse (in illness).

Thynrim, *a*. slightly old (cloth).

Thynrón, *v*. to be convalescent.

Thynréng, } *ad*. undressed (hair), [as, "balei ieng u ñiuhkhlieh
Thynrúng, } jong phi *thynreng* kumne?"]

Thyrnia, *u*, *n*. a needle.

'ti (*abbrev*. of *kti*), *ka*, *n*. hand, finger.

Tiak, *ad*. just a little; [as, "tang shu kren *tiak* u la bitar ia nga".]

Tian, *v*. to put a thing in the mouth; to thrust a thing into the mouth.

Tian-bishar, *v*. to bring to judgment; to complain; to bring to the notice of the court.

Tiap, *ad*. directly, to the very spot (reach); [as, "nga la poi *tiap* ha kawei ka jaka".]

*Tiar, *ka*, *n*. an instrument, a tool, a weapon, fittings. [*Imit*. ka tiar-ka tar.]

'tiar, (*abbrev*. of "ktiar"), *u*, *n*. a centipede, [as, "u 'tiar-sáw, u 'tiar-dieng," etc.]

Tik-shi-tik, *ad*. incessantly, [as, "mynta ha kine ki sngi ka slap *tik-shi-tik*".]

Tika, *v*. to vaccinate.

Tika-Bamon, *ka*, *n*. inoculation.

'tikdew, *ka*, *n*. the pointing finger.

'tikhún, (same as "'tiduh") *i*, *n*. the little finger.

Tikia, *u*, *n*. a small cake of charcoal used as embers for smoking.

*Tikli, *u*, *n*. percussion cap; a detonator.

'tikmie, *ka*, *n*. a thumb.

'ti-dúh, *ka*, *n*. the last finger.

Tied, *v*. to strike, to knock, to beat.

Tied-u-pyrthat, *kaba*, *n*. a clap of thunder.

Tieng, *v*. to be afraid of, to fear.

---

* Hindi.

'tieh, 1. (*abbrev.* of "ryntieh"), *ka*, *n.* a bow.

2. (*abbrev.* of "ktieh"), *ka*, *n.* mud, marsh.

3. (*abbrev.* of "stieh"), *ka*, *n.* a shield.

'tieh-bah, *ka*, *n.* a large shield used in battles.

'tieh-batur, *ka*, *n.* a bow for throwing small stones, a catapult.

'tieh-jér, *ka*, *n.* a bow consecrated to a male-child at the time of his naming ceremony.

Tiej-tiej, Táj-táj, Tej-tej, } (jem-), *ad.* sticky and soft like mud, [as, "ka ja kaba jem *tiej-tiej*".]

'tien, (*abbrev.* of "ktien") *ka*, *n.* a word, a language; [as, "ka '*tien* Bangla."]

Tieiñ, (jrong-), *ad.* like an elastic thread, [as, "haba ring ia u ata ba la tylliat bha, u jrong *tieiñ*"]—*ad.* to the full length.

'tien-bania, *ka*, *n.* an incorrect way of speaking a foreign tongue. The idea is taken from the way goldsmiths from the plains speak the Khasi language.

'tien-biria, *ka*, *n.* jokes. [*Imit.* 'tien biria-birai.]

'tien-kái, *ka*, *n.* sham words, jokes.

'tien-ngiah ngiah, *ki*, *n.* words spoken in soft and highly polished style.

'tien-jali-ja-um, *ki*, *n.* soft sweet words.

'tien-lyngkut, *ki*, *n.* laconic speech, blunt words.

'tien-tharshiah, *ki*, *n.* words which give pain to one against whom they are spoken.

'tien-woh-nia, *ki*, *n.* words spoken with a view to pick a quarrel.

Tiew, *v.* to boil, to put a cooking vessel over the fire.

'tiew, (*abbrev.* of "syntiew"), *u*, *n.* a flower.

'tiew-klong, *u*, *n.* *Dendrobium Nobile*, a species of orchid.

'tiew-knup mawiang, *u*, *n.* the ladies' slipper, *Cypripedium*, (orchid).

'tiew-dohmáw, *u*, *n.* a very small plant whose leaves are of a dark violet colour interspersed with golden streaks and much liked by women to deck their hair.

'tiew-eit, *u*, *n.* a flower (of a fruit tree) which does not bear fruit.

'tiew-jalyngksiang, *u*, *n.* the rhododendron.

'tiew-jami-iang, *u*, *n.* the violet (flower).

'tiew-japang, *u*, *n.* the bluebell.

'tiew-lapongnái, *u*, *n.* a kind of flower having sweet smelling leaves.

'tiew-lasier, *u*, *n.* a species of orchid.

'tiew-lasubon, *ka*, *n.* the tender leaf holding the flower of a certain plant of a yellowish colour resembling that of a pine-apple which is used by women to decorate their hair.

'tiew-myngngor syng-un, *u*, *n.* marigold.

'tiew-pathai-khubór, *u*, *n.* a flower, the sweet smell of which can be perceived from a distance only.

'tiew-phàn, *u*, *n.* the dahlia ; potato flower.

'tiew-riam-skáiñ, *u*, *n.* the pitcher plant.

'tiew-sngi, *u*, *n.* the sunflower.

'tiew-shyllong, *u*, *n.* a white flower resembling gloxinia which a shrub growing by the river-side bears.

'tiew-shlim, *u*, *n.* stramonium flower.

Tiew-sla, *u*, *n.* a brass pot for cooking rice, same as *khiewsla.*

'tiew-snoh-dieng, *u*, *n.* orchid.

'tiew-synteng, *u*, *n.* *Vanda cerulea* (orchid).

'tiew-thylliej-tangmuri, *u*, *n.* blythia flower.

'tiew-tyrkhang, *u*, *n.* a sweet-smelling fern.

Ting, *v.* to call a dog or a fowl or any animal, to address.

Ting-khún, *v.* to own a child as one's own.

Tih, *v*, to dig ; to discuss.

Tihár, *ka*, *n.* an evil spirit who is believed to cause a severe colic pain; severe colic.

†Tili, *u*, *n.* an oilman.

Tim, *v.* to curse; to mutter or chant formula while performing puja. [*Imit.* tim-mái.]

Tim-kñia, *v.* to call on the spirits as a Khasi diviner does at the time when he performs sacrifices. [*Imit.* tim-kñia-tim-khriam.]

Tip, *v.* to know.

Tip-briew, *v.* to be conscious, to recover, to come to oneself [*Imit.* tip briew-tip mrád.]

Tip-kein, *phr.* I do not know, I doubt.

Tip-duk, *v.* to be industrious, to be actively engaged; to be sensible. [*Imit.* tipduk-tip suk.]

---

†Bengali.

Tip-ei? *phr.* who knows?

Tip-ma, *conj.* but, on the contrary.

'ti-pdeng, *ka, n.* the middle finger.

Tip-sngi, *a.* to be well-behaved; good. [*Imit.* tipsngi-tipnong.]

Tip-thuh-tip dái, *v.* to recognise, to know.

Tir, *v.* to cut into long strips or pieces (flesh, fish, skin, etc.); (*shitir-*)much, very [as, "ka duhkha te *shitir* kciñ ia u kbér."]

Tir-shi-tir, *ad.* again and again, line after line, [as, "ki dkhiew ki mih *tir-shi-tir* ba'n leit rong la ki pylleng"; "u ia nga u shu kwah ba'n ialeh *tir-shi-tir*".]

†Tisi, *u, n.* linseed.

Tista, *ad.* regularly.

Tit, *u, n.* a mushroom; fungus.

Tit-thnat-syiar, *u, n.* a kind of mushroom.

Tiw(dum—), *ad.* completely (dark) [as, ; "ka bneng ka la sdang ba'n dum *tiw.*"]

Tla, *v.* to curse, to chide (with obscene words); [*Imit.* tla—tlep.]

Tlang, *ka, n.* winter.

Tlái, *ka, n.* a palm-tree.

Tlait, *ad.* securely (shut); [as "ki la bon *tlait* ia ka synduk.]

Tlem, *a.* spotless, pure.

Tlieng, *ka, n.* a large mat made of cane used in threshing paddy millet and job's-tears.

Tlor, *v.* to wither, to fall off as leaves or rotten substance or tears.

Tlot, *a.* weak, powerless.

Tlúh, *u, n.* a tree whose bark is very useful in making ropes, etc.

Tmang, *ad.* lonely; [as, "katno nga sngew *tmang* ba phi'm don shuh hangne."]

Tmáiñ, *u, n.* moustache;—*tmàiñ, ad.* to the brim (full).

Tmáiñ-khlaw, *u, n.* a kind of ground-creeper the leaves of which resemble that of a pine-tree, stag-moss.

Tmár, *u, n.* a kind of small bamboo.

Tmier, *ka, n.* a margin, a rim, edge.

Tmoh, *ka, n.* chin;—fellow (colloquial).

Tmòiñ, *ad.* quite (full); [as, "ka um ka la dap *tmòiñ* ha,a khiew."]

---

† Bengali.

Tmùiñ, (mih), *ad.* coming out a little only [as, "ki reng ki la mih *tmùiñ* mynta."]

Tmum-tmum, (sngàid), *ad.* pulpy, fat, [as, "u khynnah u sngáid *tmum-tmum.*"]

Tnan, } *ad.* once for all (die); hard and stiff (applied to a dead
Tnen, } body).

Tnat, *ka*, *n.* a branch, a twig.

Tnáw, *ka*, *n.* a big claw (of a crab); the wing (of a house).

Tnúm, *ka*, *n.* the ridge of a house.

To = a sign of the imperative mood which means, "*let* us," "*let* you," "*let* him," (as "*to* ia leit noh;")—*ad.* allright, very well, as "phi'n leit ai kane ka shithi?" "to," (very well).

Tok, *ad.* just, [as, "tang u shu kren *tok* nga'n shoh ia u"].

Tong, *v.* to draw (water from a well or vessel, or fish from a river); to fish.

Toh, *v.* to peck, to bite.

Tohkhat, } *ad.* very occasionally, [as, "ia kaba klet *tohkhat* te
Tohkhatlet, } mano mano ruh ia map."]

Tohkit, *v.* to enquire, to investigate.

Tohjáw, *u*, *n.* a boil.

Tohmet, *ad.* roughly, without consideration or mercy, [as, "wat leh *tohmet* ia ki khynnah bapli ki b'ym don kmie shuh"] [*Imit.* tohmet-tohjùn.]

Tòi, *ad.* otherwise, but, now at any rate, why not; [as, "u leit bakla khein tang kawei ka jingkhein ha ka eksamin, *tòi* la jop ma u;" "ban da'phi ong te *tòi* ym leit heit?"]; as a matter of fact.

Tóiñ-tóiñ, *ad.* easily, without resistance (come), [as, "tang shu shim na ka kti u shu wan *tóiñ-tóiñ.*"]

Top, *ad.* just, only, [as, "tang phi shu leit pynbna *top* shaphang kane, nga'n beh ia phi nangne na shuong".]

Tor, *u*, *n.* the lungs;—*a.* impaired, weak.

Torti, *a.* careless, not doing up to the mark.

Trái, *u*, *n.* root, Lord, master, owner—*ka trái*, *n.* principal money. [*Imit.* ka trái-ka dkhúh.]

Trái-shnong, *n.* a native of a place; a citizen. [*Imit.* trái-shnong -trái-tháw.]

Tràit, *ad.* at once (catch); [as, "ka miaw ka la kynrup *tràit* ia ka khnái"]; firmly.

Tram, (iap-), *v.* to wither, to die (of trees and bamboos) ;—*u*, *n.* a disease of the *pán* leaves.

Trang, *ka*, *n.* bachelor's house in the Bhoi and Lalung villages.

Tráp, *ka*, *n.* a small circular rain-proof frame used by the Khasis (called *ka shaladiang* by the Syntengs).

Tráw, *u*, *n.* sun-grass.

Treng, *u*, *n.* a mane.

Treh, *v.* to consent, to agree.

Trei, *v.* to work, to labour. [*Imit.* trei-ktah; trei-beng.]

Trep, *ka*, *n.* a temporary hut; *hynñiew trep hynñiew skum* (phr.) the earliest inhabitants of the world.

Triang, *u*, *n.* an eel;—*ad.* firmly (hold or grasp).

Triem, *a.* dreadful, frightful.

Trong, *u*, *n.* a tuft of hair on the head.

Troh, *v.* to clutch, to claw.

Troiñ, *v.* to dwindle.

Trúd, *v.* to scratch.

Trúd iawbei, *kaba*, *n.* white streaks on the body.

*Trup-swar, *u*, *n.* a cavalry soldier (same as *tyllup-swar*).

Tuklar, *v.* to speak, to talk or discuss confusedly.

*Tukra, *ka*, *n.* a piece, a part.

Túd, *v.* procrastinating, delaying.

'tung, (*abbrev.* of ktung), *ka*, *n.* a vetch; a small preserved fish.

'tung-rymbái, *ka*, *n.* bean which has been cooked and preserved and having a very disagreeable smell.

'tung-tap, *ka*, *n.* a small preserved fish.

Tuh, *v.* to steal. [*Imit*: tuh—thiem.]

Tuh-tnga briew, *v.* to commit adultery.

Tûid, *v.* to flow, to run (water).

Túiñ-túiñ, *ad.* hesitatingly, with fear, [as, "balei phi iaid *túiñ-túiñ* haba ong ba phi'n iaid bran"].

Tùit, *v.* to suspect, to charge falsely with, as in the word *tùit klim*—to charge one falsely with committing adultery.

†Tula, *ka*, *n.* a tola; *u*—, cotton or other similar material for igniting fire from the spark of a flint; cleaned cotton.

---

* Hindi. † Bengali.

Tule, *v.* to chide with obscene words. [*Imit.* tule—dangle.]

*Tulop, *ka, n.* pay, salary. [*Imit.* ka tulop—ka dorma]—*v.* to summon.

Tulu, *a.* having a big knob ; blunt, [as, "une u dieng uba heh ka khlieh *tulu.*"]

Tum-ki-tam, (ki—) *n. pl.* articles of furniture.

Tuma-tuma, *ad.* in pieces (to chop), [as, "ka khnái ka la dait *tuma-tuma* ia ka jáiñ jong nga."]

Tun, *pron.* thou (it is used at the end of a sentence and is applicable to women only in colloquial language).

Tùp, *ka, n.* a cannon. [*Imit.* ka tùp—ka mán.]

*Tuphán, *ka, n.* a gale ; a cyclone.

*Tupia, *ka, n.* a cap, a hat.

Tur, *v.* to advance, to rush ; to butt.

'tur, (*abbrev.* of "shyntur"), *ka, n.* a mouth.

Tur-iap, *v.* to rush desperately ;—*n. ka,* tongs (*colloq*).

*Tusbir, *ka, n.* a picture ; a likeness.

Turoi, *ka, n.* a trumpet.

T'ut, *n.* a quail (same as *tyut*).

†Tuta, *n.* a parrot.

†Tutia, *u, n.* sulphate of copper, blue vitriol.

Twa, *v.* to fall down as a wall ; to subside.

Twád, *v.* to feel by means of the hand.

Tybian, *ka, n.* floor, same as *tbian.*

Tybit, *a.* handy, skilful, tactful (same as *tbit*).

Tyng-áb, *n.* a raven, a crow.

Tyng-am, *ka, n.* the jawbone ; a loud harsh voice.

Tyng-am-dúh, *ka, n.* the wisdom tooth.

†Tyngka, *ka, n.* money, rupee. [*Imit.* tyngka-sbái.]

Tyngkâi, *v.* to reserve, to keep in store, to economize.

Tyngkâi-soh-thád, *v.* to preserve a thing carefully (used sarcastically for what ought not to be done).

Tyngkan, *v.* to suppress, to reserve.

Tyngkeng, *ad.* as if caught up between some obstacles, ["u la woh u jyrmi na ka kjat and nga la sahkut *tyngkeng.*]

---

* Hindi. † Bengali.

Tyngkhap, *v.* to insert, to infix, to hide ; [*Imit.* tyngkhap-tyngkhip], *ñiang-tynkhap, ka, n.* a tick.

Tyngkhap-máw, *ka, n.* crevice of a rock.

Tyngkhip-tyngkhap, (sah-), *ad.* behidden or unnoticed ; carefully (set aside or hidden) ; [as, "ym don dumasla mo briew na phi uba sah *tyngkhip-tyngkhap*?"]

Tyngkhúh, *v.* to hit or get the head knocked against something.

Tyngkong, *ka, n.* a platform next the door of the second room in a Khasi house.

Tyngkoh, *ad.* limping.

Tyngkra (kha-), *n.* a small fish with sharp fins close to the gills.

Tyngkreiñ, *ad.* vividly (displayed), [as, " la' u la iap hynrei ka dur jong u ka sah *tyngkreiñ*.]

Tyngkrong, (wait-), *ka, n.* a *dao* having two supporters at the back of the edge used for cutting and dressing fish, etc.

Tyngkdón, *ad.* nicely dressed (like a little girl) ; gracefully [as, "I khynnah iba i-tynnad *tyngkdón*."]

Tyngden, *ad.* firmly, strongly, [as, "ka khohwah jong phi kaba bha *tyngden*."]

Tyng-eh, *ad.* roughly, harshly, severely, [as, "da kaba leh *tyng-eh* u mut ba'n pyndúh ia kaba sniew."]

Tyngheng, *ad.* agape, spell-bound, [as "u shynreh u peit *tyngheng* ia ngi."]

Tynghong, (peit-), *ad.* agape (said of a small mouth).

Tyngngiau (same as *tynñiau*), *v.* to stuff, to cram.

Tyng-in, *v.* to flirt, to court.

Tyng-ier, *ka, n.* a platform suspended just above the hearth (in a Khasi house) where firewood is kept.

Tyngjláng, **Tyngjéng**, **Tyngjlúng**, **Tyngjlóng**, *ad.* completely (taken by surprise), [as, "u ieng lyngngoh *tyngjlong*.]

Tyngmep, *ad.* full of leaves [as, " ba'n lei ia une u jhur katne *tyngmep*?"]

Tyngmup, *v.* to speak or deal harshly.

Tyngnàn, **Tyngniaw**, **Tyngnin**, *ad.* slender, small and thin [as, " u briew uba rit *tyngnán*."]

Tyngsháin, *v.* to shine, to glare, to reflect.

Tyngshop, *u*, *n.* an effigy of a man made of bamboo work to represent the first maternal uncle in a Khasi ceremonial dance.

Tyngwoin, *v.* to go round and round.

Tylláí, *u*, *n.* a rope

Tyllái-suwali, *u*, *n.* a rope in a plough by which the neck of an ox is fastened.

Tyllan, *ad.* entirely, wholly, without reserve ; [as, " ka miaw ka bam *tyllan* snier baroh ia ka khnái."]

Tyllâwding, *ka*, *n.* a firebrand.

Tyllep, *v.* to cover completely, to hide.

Tylli, *n.* number (of things or animals) ;—*a.* solid —*ad.* wholly ; bodily, as, " phi kren ia nga kumba phi la ioh-mráw *tyli* mo ? " [*Imit.* tylli-tyllàn.]

Tylliat, *v.* to grind, to bruise.

Tylli-tyllan, *ad.* exactly (alike) ; [as, " une u khynnah uba bit *tylli-tyllan* ia la u kpa."]

Tyllong, } **Tlong**, } *u*, *n.* the stock (of maize, etc.,) ;—*n.* *ka*, the handle (of a *dao*) ; the source of a stream.

Tyllun, *v.* to revolve, to roll, to tumble.

Tyllup, *v.* to cover ;—*shityllup ka pyrthei*, *phr.* throughout the world ; the whole world.

Tymblóng, } **Tymblúng** } *ad.* like an idiot or dumb man, bewildered ; [as, "balei phi ieng *tymblóng* kumne kum u biej ?].

Tymbuit, *ka*, *n.* the elbow.

Tymmen, *a.* old ;—*n.* an old man or woman. [*Imit.* u tymmen-u-san ; u tymmen-u-kro.]

Tympán, *ka*, *n.* a *machan* (in a Khasi house) overhead where odds and ends are kept, it is above *ka tyng-ir.*

Tympem, ('nam-), *u*, *n.* one of the three arrows shot from the funeral pyre towards the north, west and south to keep off evil spirits.

Tympew, *u*, *n.* a betel leaf, a *pán*-leaf.

Tympha, *ka*, *n.* a shoulder ;—*bah-tympha*, *u*, *n.* a wall-plate.

Tymphu, ('la-), *ka*, *n.* a tree resembling a papaya tree, the branches of which are used as pipes in a liquor distillery.

Tyndah, *ad.* along with, together, [as, " u khla u bám *tyndah* shñiuh baroh ia ka blang."]

Tyndái, *ka, n.* the inside of the roof.

Tyndam, *ad.* bluntly, [as, " balei phi shu kren *tyndam* kumta ia nga."]

Tyndáw, *a.* blunt, not pointed.

Tyndep, *v.* to forget or to lose one's memory, as if enchanted.

Tyndi-tynda, *ad.* perchance [as, " ngán shu leit kein ioh *tyndi-tynda* ia kynduh pynban."]

Tyndong, *ka, n.* a short pipe, a case. [*Imit.* ka tyndong-ka tynnah].

Tyndung, *v.* to poke, to thrust, to goad.

Tynjang, (suid-), *u, n.* a lame demon who haunts the jungle. It is said that as he walks he calls out "kaw-hoit, kaw-hoit." If he meets any person he tickles him to death.

Tynjuh, *v.* to try, to test, to tempt.

Tynnad, *ad.* moderately, [as, " ka jingheh kine ki dohkha kaba la *tynnad*."]

Tynnad, (*suffix*) = pleasant, pretty.

Tynneng, *v.* to imitate.

Tynñian, *v.* to press in forcibly, to stow.

Tynrah, *v.* to thrust, to lance.

Tynrái, *ka, n.* root, source, origin.

Tynriew, *u, n.* the leaves of a certain species of palm much used on the sourthern borders of the Khasi hills for thatching. [*Imit.* u tynriew-u tyndáw].

Tynrong, *v.* to put over on the top of something ; to carry on the head ; to lighten the load of a friend by taking a portion on oneself.

Tynrûh, *v.* to poke.

Tynsah, *v.* to ram in, to elbow.

Tynsat, *v.* to put in between two things, to insert ; to inset.

Tynsong, *ka, n.* a small net-bag for catching fish.

Tyr-a, *u, n.* a species of small bamboo ; *nol-bas* (*Beng.*).

Tyrbeh, *ad.* as if some adhesive substance is adhering to something, [as, " phi wan nangno ba da ka ktieh suda *tyrbeh* baroh shirynieng."]

Tyrkhang, *u, n.* a fern.

Tyrkhong, *a.* dried, withered.

Tyrha, *a.* hot, inflamed.

Tyrjaiñ, } *ad.* in bunches [as, " ki ong ba u soh-*grape* u soh *tyr-*
Tyrjup, } *jaiñ* ha iing I Babu William, mo?"]

Tyrma, *ad.* by chance, aimlessly, [as, "phi leit iashang *tyrma* shato, la iap ho."]

Tyrnem, *u, n.* a hammer.

***Tyrpád**, ('la-), *ka, n.* a bay-leaf, *tezpát*.

Tyrpait, *ka, n.* a mashan or platform made of bamboo split or beaten flat.

Tyrpeng, *ka, n.* a shoulder.

‡**Tyrphin**, *ka, n.* turpentine.

Tyrphut, *ad.* nasty (wet); [as, " balei ba u ksew u jhieh *tyrphut* kumne?"]

Tyrpúd, *ka, n.* a big lizard.

Tyrsain, *v.* to have cramp or a creeping cold sensation (generally of the feet); " the feet have gone to sleep."

Tyrsáw, (iap-), *ad.* (to faint) out of hunger or thirst; [as, "wat leit jingleit jngái khlem da song ja ioh iap *tyrsáw*."] [*Imit.* tyrsáw—tyrsian.]

Tyrsem, *ad.* nicely (dressed).

Tyrsháit, *ad.* having the appearance of many fruits hanging on a tree; [as, " mynta ka snem u sohbha u sohmyntra *tyrsháit*."]

Tyrsiang, *a.* smooth, slippery.

Tyrsim, *ka, n.* the nail, the hoof, the claw.

Tyrsúh, *v.* to poke, to incite, to urge vehemently.

Tyrtài, *ad.* very (dirty); [as, " ki Mawshái ki dang lehsih mynno mynno phar *tyrtài*."]

Tyrtéw, *ad.* in ragged clothes; [as, " balei ba jot ka sopti *tyrtéw* kumne? "]

Tyrtho, *ka, n.* a froth; —*v.* to babble, to make an empty show in speech.

Tyrthup-um, *ka, n.* foam.

Tyr-ut, *ka, n.* the demoness who brings about misfortune to a man, *esp.* violent death. [*Imit.* ka tyr-ut—ka smér].

Tyrwa, *v.* to propose, to offer, to tender.

Tyrwieng, *ka, n.* a potsherd.

---

* Hindi. ‡ English.

U.

U, the 19th letter in the Khasi Alphabet.

U, *p.* sign of masculine, he, it, an, the.

Uba, *p.* who, which, that.

Úd, *v.* to groan, to complain, to hum. [*Imit.* úd-khñium.]

U-ei ? *p.* who ?

Uei-uei, *p.* any, anyone.

U-ei-ro-u-ei, *p.* somebody, someone.

Ullong, *same as* urlong.

Um, *ka, n.* water, juice. [*Imit.* ka um-ka wah.]—*v.* to melt, to dissolve ;—(*contr.* of kyn-um) a brother-in-law (used as a term of respect and also in the case of address).

U'm, *phr.* he not, he'll not.

Um-bah, *a.* having much water in a stream or river ;—*v.* to overflow ;—*ka, n.* flood, big stream. [*Imit.* um-bah-um-san.]

Um-biah, *ka, n.* saliva, spittle.

Um-koi, *ka, n.* a well where sacrifices and oaths are performed

Umja, *ka, n.* conjee.

Um-jakar, *ka, n.* the humours of the body ; human seed.

Um-jah, *ka, n.* cold water. [*Imit.* umjah-umtngàm.]

Um-jér, *ka, n.* dews.

Umjiat, *ka, n.* water which drains from the crevices of rocks, etc., through marshy places.

Um-jung, *ka, n.* urine.

Um-mat, *ka, n.* tears. [*Imit.* ka um-mat-um-mut, ka um-mat-ka umpung].

Um-mlúh, *ka, n.* salt-spring, salt-water.

Umpohliew, *ka, n.* a spring, a fountain.

Um-pyrdóng, *ka, n.* water in a well in which an oath, libation and rice is sprinkled in connection with sacrificial ceremonies.

Um-reit, (iong-), *a.* lively and dark (complexion).

Um-rieng, *ka, n.* fresh or pure water as distinguished from water in which something has been mixed or dissolved.

Um-rmiew, } Um-rmu, } *ka, n.* exudation on a wound or sore.

Um-sâw, *ka, n.* a flood. [*Imit.* umsâw-umsian.]

Um-shár, *ka*, *n*. cold water poured into hot water to lower its temperature.

Um-shit, *ka*, *n*. hot-water; soup.

Um-shitja, *ka*, *n*. conjee.

Um-snám-(ia—), *v*. to shed one's blood.

Um-syep, *ka*, *n*. sweat: personal income.

Um-thet, *ka*, *n*. water with which hands have been washed.

Um-thlong, *ka*, *n*. water which gathers in a pot-hole of a stream.

Um-thra, *ka*, *n*. water which issues before the delivery of a child.

Úm-úm, (s'aid-), *a*. lukewarm, warm.

Umwi, *ki*, *n*. people living in the country through which the stream Umwi near Jarain passes.

U'n, *phr*. he will.

Une, *p*. this (near me).

Uno ? *p*. which ?

Uno-re-uno, *p*. someone, somebody.

Uno-uno, *p*. whoever, any one.

Ùr, *v*. to slip, to fall;—*ad*. with a rumbling noise; with a warm sensation. [*Imit*. ùr-háp.]

Urlong, *v*. to happen, to come to pass (as predicted or expected).

Ur-met, *ka*, *n*. menstruation.

Urwir-urhap, *v*. to reside as an alien in a place.

Usa, *v*. to dress and smooth the plastering of a wall by means of a piece of board.

*Ut, *ka*, *n*. a camel.

Ut-shi-ut, *ad*. slowly, hesitatingly; procrastinating, dilatory; [as, "ka jingkhreh *ut-shi-ut* nadúh mynno ym lah dep shúh".]

Uta, *p*. he (out of sight).

Utai, *p*. he (within sight).

Utai-tai, *p*. he (there within sight).

Utei, *p*. he (up there).

Uthie, *p*. he (down there).

Uto, *p*. he (near you).

Uwei, *a*. one.

---

* Hindi.

Uwei-la-uwei, *p.* someone else.

Uwei-u-ár, *p.* some other person.

Uwei pat, *phr.* another.

W.

W, the 20th letter in the Khasi Alphabet.

Wa ! *interj.* denoting surprise, hallo !

Wab-wab, } (jem-), *ad.* flexibly, pliably, [as, "une u shken u long
Web-web, } uba jem *wab-wab.*"]

Wak, *ad.* abruptly ; asunder, [as, "u phái noh *wak* na ka lynti kaba beit" ; "u David u kád *wak* ia ka shyntur u sing."]

Wád, *v.* to seek, to search, to look for. [*Imit.* wád-thúd.]

Wadar, *u, n.* a Wahadadar ; a president ; a president or ruler of the Shella confideracy.

Wád-buit, *v.* to find out the secret, plan, trick, etc.

Wád-dong, *v.* to seek an excuse.

Wád-lád, *v.* to seek a means or an opportunity.

Wád-nia, *v.* to seek a pretext for controversy ; to find out suitable arguments for prosecuting a case.

Wád-phoi, *v.* to seek a quarrel.

Wang, *u,* or *ka, n.* a taro-stalk (*Colocasia antiquorum*);—*ad.* ajar wide open, [as, "u plie *wang* ia ka iing."]

Wang-wang, } (kyllúid-), *ad.* very (loose) ; [as, "kine ki juti ki
Weng-weng, } kyllúid *wang-wang* ha nga"] ; weakly.

Wah, *ka, n.* a stream, a river ;—*v.* to suspend, to hang. [*Imit.* ka wah-ka um]

Wah-bah, *ka, n.* a large river. [*Imit.* wahbah-wahsan.]

Wah-dúit, *ka, n.* a rivulet, a streamlet. [*Imit.* wahdúit-wahrit.]

Wái, *v.* to finish up, to cease, to bring to a close.

Wái-wái, (tlot-) *ad.* weakly, [as, "nga dang sngew tlot *wái-wái* mynta ba'n iaid jngái,"] [*Imit.* wáiwái-witwit.]

'wái (*abbrev.* of "kwái"), *u, n.* an areca nut ;—(*abbrev.* of "khwái"), *u, n.* a fishing hook.

'wái-kháw, *u, n.* a fresh areca nut.

'wái-dong, *u, n.* rolled or prepared betel-nut ; a *khili* (Hindi.)

Waiñ, *ka, n.* wine ;—*ad.* easily (bent) ; (as, "u prek u la dor *waiñ*"); of a proper length (as, "u ksái uba jrong *waiñ*").

'wái-sohlapér, *u*, *n*. the fruit of a small kind of palm.

'wái-sohpari, *u*, *n*. dried areca nut.

Wait, *ka*, *n*. a *dao*, a heavy large bladed knife.

Wait-bnoh, *ka*, *n*. a *dá* with a crooked head.

Wait-khmut, *ka*, *n*. same as "*wait-bnoh.*"

Waitlam, *ka*, *n*. a sword.

Wait lyngkái, *ka*, *n*. a *dá* having a tapering point.

Wait-lyng-en, *ka*, *n*. a *dá* with a convex edge.

Wait-lyngngùn, *ka*, *n*. a straight heavy *dá* used in felling trees and in dressing timbers and planks.

Wait-tyng krong, *ka*, *n*. a *dá* with two legs or props attached to the back thereof, used in dressing fish, etc.

'wái-um, *u*, *n*. areca nut preserved in water, in a well or vessel.

Wái-wot, *ad*. finally, [as, "u kren *wáiwot* ynda la pynjew eh ia u bad u leit noh thiaw sha la shnong."]

Wallam, *v*. to bring, to fetch. (Same as *wanlam*).

Wan, *v*. to come.

Wankái, *v*. to come on a visit. [*Imit*. wan-kái-wan-iáid].

Wan-doh, *v*. to be full in flesh, especially after protracted illness, [as, "mynta u la *wandoh* pat, tói, u la sah kat i nap".]

Wan-dur, *v*. to be in the proper shape, symmetrical. [*Imit*. wan-dúr-wandàr.]

Wan-met, *v*. to become full in flesh, to become strong. [*Imit*. wanmet-wanphád.]

Wan-on, *v*. to accompany a person on his journey.

Wan-rwing, *v*. to go to any place and return back the same day.

Wan-sháw, *v*. to come and fetch a person or thing.

Wan-tàn, *v*. to come to meet a person on the way.

Wan-wir-wan-háp, *v*. to reside as a stranger and not as a citizen.

Wár, *n*. the people living in the southern low lands of the Khasi and Jaintia Hills; [*Imit*. u Wár-u Riat.]

Wàr, *ad*. far behind, spaciously, [as, "ieng kyllúid *wàr*."]

Waris, *n*. a successor, an heir.

Wat, *v*. (*Imper.*), do not, don't;—*ad*. even[as, "*wat* u masi ruh u tip la u kynrád."]

—wat (suffix)=times, as, shi-*wat* once, ar-*wat* twice, etc.

Waw ! *interj.* alas ! dear me !

Weng, *v.* to remove, to take away.

Wei, *adj.* one ;—*conj.* since, in asmuch as, [as, "*wei* phi la kular topyndep mynta.") ;—*v.* to pour.

'wei, (*abbrev.* of "thwei"), *ka, n.* a pool.

Wêr, *v.* to invite, to hire.

Wêr-kynbat, *v.* to weed.

Wèr-wèr, *ad.* as a rumour, (as, "nga sngew *wèr-wèr* kumba ka sor Laban ka'n leit noh mo ?")

Wet, *v.* to put a strap round to carry, to fasten a "*star*" or head strap into a knot.

Wia, *ad.* with a whiz, (as, "ka khlieng ka suh *wia* na jrong".)

Wiak, *ad.* just, a little, (as, "tang shu lait *wiak* u la shoh ia ki.")

Wiang, *v.* to set fire to (a house or jungle)—*ka, n.* a (brass) plate.

Wiar, *v.* to bark.

Wiat, *v.* to draw (a bow string), to smile.

Wiat-samrkhie, *v.* to smile.

'wieng, (*contraction.* of "*tyrwieng*"), *ka, n.* a potsherd.

Wieh, *v.* to dip, to steep ;—*u, n.* earth-worm. [*Imit.* u wieh-u ktiar].

Win, *v.* to be uproarious, to be in a tumult, to move.

Wir, (iáid-), *ad.* astray, as a stranger.

Wit, *a.* hindering, obsructing ;—*v.* to be in the family way.

Woh, *v.* to fasten with a hook, to hook.

Woh-dáw, *v.* to seek a plea for argument. [*Imit.* wohdáw-woh-dong.]

Woh-nia, *v.* to object, to criticise.

Y.

Y, the last letter in the Khasi Alphabet.

Ym, *ad.* not.

Ym banse, *phr.* to be obliged to, it cannot be helped.

Ym don bak, *phr.* not to have authority to do anything, not to dare.

Ym laplieng, *phr.* to be in a mighty hurry.

Ym lei-lei, *phr.* it will not fare ill, it will not go wrong; it will be all right.

Yn, *aux. v.* will, shall.

Yn lei, *phr.* it will do no harm, it will be all right.

Yn sa, *phr.* it will.

Ynda, *conj.* after, when, till.

Yn-nái, *ad.* no, not, I do not want it; (as, "phi'm ia bám ja?"—"Em phi, koit, *yn nái.*")

Yngkúid (sati-), *ka, n.* a magic ring.

Addenda.

Bajikór, *u, n.* a juggler.

Karikór, *u, n.* a mechanic.

Kyrhúh, *v.* to roar, to thundet.

Ïwjit, *v.* to have the small of boiled food which has been left for a long time.

Lyngknep, *ka. n.* the area.